Been Nowhere, Done Nothing.

The Lockdown diary of a menopausal woman

written by Jan Coulson

This book is dedicated to my friends who took the time and cared to listen to my rants and ravings.

And for Greenie and Anna - my darling girls.

Authors note

This second book started off as a menopausal rant about the early stages of Lockdown, a follow on from my first book. I thought it would only last a couple of months, but it turned into a sixteen month personal saga throughout the strangest time I hope any of us will ever have to live through ever again. Aided and abetted by the fluctuating menopause symptoms, it was never meant to be this long and there were days when I thought I would never finish it, like all of us I feared Covid would never end.

This is why as the book progresses I change from daily to weekly to monthly entries. I honestly felt like it was Deja Vu on a regular basis and I did not want to write a complete repeat of the first, second or third Lockdown. Though in point of fact it was almost a repeat performance.

I kept a notebook permanently with me to jot down every event that made any sort of impression on my tiny brain as and when it happened and it is all in chronological order. Some of the things that registered with me some people may not even have been aware of, yet I am pretty sure my brain skipped over some far more important and significant occurrences. The reality was that those events just did not make any sort of impression on my subconscious and passed me by.
Most of the Covid data is from the World Health Organisations website and was correct on the day of writing.

This is the Covid Lockdown through my bewildered, emotional and angry eyes as I saw it at the time and is purely from my point of view and no reflection on anyone else's opinions or thoughts.

As in my previous book I have changed the names of some of the characters, but I can assure you that this is all true and really happened.

Special thanks to Peter for all the technical assistance,
I would never be able to publish this without his help.

Thanks to my clever friend Kirsty Scarrett for yet
another fantastic front cover.

And thanks to all of you for taking the time to read this.

1. Recap of a difficult year 2019

The Menopause. What a bloody awful time for any woman.

When you transfer from cool, sophisticated, confident, intelligent woman to emotional, forgetful, confused, old lady.
When your once hourglass figure starts to slide downwards and settles somewhere around your knees.
When your looks start to fade and lines appear all over your once baby smooth face.
When you start growing inch long black hairs on your chin but can't actually see them and your husband is constantly launching himself at you with a pair of tweezers because he can spot them a mile away.
When you never get a decent nights sleep and constantly feel like you are floating through the days in a constant bubble of paranoia and confusion.
When you flit between vicious rage and floods of tears on a hourly basis.
When you cannot recall a thing unless you have written it down, and that's only if you have actually remembered to write it down in the first place.
When your diminished fluffy brain cannot retain one small piece of information and you ask the same question over and over again with no recollection of the answer - whatsoever.
When your body temperature is permanently on BOILING HOT.
When you worry about the tiniest, weeniest, minutest things.
And sadly, when things start to go wrong in your once perfect life and you cannot quite figure out how to make it right again.

At the time of writing this book, I am entering my sixth year of hormonal madness. You would think that by now I would be used to behaving like a complete fruitcake, but no, it doesn't really get any easier. Apparently I could have another six years before the symptoms disappear altogether, oh goody, that's something to really look forward to. I do though have occasional days when I feel that maybe I am starting to emerge from this hormonal nightmare but then something happens and the way my body responds tells me I am not quite out of the woods yet. So along with every other woman on the planet who is suffering with it, I fight my way through every night and day, hoping and praying that it will come to an end and I can have my old life back. And Peter, my husband, wants his happy, funny, glamorous wife back, not the miserable old harpy that he currently lives with.

The menopause has been very topical for the last few years, it doesn't seem such a taboo subject to converse about anymore. But then there are so very few subjects nowadays that are not discussed at length by someone or other, subjects that someone on the planet will take offence at, so in fact the menopause actually seems a fairly safe topic to talk about. There have even been several articles written about this particular issue in the Tabloids, so it must all be true. Certainly the males who work with me in my office know everything about it, they are extremely well informed. We discuss it constantly amongst us ladies, of which four of us are of menopausal status, as an Arctic wind whips across the desks courtesy of the freezing air conditioning. Our male bosses drunken wind up speech at the Christmas party about how women just have to work their way through it went down like a lead balloon. He was very lucky not to get his face smashed in, and that would have been by the more genteel lady in the office. The rest of us wouldn't have been quite as compassionate. In his bolshy drunken state, fortunately for me, he cannot remember what I called him! (Four letters, starts with C ends in T.)
I know, wash my mouth out with soap!

It feels like a million light years ago but was actually only in February 2019 when I set off on a solo Asian adventure, travelling through Burma, Thailand and Laos, ending up spending two months in the town of Hoi An in Vietnam. I had previously visited there 7 times, my husband and I have been there together for several wonderful holidays. There is something magical about the place which I find quite hard to explain whenever anyone asks me why I love it there so much. It is certainly not for everyone, I can think of a couple of people I know who would find it their kind of Hell. On the surface it is extremely hot, unbearably humid, it rains constantly for three months in the Autumn, it's dirty, smelly, full of rats, stray dogs & rubbish and the traffic is a complete nightmare. But if you make an effort with the locals, take time to drink it all in and absorb the atmosphere, it begins to get under your skin. For me, I fell in love with the place on my first visit. I have tried going to other places on holiday since but always seem to gravitate back there. You can cycle out into the peacefulness and stunning scenery of the lush green paddy fields or to visit Hoi An Old Town at night is one of the most beautiful sights you could possibly see. It is very different from anywhere I have ever visited and as far as I am concerned there is nowhere else quite like it. The food is amazing, the shopping is fabulous, there are some lovely beaches along the coast road, the accommodations are surprisingly good and it is still a relatively cheap holiday destination.

It is also currently one of the safest places on the planet to travel to - no terrorism or crimes against tourists there, (apart from being ripped off money wise if you don't haggle when making a purchase or getting completely flattened by a motorbike when crossing the road).

During my big trip I met some wonderful and interesting people (and some downright weirdo's) and had seen some incredible sights. I was away from my home, job and husband for three whole months. Also having been married three times (stop it, I know what you are thinking), I had always been too busy looking out for someone else's needs than to really think about something I would like to do. That trip was the first real taste of freedom I had experienced in my entire adult life and I absolutely loved it. It was also the first time I had ever completely pleased myself.

When I left school (a hundred years ago) going away to college or university wasn't really an option, you left school at 16 and got a job: any job. Only three people in my school year out of 150 students went off to University, nowadays everyone goes, sometimes just for the social life. Believe me, I worked at a University for 5 years and know exactly what the students get up to in their leisure time. You try talking to any of the cleaning ladies in the Halls of Residence, they could tell you a thing or two which would make your hair curl!

During my Asian sojourn I changed as a person in more ways than you can possibly imagine. I realised that you are not over the hill in your fifties, despite the horrendous changes the female body goes through. Life doesn't just finish at the big 50. I met loads of single women of all ages who were travelling on their own having a big adventure. I found that travelling solo made me utterly fearless, I now totally understand teenagers on their gap year, why they are game for anything. I felt like I was back in complete control of my own life and had a fantastic time. But boy did I pay for it when I came home, crashing back into the realities of a mundane job and sedate life in a Central Bedfordshire village.

I arrived home at the end of April and for the best part of the Spring and Summer I spent every day wishing I was back in Vietnam. I had loved the simpler life there, my beautiful house here and all our possessions didn't feel important anymore, I had befriended some of the locals and fallen totally in love with them. Having never had any children of my own, that maternal feeling was something I had never experienced before and I missed those girls so much when I came home, especially Greenie and Anna. Anna had just got married and had a baby and we were dying to see each other again.

Looking back, I think a cruel combination of the sometimes debilitating menopausal symptoms and a deep depression had me in a vicious grip for the latter part of the year. I didn't go out much, didn't talk to my friends as often and virtually stopped doing everything I used to enjoy. I looked absolutely normal on the outside but internally I was a wreck and no-one knew I was fighting with demons every day.

I stayed hidden in the house most weekends, was completely miserable and felt physically ill a lot of the time. My husband just acted like most men do and did a disappearing act, doing his own thing because he could not deal with the worsening situation at home and my complete and utter madness. If he ignored it it might go away. This in turn made me even more depressed and insular, which in turn made Peter go out on his own even more.

Crisis point between us was reached the week before Christmas which led to a very miserable Yuletide experience in our house. I couldn't be bothered to put up the tree or make any decorations or generally make any effort at all. The oven broke on Christmas Day, one hour after putting the turkey in.

I felt like that bird. Completely raw, slaughtered and stitched up.

Strangely enough this huge meltdown was the rocket up both of our arses that we possibly needed. It was either sort it out or let the menopause win and destroy a very strong 20 year marriage. Getting my husband to speak about his feelings is like pulling teeth and we had some very difficult and arduous conversations I can tell you. I threatened to beat it out of him with a big stick if he didn't talk to me. There were days when I thought I could not carry on with our marriage and wanted it all over, my thinking was that maybe I could cope with the menopause better on my own. During this time we hardly left the house and saw no-one over the festive period. In a strange way it would normally have been the perfect Christmas for us two busy people, locked in the house with just each other for company for a fortnight, but this time emotions were running high.

We managed to get through Christmas and into 2020 with a slightly fresher outlook. Peter wanted everything to go back to how it used to be instantly but that was never going to happen. This was going to take a lot of work, I just wasn't sure whether I had the energy left inside me, it was gone, all my strength had been zapped.

Thank God for my friends - you know who you are - thank you so much. Being able to cry, scream and rant in front of them, helped to get some of the pain and frustration out of my system.
Peter discussed the situation with no-one. That's men for you.

There is nothing like a bit of emotional stress to aggravate the menopausal symptoms. Hot flushes, night sweats, mood swings now tempered with floods of tears, crippling depression, anxiety about the future, sleepless nights, thumping headaches : they all ramped up with a vengeance. I could have screamed from the roof top but I am not sure anyone would have noticed. There were a few days when I could have jumped off the roof top - someone might have noticed then as they scraped me off the pavement!

Work initially helped me through, getting up in the morning, wearing something smart and putting on the warpaint, made things seem more normal. Makeup is like a mask you can hide behind and mine was getting thicker and thicker by the day, you could scrape it off with a trowel. My eyeliner was getting decidedly darker and some days I looked like a Goth. Fortunately the people in my office were a fantastic team and we still managed to have a laugh most days to lighten the emotional pressure. The only problem was that we were completely overloaded as we had taken on work for the South of the country as well as our own area and things were starting to get a bit stressful. I work in an events office and we were in effect doing half of the countries admin work, apparently on a temporary basis (yeah, I didn't believe it was going to be temporary either). At least it took my mind off of my hormonal misery during the day. By the time I got home every evening I was totally exhausted, my eyes which had been glued to a screen all day were drooping with tiredness. My bed beckoned me every night, if I could sleep I could forget about everything else. Unfortunately, as most menopausal women know, sleep doesn't come easy even when you are completely knackered. I used to pass out the minute my head hit the pillow and then be wide awake at 2am fighting with the gremlins running around in my brain until 5am when I would drop off again only to get rudely awakened by the alarm at 7am.
No wonder I was miserable, I was physically and mentally exhausted.

And Oh dear, I was disappearing for three weeks at completely the wrong time for the increasing workload.

Just a week before the Christmas saga had begun, I had booked a flight to Danang on 28th February so I could visit my friends in Vietnam. I had only been allowed to have three weeks off work, they wouldn't let me have any extended leave this year despite putting in a request, so I had to make do with the shorter time. At that point Peter didn't seem very interested in going, so I was off there on my own again.

To be absolutely honest, after the shit 8 months I had just gone through I really needed some time on my own again to rediscover ME. I had got lost somewhere in a very dark place and needed to find my way out into the sunshine again.

I thought I was being very clever going with a different airline from last year as it was the shortest flying time to get there. (Not so clever as I will relate later). It was nothing to do with the cost of the fare, with most airlines it was more or less the same price. I used to have an irrational fear of flying which seems to have recently abated (I don't seem so worried that we are going to crash anymore) but I just wanted to go the quickest route. It is such a long journey to get there, you cannot fly direct. So I settled for three hours at Heathrow, 10.5 hours flight to Hanoi, a 3 hour stopover and then a 1 hour flight to Danang - Total journey time of 17.5 hours.

So throughout a miserable but fairly mild January and February I set about shopping for gifts for my Vietnamese friends and the new baby, whose English name was La Vie. I have to say I got a lot of enjoyment out of buying those clothes and matching up the pretty little outfits. The sales were on and I bought loads of cheap clothes and toys. (Probably half of them had been made in Vietnam and I was just taking them home). I bought handbags, purses, jewellery, trinket boxes, hair slides and chocolates - lots of chocolates, for Greenie and Anna. More chocolates and sweets for Greenies children and even more for the staff at the hotel. For my friend Linh, who owns a beauty and massage parlour, I brought her industrial sized body lotions and foot scrubs.

Unfortunately all of these gifts weighed a tonne and this was the start of finding out that I wasn't very clever. This airline only let you check in 23 Kilos as opposed to 30K on the airline I had flown with last year. It was certainly starting to look as if I would only be able to take my toothbrush and a clean pair of knickers for myself.

At the end of January, Peter decided he would come out for twelve days but would fly with a different airline that allowed a bit more luggage weight. So problem solved, I packed up a massive suitcase for him stuffed full of all the goodies I had purchased, along with a few paltry items of clothing for him, which weighed in at 29.5 kilo's. In my own 23 Kilo suitcase I managed to pack all of my clothes, toiletries, shoes and a few little presents for the girls and new baby. That seemed completely fair to me.

Because I had stopped going out for such a long time I had recently returned to aerobic classes in January with my much younger and beautiful friend Rachel, something I always used to enjoy. Maybe not the best thing to do with dodgy knees and hips at my age, a gentle pilates class might have been better in retrospect. I did take it very gently to begin with, but on only the second class I felt something snap in my right knee. Because I ended up walking a bit lopsided, overcompensating on my left side, I then hurt my lower back. For six weeks I was hobbling around wearing a very sexy knee brace - NOT. Going downstairs was pure agony, just getting out of bed in the morning was a physical feat.

Talk about feel my age, my body was slowly falling to pieces. All my joints constantly grated and ached, nothing seemed to work properly anymore. Combined with the constant change in body temperature, I think my body was what you might describe as TOTALLY KNACKERED. I would never have got through a MOT. I only mention this because I did not go to the Doctors about the knee pain after being given no help whatsoever with my menopause at the GP's, I just could not be bothered with them. I realised I had left it too late to get any proper pain killers and sitting cramped in an airplane for 10.5 hours was going to be awkward and uncomfortable to say the least.

In the meantime something called the Covid 19 virus was circulating around Asia having been spread from China allegedly after someone ate a bat. People were dying and whole cities had gone into Lockdown. Considering the Chinese eat every type of animal on the planet, I was surprised they hadn't poisoned themselves before.

There had been a few cases of the virus in Northern Vietnam but the authorities there had immediately sealed all the borders and it looked liked it had been contained. All incoming flights from China and Korea had been cancelled, which meant that Hoi An would not be sinking under the usual heavy weight of tourists. You would be able to walk around the Ancient Town without millions of people jabbing their selfie sticks in your face, spitting on your feet and generally getting in the way.

So on 28th February, with the Coronavirus merely a tiny speck on my horizon, I naively set off for Vietnam.

I don't entirely approve of some of the things I have done, or I am, or I have been, but God knows I'm me - Liz Taylor

2. Vietnam Re-visited 2020

Friday 28th February 2020

I arrived at Heathrow Airport at 7.30am. Everything was extremely
quiet with only a few people milling around, which considering this is
one of the busiest airports in the world should have told me something.
But no, nothing had registered with my soft marshmallow brain at that
point, I was so desperate to get to Vietnam to see my friends I would
have leapt through a ring of fire, eaten a live hamster, swallowed a
sword or crawled across a bed of nails - naked.
Peter and I are sitting having coffee in Cafe Nero after having checked
me in, where there are a handful of people wearing face masks which
seemed a novel way of eating their breakfast.

The young chap on the check in desk has given me an interesting and
annoying piece of information. Apparently when I arrive in Hanoi, I
have to collect my luggage, clear Immigration, change terminals and
check in again for my ongoing flight. I don't understand this as I have a
ticket, two boarding passes and am checked through all the way to
Danang. This never happens with other airlines, you check in and meet
your luggage again only at your final destination.
This happened to me last year when I flew from Luang Prabang to
Danang and it was a complete pain in the arse. I assumed it was because
I flew into Vietnam with one company and had to change airlines to fly
onward to Danang. This time I am going all the way with the same
company and thought I would not have any of this hassle. The young
man confidently assures me that there is a free service at Hanoi
International Terminal to take my baggage to the Domestic Terminal so
I do not have to lug it onto a bus like I did last year. Partially mollified,
I accept the situation but was beginning to realise I definitely had not
been very clever flying this route.

When it comes to the time to say goodbye to Peter, it is a difficult and
emotional moment. I am so excited, I can't wait to go, but it has been
such an awful time and I am leaving him behind again. But let's face it,
it is only a week until he joins me, I think we can survive the short
separation. There are a few tears from us both, then he is gone and I am
alone in the security queue. As is quite usual for me I set off the alarms
and have to suffer the indignity of being frisked by a very thorough

young lady who felt up all my female parts in full public view. On any other day I might have enjoyed it!
I also forget to pick up my iPad and nearly leave without it. There must be a simpler system of checking passengers luggage than basically making you empty your bags, pockets and half undressing in public.

Once I make my escape from the security scrum there is nothing notably unusual about Terminal 4 today, maybe there are a few less people around but everything is open for business. All the designer shops with their smartly dressed sales people are trying to entice me in. I always think that Heathrow shopkeepers look like they are dressed by '*Armani*'. I am kitted out entirely in M&S from head to toe and have no interest whatsoever in £300 shirts or £2500 handbags. I sit myself down, where I can keep an eye on the departures screen, waiting for my gate to show up. Previously at this time I would be getting myself in a complete stew about the journey. I always feel sick, nervous and terrified before any flight, I always convince myself that this time I am definitely going to die. But since last years trip this terror has disappeared, I still don't enjoy flying but I am not so worried or tense anymore. Today I just want to get it all over with and feel quite relaxed. I managed to log on to Heathrow's Wi-fi and play games on my iPad. That shows just how far I have come in the last year, that I can sit in an airport lounge and lose myself in something else other than my sheer panic about the journey ahead of me.
It also proves that the small lump of tumble dryer fluff that has replaced my once active brain can handle a small piece of technology.

My gate is called and I take the 3 mile walk to get there. There is quite a crowd of passengers milling around and I do a quick head count, around 350. That can't be right, we are going on a Dreamliner, it only holds 280 people. I realise that half the passengers are going to Russia and have sat in the wrong seats. They all suddenly disappear in a bit of a flurry and there are about 130 of us left. The flight is called and we are loaded in record time. I am in the back row and Yippee, have it all to myself. I wipe down all my seats, screens and use my hand gel before I get comfortable (this is quite a usual thing for me to do on any flight). Looking around the cabin, the plane is half empty, it is pretty much all Westerners with very few Vietnamese. You can easily spot the Viets as they are all wearing face masks which again is quite usual for them. So far everything seems perfectly normal.

Everyone settles into their seats, we have all watched the funny little cartoons that make up the safety briefing and the enormous plane takes off bang on time. There is very little engine noise as we go up and because the plane is so big it doesn't bounce around much on take off. I am a little bit tense to begin with but as soon as the seat belt sign goes off I relax and put my feet up. It takes the crew a little bit of time to get organised and we do not get a head set until 30 minutes into the flight and it is 2 hours before we get a drink or anything to eat. But it is quiet with no screaming babies, uncrowded and I can stretch my painful knee out and lay down.

The first time I flew with this particular airline was 7 years ago and it was a truly awful experience. This time the plane is shiny and new, the service is much better, the food is edible and the TV screens work properly with a massive selection of entertainment. Last time they only had 6 English speaking films played on a crackly loop, so if you went to the toilet you missed part of the film and I was never sure exactly what the food was as it was unrecognisable and stone cold, you really needed to take a packed lunch with you.

I have never been on a Dreamliner before, it was a new experience. It has big windows with no shades, there is a button where you can change the colour of the glass in the window, so you can pretend it is dusk or dawn, whichever time zone you want to get into. As it was only 11am when we took off I wanted daylight for a bit longer but most of the passenger changed theirs to dark and immediately fell asleep. How do they do that? What drugs have they taken that makes a person who has only been out of bed for a few hours fall instantly asleep the minute we leave the ground? And more importantly, where can I get some of those substances? It is always a mystery to me how anyone can sleep bolt upright in an uncomfortable seat with the noise of a jet engine roaring in their ears.

Thoroughly relaxed, I trawl through the films and come across "Hustlers'. Now I am not a big fan of Jennifer Lopez, I think she should stick to singing and dancing and give the acting a miss. But she is amazing in this film not for her acting skills but for her body and pole dancing ability. My jaw dropped open when she did the splits and bounced up and down in a very suggestive way, showing her shapely arse in all of it's perfect glory covered by a tiny white thong. I was in total awe of her; she is 50 years old and looks utterly amazing. I do wonder how she will cope with the misery of the menopause? Or do beautiful and famous people not suffer from it?
I must have dozed off at some point, probably exhausted from watching all the bumping and grinding, as I woke up as the film was finishing and had missed most of the story.

Saturday 29th February

I switched the screen off and miracle of miracles went to sleep for three hours - probably helped by the two gin and tonics and two bottles of red wine consumed with my pasta dinner. This never happens to me and it shows how calm and relaxed I was at this stage, when I woke up we were over half way there. I watched another film called *'Knives Out'* which had the normally gorgeous Daniel Craig speaking in the strangest American accent in the starring role. I then selected the Oscar winning *'Parasite'*. Now I don't know about you but most of the Oscar winning films that I have ever watched are complete rubbish in my opinion. Three times I have tried to watch *'La La Land'* and have never got past the first 10 minutes before I fell asleep. As this film was Korean with subtitles, I didn't hold out much hope for it. But as I had nothing else to do I decided to see what all the Hollywood hype was about.
What a strange film, it was surprisingly entertaining if a bit weird. There were obviously Korean jokes in there which us Westerners do not understand but it was very amusing. I was still watching it as we started to descend into Hanoi when the crew abruptly switched all the screens off, so I missed yet another film ending. A lot of airlines let you watch the TV right up until you arrive at the gate but not this one apparently; there's probably a law against it. But hooray we were there and half an hour early.

It was still dark outside but as we taxied off the runway what was very noticeable was the amount of aircraft parked up. Now I know what you are thinking - it is an airport, there should be airplanes around. But there were lots and lots of planes sitting around in total darkness, nothing seemed to be leaving or being prepared for flight and there seemed to be very few ground staff around. Hanoi International Airport was a bit of a ghost town. Maybe it was because it was 4.30am and we were early.

You can tell at this point I was being very naive, I was in Asia now and this was where the Coronavirus had originated.

As we left the aircraft there were eerily gowned and masked staff assessing the body temperature of all arriving passengers. Oh shit, my body temperature regularly runs on boiling hot, what if I have a hot flush and it sets off all the alarms!! Fortunately they did not pick up any signs of global warming coming from myself and I was allowed into the Immigration Hall. Some poor woman off of the plane, who's face was glowing bright red, got pulled out of the passport control line and was escorted off somewhere by a uniformed official. I don't know where they took her but I never saw her at the luggage carousel nor did I see her leave the airport.

It doesn't matter into what country in the world you arrive, there are never enough officers in Immigration and this morning was no exception. It drives me nuts that after any long flight you then have to wait ages to get through passport control. Only two booths were open, so the half hour we had gained on the flight was then lost standing in a queue waiting for some stoney faced Immigration officer to give you admittance to their country.
Of course, some people had not arranged their Visa's in the UK and were in the wrong line and were marched off somewhere else to get in a different queue. Come on people pay attention, this is a Communist country, they are very officious and have a strict system for everything. You cannot do a shortcut if you get in the wrong line, you have to be in the correct one. I am not at my best early in the morning and with airports not being my favourite place I do get a bit ratty with stupid people who don't read the signs and then hold all the organised people (me) up.
With my visa supposedly checked and stamped I was allowed entry into Vietnam.

I met up with my luggage : always a big relief. We were the only aircraft in and it was already going round on the conveyer as I descended the escalator from Immigration. I can always spot my bags from across any airport, they are bright orange for exactly that purpose. I wandered around the Arrivals Terminal looking for the imaginary baggage service to get to the Domestic Terminal. I could see most of the Westerners off of my plane were in tour groups and were being directed to their transportation by the local guides. Outside of the terminal there was no-one: no buses, no taxi's, no people and definitely no baggage service - I was on my own. Fortunately as I had received some experience of Hanoi airport during my adventure last year, I knew that somewhere there was a free bus which went to the Domestic Terminal. So I set off dragging my luggage to locate the bus stop as I could vaguely remember where it was.

So there I am at the roadside, completely alone in the darkness at 5.30am, waiting for a bus that may or may not arrive. I kid you not, Noi Bai, Vietnams Capital City International airport was totally deserted and it was a bit spooky.

After about 10 minutes, a young man joined me in the queue along with two elderly English women (who didn't have a clue what they were doing or where they were going). Hurrah, twenty minutes later a bus turned up. Thank God for the strong young man. These user un-friendly buses have three narrow steps, which are each 1 foot high and 1 foot wide, trying to get up them with a large heavy suitcase whilst gripping your hand luggage is no mean feat, and you need Herculean strength. The young man was put to good use by us wimpy females, bless him. The driver set off like he was on a race track, the suitcases toppled over and were sliding around on the floor, one false move with the door and they would go flying out into the road.

Arriving shaken and stirred at the Domestic Terminal, the lights were on and there were more positive signs of life, mainly Vietnamese passengers with a smaller sprinkling of Westerners. All the Vietnamese (without exception) were wearing masks and rubber gloves. I felt a bit left out so I used my hand gel copiously to show willing.

Now as I said before I have had dealings with Hanoi airport before, it's not your usual system. At the Domestic Terminal they only show flights up on the board two hours before they depart, so my flight, which was allegedly at 8 am, was not showing yet. I found the airline customer services help desk and asked if I would need to go through a full check in or just through the luggage drop. The very bored and unhelpful customer service lady (I am sure she was the same one from last year) informed me I could drop my luggage at any desk and waved me in the vague direction of the check in area.

Was this a good idea I asked myself, but I really needed to get rid of my suitcase, so I wandered over. Yes, they could check in my luggage to Danang despite my flight not showing on the departures board yet and promised me faithfully that it would end up on the correct flight. Fingers crossed, I handed my suitcase over to them, wondering if I would ever see it again. I checked the luggage tags, yes they said Danang, there was hope that it would be put on the correct aircraft. As I already had a boarding pass and there was nothing else to do, I skipped off to the departure lounge. Yes I could actually skip now that I didn't have to drag my suitcase around.

The Vietnamese security experience was more long winded than Heathrow but without the getting touched up bit! I had to take off all of my jewellery, shoes & belt, the iPad and phone had to go through separately. In the end I had four trays to collect at the end of the conveyor, you know what it's like - such a faff, making sure you have everything. It's hard enough remembering to take my lunch to work let alone trying to remember what went in what tray and whether it all has come out of the X-ray machine.

Fully dressed and with all of my possessions in tact, I wandered off to find myself a seat and wait for my flight gate to appear on the departures board. The airport is new, very shiny and a bit tacky if you get my drift, a bit like cheap tinsel on a Christmas tree. Most of the shops in Domestic are of Vietnamese origin and sell some very odd things that I cannot imagine that anyone would want, as well as the ubiquitous duty free shops.

I asked a young waiter if he would help hook me up with the free Wi-fi. Oh he was so bored with my request, rolled his eyes and I could tell what he was thinking. Well it's not my fault I can't read Vietnamese. With the Wi-fi connected I plonked myself down in an uncomfortable red plastic seat, turned the iPad on and played a few games whilst I waited and waited. My flight details at last came up on the departure board and then disappeared again immediately. It then came up with a new time and disappeared yet again. Eventually it came up with another new time. I am sure this airline just make it up as they go along, it is like playing airport bingo.

There were only about 40 people at the Gate when they finally started to load us, so I was thinking that the flight must be empty. But oh no, the flight suddenly filled up with Vietnamese families, all rushing so as not to miss the plane, dragging all their bags through the cabin and generally faffing around looking for their seats. You could enter the plane at both ends and it seemed like the people seated in the front had got on through the back and vice versa, complete chaos. I shut my eyes and did a bit of deep breathing. I can now cope with the big planes but the smaller ones still leave me a little bit trembly. I had completely lost count of how late we were running and just hoped my driver would still be waiting for me at the other end.

Seat belts on, trays folded away, head rests up, emergency exits pointed out, we bombed off down the runway and finally parted company with Hanoi airport.

I spent so long in this airport last year I had thought about applying for Vietnamese citizenship.

Mental note to self - DO NOT DO THIS ROUTE AGAIN.

At least it was a smooth flight and only lasted 1 hour. As we hit the runway with a massive bang at Danang I felt an enormous sense that I had come home.

Because I had already cleared immigration at Hanoi, I was out of the airport and into the warm sunshine within 25 minutes of landing. Unfortunately there was no driver or car waiting. I was not staying in the same superb hotel as last year, as all the staff there had been laid off whilst they had a refurb and all found other jobs. So Greenie had booked me into the hotel she was currently working in. On the Internet it said is was a 4 Star, it looked OK on the website and she had done me a deal at £23 per night including breakfast, which seemed very reasonable. She had also been in charge of organising a car for me of which there was no sign.

Arrival halls in foreign airports are always a bit bewildering and Danang is no exception. There were lots of drivers shouting and waving hotel signs at me but there was nothing with my name on. I wandered around for five minutes but could not see anyone, I was just heading for the taxi rank when a young man came running up to me waving a sign with my name. It turns out that as the flight had been delayed he had been having a crafty sleep in the car and missed my arrival.

Loaded into the hotel 4x4 car, we set off into the perilous traffic of Danang City. But hold on wait a minute, it wasn't that bad. There did not seem to be as many vehicles on the roads, maybe because it was lunchtime.

Driving along the coast road, I could see all the unfinished hotels and apartment blocks that were going up last year. There is a huge amount of foreign investment along this bit of the coast. That was strange, some of them looked like they had been abandoned and there were no workers on site. We drove past the enormous finished Ving Pearl resort that is always full of Chinese and I could not see a single person around. The casino car park next door was also completely empty, it is always full even in the middle of the day. This was obviously the result of the Chinese and Korean guests staying away - it suddenly dawned on me that they are the main source of income for this part of Vietnam and the locals will suffer if they have no Asian visitors. So this Covid 19 thing could still have serious consequences for the Vietnamese people despite the authorities managing to keep the disease at bay.

You can tell at this point, I was still away with the fairies, elves and pixies, it had still not hit me how serious this could be for everyone. But at that time I don't think anyone on the planet could have predicted how the Coronavirus crisis would all unfold.

Putting all of this niggling apprehension to the back of my mind, I settled back in my seat, I felt OK not too jet lagged, I was just so glad to be here again.

We pulled up outside the hotel and a very sweet young man called Jimmy took my luggage and a cute girl called "Puca (I know, strange name, apparently it's something to do with Pokemon) checked me in. All of the reception staff were wearing masks and looked like they were about to go into surgery. I was informed by Puca that I was a very special guest and they had been told to look after me by Greenie who would be in later on.

Well that was all very nice, until I saw my bedroom. Now there wasn't anything actually wrong with it, it was just a bit on the small side. Last year I had a beautiful big room with a lovely view and gorgeous bathroom. This 'sea view' room looked out over a scruffy road, I could just about make out the sea over the top of the trees. The bathroom consisted of a toilet, sink and a shower head, what you would probably call a wet room. I couldn't see how the water would not make it's way into the bedroom every time I had a shower as there was no barrier to stop it and I would be slipping around on the wet floor. Water on shiny ceramic tiles is an absolutely lethal combination (it's only when you get older that this sort of thing even crosses your mind). The room looked clean enough but it was just a bit bland and boring. There are some gorgeous hotels here for around the same price and this was a bit of a disappointment. It would probably be OK for me but I couldn't see how Peter was going to be able to fit in there as well.

As it was Greenies choice, I didn't want to make a fuss and upset her, so I unpacked everything, got changed and headed for the beach.

Downstairs I bumped into the hotel manager who also used to work at last years hotel, he gave me a big hug and welcomed me back. He also told me I was a special guest and the staff had been instructed to look after me. Slightly mollified by the fact that the hotel would make up for in service what they lost out on the bedrooms, I walked up to Cua Dai beach.

Now Cua Dai beach is a complete mess. Anyone who does their homework in advance of coming here should know this. Unfortunately my hotel's website shows a funky beach club and pristine white sandy beach, unfortunately this is 2 miles away and not across the road as the site leads you to believe. Greenie says that guests are always complaining about the state of the local beach and to be honest I can see their point. I have advised her to get the management to take those photos off the Internet but they haven't, so they constantly get complaints all the time about the state of the beach across the road. It is not the fault of the hotel that the Winter Typhoons have destroyed the beaches along Cua Dai, but they are slightly misleading visitors with the pretty photographs on their website.

The first thing that strikes me as I walk up to the beach is how few people and vehicles are around. It's Saturday afternoon and usually the beach is full of local families enjoying their day off. There are a few people splashing around amongst the enormous green slimy sandbags that are trying to keep the sea at bay and failing miserably. Further up the beach I can see some black plastic bundles sitting like enormous rocks on the beach and an abandoned crane.

It is a complete eyesore. Last year there was still a little bit of beach left with a few umbrellas but I can see that it has completely gone and been washed away. There are a few sun beds perched up on the top of a bank of cement bags covered in astro turf, very classy, so I pick one of those and sit myself down. The minute my bum touches the canvas a tiny lady appears from nowhere and charges me 50,000 Dong (£1.75) for using her bed. It looks like I am her only customer, there is no-one else around. Now is it because the tourists are avoiding this ugly beach and have gone further up the road or is there something else going on? It is all too much for my tiny brain to process at that exact moment and tiredness overwhelms me, after slathering myself in Factor 30 sun screen, I immediately doze off.

When I wake up two hours later, the sun has lost it's heat and I feel distinctly chilly. Not a normal sensation for me! Looking around there are now a lot more locals on the scruffy beach, a group of kids are running around in the surf, the DIY restaurants have turned up on the back of motorbikes and the restauranteurs are laying out their plastic furniture for evening dinner. All perfectly normal.

I decide to head back to the hotel as the sun is starting to go down and the mosquito's will be out in their zillions. As I am ambling along trying to avoid breaking my ankle on the broken and uneven pavement, I hear a loud wolf whistle. I completely ignore it, I know it can't possibly be aimed at me until I hear someone shout my name. Looking around, I see a short bald bloke wearing a huge grin riding a rickety bicycle towards me. OMG talk about a coincidence, it's Danny from last year. I met him in a local bar and we got drunk together several times and even went out for lunch on my birthday. I was going to message him to see if he was still here, he was working at a huge building project just outside of town and obviously is. He's in a bit of a rush as he has a massage booked, so we agree to meet for a drink on Sunday afternoon down in the Old Town.

When I get back to the hotel I find my friend Eric working on reception and wrap him up in a huge bear hug. He has filled out in the last year and I can see he has also had a proper haircut, he must have stopped letting his mum cut it around a pudding basin. I can't see Greenie but Eric says he will take me up to the Spa where she is on shift.

I walk into the fragrant coconut and lemongrass smelling spa and Greenie spots me. She comes flying over and launches herself into my arms crying her eyes out. It all gets a bit emotional and I can see Eric rolling his eyes, like all men do whenever women are overcome with tears. She is completely overwrought, sobbing her heart out and is hanging on to me for dear life.
Once she calms down, we yak away ten to the dozen whilst poor Eric slips unnoticed out of the door. I give her the handbag stuffed full of the little bits and pieces I bought for her. She says thank you without really looking at it and puts it to one side. Now I learnt last year that this is normal behaviour for the Vietnamese, they don't usually show emotion and rarely say thank you. This doesn't mean they are not grateful, it's just that they express themselves differently from us.

She informs me that reception have given me the wrong bedroom, she had chosen my room but the previous guests had not checked out when I arrived so they gave me another room to have a rest in whilst they got it ready. I wish reception had explained that earlier as I have totally unpacked all my luggage. She goes off to get the key and we move my stuff to the other room, fortunately it is on the same floor. This room is much better and lighter, still a bit on the small side but does have a much bigger bathroom with a bath and separate shower. Unfortunately the curtains and cushions are a bit grubby and the nets have moth holes in them. There is also something splashed up the wall by the bin which hasn't been cleaned up properly. But the good thing is that it is away from the lifts and stairs so hopefully will be quiet.

I decide to have a bath, which turns out to be a never repeated experience as I don't think I will live that long. The bath is one solid piece of marble and was enormous. God knows how the builders got that up the stairs, it would not have fitted in the lift. Unfortunately it took 45 minutes to fill it up a quarter of the way, when I gave up waiting and got in anyway. I can barely immerse myself under the water and it is a disappointing experience, but at least I feel like I have washed away some of the jet lag. I rang Peter and his mother, Maureen, to let them know I had arrived safely and then went downstairs in search of some dinner.

As I leave the hotel to find a restaurant, I am asked three separate times by Greenie, Eric and Jimmy where I am going. This is quite normal behaviour for Vietnamese hotel staff, they always want to know where you have been, where you are going and what you have been doing. I do wonder if it's because they need to know in case the authorities ask about their guests, they do have to keep your passports and register you with the police, but it's probably just because they are being nosy.

I walk along the beach road and go into The Blue Wave Restaurant. Peter and I have eaten here before and I know the food is good. There is a whole line of shops, massage parlours and restaurants along here and they are all open, but most of them have very few customers. There are some people wandering around but it's not what you would call buzzing for a Saturday night.
I have a mango and prawn salad, followed by crispy prawns and three bottles of La Rue Beer. I always know I have arrived in Vietnam when I drink my first La Rue. Unfortunately I am not used to drinking beer, I normally drink wine, and along with the jet lag, it goes straight to my head. I feel a bit tipsy when I leave the place and struggle to walk in a straight line along the cracked pavement in the pitch dark. I safely arrive back at the hotel without breaking any bones and with a chorus of 'where have you been' from the reception staff I make for my bed and crash out in my freezing cold air conditioned bedroom.

Sunday 1st March

Next morning, after a really decent nights sleep with only a couple of sweaty moments, I am awoken by the sound of children screaming. Oh goody, just what I need. I am up on the top floor but the acoustics are obviously very good as I can hear the kids at the swimming pool crystal clear and the sound of chinking plates and cups coming from the restaurant three floors below me.

After the rude awakening I arise refreshed and excited, ready for whatever the day will throw at me. It's a good thing as Greenie is picking me up at 10am on her motorbike to take me to Anna's house. If you have ever been on the back of a motor bike you will know the exhilarating feeling. Peter has two big powerful Indian motor cycles and I am used to riding pillion and usually feel quite safe. In fact I feel safer

on the bike than in the car when he is driving, on the bike he can't eat a sandwich, send a text or pet the dog, but going on a motorbike in Vietnam is a completely different ball game. The traffic is total chaos and the bikes do not stop for anyone or anything - we will either kill or be killed!
Just what I need for my first morning here! Break me in gently why not?

Breakfast is a bit mediocre and by the time I get into the restaurant (I am always last for breakfast) most of the buffet is empty, which is odd as breakfast doesn't officially finish until 10.30 and it's only 9.30 now. I ask for an omelette with everything except meat and get one containing nothing but ham. I eat it anyway, I am not a vegetarian, I just don't like the taste and texture of meat, especially roast meat, but I will eat a bacon sandwich. I especially do not eat meat in foreign countries and instantly become a vegetarian whenever I go abroad.
The staff are pleasant enough though and are all wearing face masks and gloves. My waitress is called Angel and is very sweet but doesn't speak much English, not that I would be able to hear her speaking much from underneath the mask. The tea is like gnats pee, served in tiny cups no bigger than a thimble - I end up having four cups which hardly touch the sides. I must remember to bring my own tea bags down tomorrow and buy a proper mug in town.

I am not sure what to wear to Anna's house, having never been there before. Do I go casual or smart? It's all a bit of an odd situation with her. She had the baby on November 4th and she has not left the house yet, Anna has only been out a couple of times since then as well. She is back living at her parents house having moved out of her in-laws when she gave birth. There has been no mention of the husband for months, so I am a bit baffled by it all. Some of her messages do get a bit lost in translation so hopefully today I will find out what is going on.
I finally decide on an outfit of long shorts, a smart T-shirt and flip flops, the normal safety apparel for riding on the back of a motorbike!

Greenie turns up wearing a floaty dress and sandals with her two year old daughter, Kitty, in tow. Kitty stands in the footwell holding onto the handle bars whilst I hoist my big arse onto the back. Fortunately I have brought a cycle helmet with me to use as a crash helmet, it might offer some protection if I fall off. I am clutching my handbag and a large gift bag for Anna, so it's a bit difficult to hold on to anything. Once balanced we set off. It's a lovely day, sunny but not too hot. Once we get nearer the town everything looks perfectly normal, there are lots of people around and the roads are busy with motorbikes and bicycles, but not with buses or coaches. It was normally a small miracle that you did not get mowed down by a tour bus on the Cua Dai road. Last year there were hundreds of them thundering up and down, day and night, now there appears to only be a few small hotel shuttle buses around.

We turn off the main road and head out of town. I think I know the Old Town pretty well, but we are now in the suburbs and I am totally lost. There is a local market on and Greenie weaves in and out of the stalls that are selling just about everything, it is complete chaos and I love the frenetic atmosphere. You can't go faster than five miles an hour so I am not afraid of falling off or having an accident. Good thing really. We pull up on a busy street and Greenie rings Anna as she isn't quite sure which house it is. I swing my leg over and notice that the the motorbike rises up considerably without my hefty weight on the back suspension. I look down the road and spot Anna waving frantically at me, I can't hold back any longer, I run down the road (not a pretty sight at my age) and sweep her tiny frame up into my arms. She starts sobbing uncontrollably and it takes a few minutes for her to stop crying and breathe properly, I am literally holding her up she is so distraught. She had a terrible time with the birth, an emergency caesarian, problems with breast feeding, the baby had to go back to hospital with several infections and I feel that she hasn't been able to talk to anyone about it, (and where is the husband??). The Vietnamese don't do emotions very well and I know from her messages and phone calls that she needs to talk about her experience and this is obviously the first time she has properly let it all out.
What is it with me and these girls? I am standing in a busy street, in the middle of I do not know where, clutching a tiny dark haired girl (who looks a bit like a smaller version of Thelma from Scooby Do), who is wearing a strange outfit of Blue Kitty pyjamas both bawling our eyes out. We are then joined by Greenie who joins in as well!! What a enormous surge of hormones!

Eventually everyone calms down and after slipping our shoes off, we enter Anna's parents house. It is quite big and apparently is three houses joined together, a huge extended family all live there. It looks like most Vietnamese houses: as if it is not quite finished, covered in mildew and could do with a coat of paint. The walls are not painted and are just raw plaster and there is a plain concrete floor in the room we sit in. There is not much luxury here despite the size, apart from the obligatory flat screen TV that all the Vietnamese seem to have. They might not have many possessions but they all have a colour TV in their homes. There is not much furniture and I end up perched on a tiny metal stool with my bum cheeks hanging over each side, whilst Anna & Greenie sit on the ornate wooden sofa. The baby is laying quietly in a bamboo crib, she is gorgeous with long black sticky up hair and huge dark eyes.

Now Anna has calmed down the first words out of her mouth are: 'Jan, why have you got so fat?'
Thanks Anna, I know I have put on a stone in weight since they last saw me, but I am not quite Billy Bunter yet. When they met me last year I had been travelling for a month, eating no rubbish and the pounds had fallen off. I was much thinner then, now I am probably back to my normal weight. I don't take offence, I know she doesn't mean it like it sounds. She probably doesn't know the English for ' You have put on a few pounds but it really suits you'.
She shows me her hand and fingers which are bent at a funny angle, a bit like my mothers hands which are riddled with arthritis. She says it happened after La Vie's birth and she is due to have an operation in the next few weeks to correct it. I have never heard of giving birth causing problems with hands and fingers, it is very odd.

Greenie and Anna chat ten to the dozen, they stop after each sentence and translate into English so I know what they have been saying. Anna has not spoken English to anyone except me since last August so Greenie does most of the translating. The subject of husbands comes up. Greenie says she hopes that one day she will have another baby with a new husband and I can be grandma to it. She pays for everything in her house and her husband gambles most of his wages, I get the feeling all is not quite right in their relationship. Anna says she has her daughter now and that is all that matters to her. Obviously husbands are not too popular around here. I get no further information but can tell that something is not quite right with either of their marriages.

I hand Anna the gift bag, which she takes from me without a word of thanks and puts to one side - I know it's odd behaviour but I am used to it by now.
We are then joined by Anna's grandmother. She cannot be that old, I would estimate around 75, but I kid you not she looks like an ancient Egyptian mummy that has just been dug up. The dead Pharaohs in the British Museum look healthier than she does. Dry wrinkled crispy brown skin is literally hanging off of her tiny skeleton. Anna's mother then joins us, she is preserved a little bit better, bearing in mind she is probably about my age or even younger, she looks at least 25 years older than me. The grandmother vividly remembers the American war

and they have both had a very hard life, constantly working outside in the strong sun and humidity, no wonder they look a bit weather beaten and their skin is the texture of my bikers jacket.

I whip up the courage and ask Anna if I can hold La Vie, I am literally dying to get my hands on her. My friends would all laugh like mad if they saw me, I'm not normally over keen on children at the best of times, as I always say; I definitely couldn't eat a whole one. We make eye contact and she stares at me fearlessly with the biggest brown eyes, she doesn't cry but she doesn't smile either when I hoist her into my arms. This seems to be the norm for Vietnamese children, Greenie's daughter Kitty doesn't smile much either, mind you at this moment she has her face full of sweets that Anna's grandmother keeps feeding her. I ask Anna what La Vie's Vietnamese name is. It's a complete mouthful and the only bit of it that I can get my tongue around is the last bit - Dang.

There now follows a photo session of epic proportions:
 Me with La Vie.
Anna with La Vie.
Greenie and Anna
Greenie and Anna with La Vie and Kitty
Grandmother with La Vie
Me with Anna
Me with Greenie
Me with Greenie and Anna
The Vietnamese also love a selfie so both girls take pics of themselves as well. It's exhausting, all that posing but they love it.

Grandmother and mother then cart La Vie off to bed and I am left with the girls and Kitty. Kitty is an intriguing child, she won't make eye contact with me and is very serious, Greenie says she is not a good mixer. No kidding.
 Greenie suggests Anna opens my gifts. They lay all the baby clothes out and coo over the dresses and outfits. Anna says it is all so much, but I can see she is chuffed to bits with it all and the handbag and other trinkets. Thinking about it, there was only about £50 worth of stuff there but of course that is a months wages out here and she is a bit overwhelmed by it all. Probably no-one has ever given her so much at one time. It really brings home the huge financial difference between them and us. £50 is nothing to us Westerners, I pay that for a haircut, but it's an enormous amount to them.

Kitty starts getting a bit fractious and Greenie says she needs her nap so we decide it is time to leave. It's been lovely seeing Anna and I feel more contented than I have done in a long time. I know what you are thinking but I cannot easily explain how I feel about those girls - I don't understand it myself. Anna seems OK apart from the dodgy hand, maybe a little fragile but my mind is put at rest, at least she is staying with her family and not with the invisible husband's.

We get back on the bike and Kitty immediately falls asleep standing up with her head resting on the speedo!!! On the way back we divert off to Greenie's house so she can put Kitty to bed. We pull into the yard of a very big house which I have cycled past loads of times, I never knew she lived here. She lifts Kitty off and takes her inside whilst I have a look around the large scruffy garden. There are some enormous colourful cockerels in cages dotted around, apparently Greenies husband breeds them for gambling and cockfighting. Hmm, I am beginning to see why she moans about him all the time. She comes out of the house really furious, he has gone out and she has no idea where he is, he was supposed to be looking after the children but has left his elderly mother to do it. We get back on the bike and she delivers me safely back to the hotel whilst she goes off in a fluster to sort out her domestic issues.

I get changed and crash out by the pool for a couple of hours before I go into town. I promptly fall asleep the minute I lay down in the warm sunshine. I have to say the weather feels perfect, the humidity seems very low at the moment and I am coping with the heat really well. I only had a few hot flushes during the night and all my aches and pains have already eased after just one day; maybe it's because I am more relaxed than I have been for months. Last year the humidity here went through the roof and I could not control my thermostat some days. I tell you, it's very tiring to keep changing temperature all the time, it wears you out.

I get showered and changed and jump in a taxi to go into town. All the staff want to know where I am going as usual. I tell them I am going for a pizza, this seems to placate them and I think I get away without a full detailed report going to Greenie.

When I get dropped off in town, I change up some Sterling into Vietnamese Dong and for a few hours I am a millionaire as I have 2,000,000 dong in my bag (about £70). I wander off through town to find the wine bar where I am meeting Danny. I went in here quite a few times last year, it is in a hidden place, you would never know it was there (if you didn't know) and is never packed out. I go in - the place is completely empty and I am the only customer, mind you it is a bit early. I sit myself down and order a glass of red. This bar is one of the few places you can get a decent glass of wine for a reasonable price in the Old Town. A glass of Chilean Merlot is about £3 in here as opposed to a glass of the local brew which tastes like lighter fuel but only costs £1.00.

I sit on a very low squashy sofa (which I know I won't be able to get up from easily) watching the world go by from the veranda. Nothing seems to have changed down here in the market, everyone is still hustling, especially the older women selling their fruit and veg and the motor bikes are causing havoc as usual.

There is a particular smell about this place, an interesting and eye watering combination of petrol fumes, rotting veg, cooked food, sewer drains and heat. Sometimes when I am at home, I occasionally catch a whiff of something and if I shut my eyes I can transport myself right back here to this exact spot.

Danny eventually turns up 15 minutes late and makes a big entrance with the staff, he is also drunk as a lord. He has been drinking in town since 10am and is completely plastered. I give him a big hug and a peck on the cheek, he holds onto me a bit too long, or it could just be that I am holding him up. Oh dear this is going to be an interesting afternoon!!

He is completely dishevelled, unshaven and is so drunk he can't sit up straight and ends up half laying on the sofa with his feet on the table. The bar owner doesn't seem to mind, I think Danny's custom keeps his business financially viable. We do manage to catch up with some of each others lives over the next two hours, interspersed with Danny periodically sliding off of the sofa onto the floor.

As it turns out his brother and elderly parents are arriving the same day as Peter, blimey he will have to rein himself in for a few weeks and behave himself. When I met him last year he had been here for about six months and was absolutely loving it, living his best life. Now I detect a much more cynical view of the place and I can tell he is fed up with dealing with the locals, especially from a business point of view. He keeps telling me not to get too involved with the girls and to tell Anna and Greenie to mind their own business as to where I am going or what am doing.

Around 6pm I suggests he goes home to bed as by now he was talking complete bollocks and I really needed to eat something after the wine. I

wander off through the market, noticing with amusement that he had come on his bicycle. I stand and watch him amusedly as he wobbles unsteadily up the road, weaving in and out of the motorbikes.
I hope he falls off and breaks something.

I wandered through the pretty narrow streets of the town, it does seems very quiet. Normally at this time of night there would be huge groups of Chinese and Korean tourists being shown around the town or taking lantern boat trips up and down the river. All the restaurants, bars and shops are open and there are a few boats still operating, it is actually very pleasant that there are fewer people around. You can enjoy the town a lot more without getting jostled and rudely pushed about.

I do end up having a pizza for tea but they have run out of anchovies so it is a bit bland but fills a hole. The normally excellent free Wi-fi is a bit hit and miss around the town and I cannot get through to anyone at home, so I have a solitary evening in the restaurant watching the world go by from the balcony. A taxi takes me back to the hotel and I lay in bed watching TV until I nod off. Around midnight I woke up feeling really sick and a bit panicky. I normally don't drink much alcohol at the beginning of a holiday, I always wait until I have adjusted to the heat and timezone, but I had drunk two large glasses of wine on an empty stomach and hadn't drunk much water today and now my body was complaining.
It's weird how you can talk yourself out of being sick when you don't want to be. I roll over, go back to sleep and don't wake up until 8.30am.

Monday 2nd March

I have another mediocre breakfast this morning where again there does not appear to be much left by the time I get down there.

This morning I am venturing out on a bicycle. Bearing in mind I have not been on a bike since I was here last year, this could be an interesting experience. The bikes at this hotel at least appear to be in better nick that anything I went on last year and Jimmy blows the tyres up for me as an added bonus. The brakes are a bit dodgy but do actually work after a few seconds squeezing hard.
I decide to wear my sexy knee brace as I do not know how this is going to go. My knee doesn't feel too bad today, the warm weather must be doing it good, in fact most of my usual aches and pains have definitely abated. Which is completely weird as my joints hurt every day at home, I have only been here two days how can they feel better already?

Wearing my stylish cycle helmet I set off, a bit wobbly to start with but I soon get the hang of it, they always say you never forget how to ride a bike. There is hardly any traffic on the main beach road, just the odd taxi or motorbike which give me a wide berth. Last year you took your life in your hands cycling along here but now there is nothing to avoid. Apart from a few Western tourists ambling along the broken pavement, there is no-one around.

I arrive at Hidden Beach. This is about two miles from the hotel and slightly off the main drag, hence the name. As I freewheel down the narrow track, praying that I do not need to apply my dodgy brakes in a hurry, I can see there is a lot of new construction going on. This beautiful sandy beach is in a lovely spot and someone has decided it would be a good place to put up a big hotel and spa. It's going to ruin it. Sure enough, Hidden Beach is packed and evidently hidden no longer, I am lucky to get a sun bed there are so many people there. This is obviously where all the tourists are hanging out.

Settled down in my little spot I lay back to soak up the sunshine. It's sunny with a nice breeze blowing, just perfect weather. I know the sun is supposed to be bad for you but I look half a stone lighter and so much healthier with a tan. It's a shame my body doesn't look quite so good in a bikini this year, mainly due to the the amount of alcohol and chocolate I have consumed in the last 10 months. Eating and drinking had been a small way of shutting out some of the negative feelings and it was very comforting. I can certainly see why some people balloon in weight when they get stressed. Looking around there are some very large young girls wearing microscopic bikinis twice the size of me jumping confidently around in the surf, what am I worrying about, I look like a supermodel compared to them. (A very old supermodel).
I lounge around at the beach for 5 hours, listening to music on my iPod, mulling the last year over in my head. I have a feeling that this trip could turn into a cathartic and healing experience for me and I will go home happy and relaxed, a complete new woman.

Ha, shows how much I know!

On the way back to the hotel I go to see my friend Linh. She owns a beauty parlour up on Cua Dai Beach, but I know she lives just behind my hotel at number 68, whatever the road is called. Last year she was talking about relocating her business and I don't want to cycle all the way up to that beach to find she has closed up shop.

I am in luck, she is at home and thrilled to see me. She drags me into her house where her two teenage children are laying on the sofa playing on their phones whilst the TV blasts out some hideous loud Vietnamese game show. Just like normal teenagers the world over.

As it turns out she has closed the shop and has not worked for four months. She shows me the shop: it is piled up on the forecourt of her house.

And I mean the whole shop; even the roof and floor.

We sit in her house on the uncomfortable wooden sofa (they are found in most homes) and she talks non-stop about the Coronavirus, she seems completely obsessed with it. The schools are all closed which is why the kids are at home and they have no idea when they will reopen. She says everyone is terrified of catching it and it is the only topic of conversation around town. I tell her that as Vietnam has such a low amount infections, she shouldn't worry, they have it contained.

At that time they only had 22 cases in a country of 90 million and they were all up in the North region, I really couldn't see what she was worrying about. She rattled on about how businesses are suffering, now this I can understand. With the huge numbers of Asian visitors down to almost zero, most of the big hotels will be empty which means they will have to lay off staff, (her husband is a chef at one of the beach hotels) which will in turn have huge consequences for the locals.

As she had nowhere to give me a massage, she took me along to her Aunties salon which was practically next door to my hotel. Her aunty was lovely and very attractive to look at, she had a slightly different look about her than the other Vietnamese ladies, almost Spanish looking. I booked a massage for the following day which she would allow Linh to do in her salon: I would pay her and she would then pay Linh. Everyone seemed happy with the arrangement. I mentioned about my bad knee and Linh ended up rubbing a bit of tiger balm into it. The Vietnamese put tiger balm on everything: headaches, cuts & grazes, strains, sprains, broken bones, they think it cures all aches and pains - it helps my knee a bit but makes my eyes sting like mad and sets off a sneezing fit.

After a shower, where I had to wear hotel flip-flops to save breaking my neck slipping around on the wet tiled floor, I got the hotel shuttle bus into town. On the way I got chatting to an English couple who had just arrived, this was their first visit to the Old Town and wanted to know where to eat that was 'safe'. I have never had an upset stomach in Vietnam (nor has Peter and his stomach is very delicate), as far as I am concerned everywhere was safe. I pointed them in the right direction for

the main restaurants and I headed for Cuisine Dannan, a favourite eatery of mine, which is on a street several roads back from the centre. On the way there I managed to purchase a cheap mug for my morning cuppa decorated with a natty little slogan - 'Keep calm you are in Vietnam'.
(As it turns out, a totally inappropriate motto for my visit).

At the restaurant, the staff that I was friendly with last year no longer work there and the food wasn't that great either. A big disappointment, normally the food and the service in here are amazing. I had dreamed about their sweet and sour prawns for nearly a year and now it all tasted a bit bland.
It begins to dawn on me that there is definitely something wrong in the town for the restaurants to not have the right ingredients, to serve mediocre food or give bad service. The Vietnamese are normally extremely efficient and usually there is no such thing as 'off menu'.
You can see I was being a bit dippy and it was still a bit of a mystery to me at this point as to what was going on.

After my boring and tasteless dinner I take a proper walk around the town. There are still a lot of Westerners around especially in the centre by the Dragon and Japanese Bridges, but as you walk away from there, the side streets only have a scattering of a people, a few of the shops are closed as well. This tiny place had 5 million visitors in 2018, the figures have not been released yet for 2019, it is normally crammed with tourists. The realisation was starting to hit me that something was not quite right!

The penny had now dropped and the eagle had finally landed in my brain.

When I got back to the hotel and on the Wi-fi, which again was a bit hit and miss, I had a million messages from Greenie and Anna - guess what? Wanting to know where I had been all evening and what I had been doing.
I manage to catch up with Peter, he informs me that a lot of airlines are beginning to cancel flights across the world but his flight out is currently still going. It also seems that this Coronavirus is starting to get a bit out of hand in Northern Italy.
Italy was thousands of miles away, I can't see how that could possibly affect us here.

Tuesday 3rd March

I slept like a log and got up so late that there was nothing left at all to eat at breakfast. The restaurant looked like a cloud of locusts had been through it. I ended up having two mugs of tea and a cereal bar I had brought from home. I saw the couple from the evening before, they had a lovely evening in town, had not had a bad stomach during the night and were now off on a tour to the Marble Mountain. Good luck with climbing all those steps in this heat!

It was a bit cloudy this morning but very warm. I cycled off to the busy beach, I was definitely getting the hang of cycling again, and my knee seemed so much better. The combination of the cloud and wind was lethal today and I ended up glowing red, especially around my ankles, but I did manage to get two litres of water inside me.
 Listening all day to my iPod, I heard songs that I hadn't heard for ages, listening properly to the words they fitted in with my horrible year I had just gone through. Blimey I was being so maudlin. Fortunately I had my head buried under a hideous green Vietcong sunhat so no-one could see me bawling my eyes out.

I managed to have a quick shower at the beach, (yes they even have showers there; they don't have a door but they do work), before meeting Linh for my first massage of the holiday (my only massage of the holiday as it turned out).
It felt fantastic. Linh is tiny, smaller even than Anna, but she has the strongest hands and knows exactly what she is doing with tired, European bodies with taught knotted muscles. As I lay practically naked on the table whilst she climbs all over me, I begin to feel some of the stress of the last few months beginning to leave my drained and exhausted body.

Thoroughly relaxed and feeling light as a feather, I float back to the hotel where I receive a message from Danny, asking if I would like to meet him for dinner in town. Promising that he has been working all day and is stone cold sober, I agree to meet him in the wine bar. Greenie and Eric are on double sentry duty on reception tonight and I get dual grilled about where I am going. Nothing gets past them, they should definitely work for the security services - perhaps they do.

My taxi driver is called Mr Chin. This I find very amusing as we have a bit of a private joke in the office about a customer of the same name who likes one of my colleagues. I send my friend a message to say I am with her fella - LOL.

I find Danny perched upright this evening (a very good sign), sitting on a bar stool, his freshly shaved bald head shining in the lights, drinking a pint of lager and looking the picture of health unlike the untidy wreck I saw on Sunday. He also smells divine, unlike me who smells very strongly of insect repellent and DEET.
I order a glass of wine and we sit and chat. As we talk, he doesn't stop moaning about the Vietnamese, how bored he is with his job and all the red tape that goes with it. I am now firmly of the opinion that he is completely fed up and his love affair with Vietnam is over - he really needs to go home. He agrees wholeheartedly with me, but as he is receiving a huge salary every month he wants to stay for as long as they keep paying him.
I don't know about this, money doesn't really make you happy, especially as you get older. I took a huge pay cut when I walked out of my last horrible job, I wouldn't go back there if they paid me £100,000 a year. Don't get me wrong, it is great to earn a nice salary but if the job makes you completely miserable it is time to call it a day. I am much happier where I work now (despite the depleted income).

There must have been something in the wine as for some strange reason I end up telling him all about my hormonal situation. To my horror and embarrassment I start crying and then can't stop. In full public view, I end up sobbing my heart out. It was almost as if I was having an out of body experience. It felt like I was watching someone through a window completely breaking down in public and I was willing them to pull it back together. Unfortunately that person I could see was me. Danny actually handled it quite well for a man (and he is a proper mans man - definitely not in touch with his feminine side) and he doesn't head for the nearest exit. He gets me another drink, turns on the humour and ends up making me laugh like a drain.
Mini menopausal crisis averted.

With my composure firmly back in place, we ate dinner in a lovely restaurant overlooking the river which was lit up with colourful lanterns and floating candles. We talked about every subject under the sun: politics, music, family, work, theatre, cinema, on and on we yakked. When he is relatively sober he is really good company and I like him a lot.
After dinner we went to an Irish bar across the river that had a Phillipino band playing Western pop songs - badly. By this time I had

already had two glasses of wine and two bottles of beer, and I ended up having another 3 in there. I completely lost count of how many drinks Danny had, he drinks like a fish. (I know it was a lot because I paid the bill). By the end of the evening the band were beginning to sound fantastic and I was having a really good time.

We eventually left the bar and staggered up the road in the pitch black as all the street lights and lanterns had been turned off, I had no idea what the time was. We fell into a taxi and literally tipped Danny out of the car at his apartment. All evening he had been very entertaining and amusing and I cannot remember the last time I had enjoyed an evening out so much. I sneaked into my hotel, past the KGB night reception staff, fell into my bed and instantly passed out.

Wednesday 4th March

Next morning there is not a crumb of bread left at breakfast, they had run out again. I was really starting to get a bit fed up with the bad service at this hotel. No-one had cleaned up the spillage in my room and I cannot seem to get any hot water out of the shower, it is just lukewarm. I am going to have to complain to reception which I really do not want to do as I know Greenie will get upset and she will take any criticism from me personally.

It is warm and cloudy again today as I set off on my bike for the beach. The Wi-fi up there is unreliable and I get a bit of peace from the incessant messages on WhatsApp. On the way back I decided to ride the route through the Paddy fields, I remember every inch of the paths and tracks around here as I cycled through them everyday last year. This is quite surprising as I can't usually remember my way (after 22 years) to my in-laws house in Cambridge but I can find my way around here again with no problem. There are lots of locals out with their children flying colourful kites high up in the sky as the sun starts to go down, it's a wonderful sight. They are all different shapes and sizes and some are soaring so high they must get picked up on the airport radar.

When I arrive back at the hotel I have another stack of messages from Anna and Greenie. Anna has dressed La Vie in one of my outfits and sends me lots of pictures, she looks really cute.

I am absolutely dripping after the sweaty effort of the cycle ride and am just about to get into the lukewarm shower when the phone rings, it's Greenie. She is downstairs on her way to a wedding and wants to show me the outfit that she is wearing. I drag all my filthy clothes back on and go down to meet her. She is draped in a very sexy green dress accessorised with the bag, necklace and earrings I bought her. She is also accompanied by someone who is not her husband. She doesn't introduce me to this man but I met her husband last year and this is definitely not him. Hmm what is she up to? She leaps on the back of his large motorbike, not easy in a tight outfit like that and they roar off down the road.

Oh well whatever she is playing at, I hope she enjoys her evening!

I end up alone in the restaurant next door for an early dinner where I have a decent meal and treat myself to a glass of the local wine - Dalat Red. I got slightly addicted to this last year and now remember how truly awful it is. I resist the temptation to have another as my vocal chords seem to have been temporarily damaged.

I end up watching a Star Trek film (??) in bed at 8.30pm, sending loads of messages and pictures on WhatsApp and Instagram to my friends and family.

The Wi-fi is behaving itself this evening and working really well. I suggest to my friend Carlos that he gets together with Greenie as she is on the look out for another husband. I send him a glamorous picture of her: he asks me to post her first class to his house, immediately.

Thursday 5th March

This morning I feel totally knackered and can hardly get out of bed. This is quite common for me on any long distance vacation, I have been here 5 days and the jet lag is still playing games with my body clock. When I eventually arise it is so late I can't be bothered to go to breakfast as I know there will be nothing left to eat. I do sum up the courage to tell reception about the hot water issue in my room and they promise to send someone up to look at it. I leg it out of reception as fast as an Olympic athlete before Greenie appears.

I decide I am going to do a long bike ride this morning and give the beach a miss today as I am a bit red and sore in places. I set off along the Cua Dai beach road towards the port. There is hardly anyone around and no traffic apart from the occasional motorcyclist. I decide to ditch the cycle helmet, I don't need it and it's just making me hot and sweaty.

I get as far as the VinPearl resort. This property was just a scrubby piece of land two years ago, in 2019 this gorgeous hotel opened, mainly for Asian clientele. Parking my bike in the almost empty car park, I wandered in for a look around. The vast lobby was totally deserted. There was not a soul around, no staff, no guests, no-one.

The reception area was enormous and beautifully decorated, I could see that there had been no expense spared on the decor. I went outside to the sumptuous pool area, there were luxury sun beds and cabanas dotted around but again no people present. It was a bit like the Mary Celeste. Suddenly I spotted movement, but it was just the pool boy doing some cleaning. He smiled but did not ask me what I wanted.

Whenever I am at work and someone I do not know asks me anything, if they are not wearing an ID badge I always ask them who they are. Not sure if that is a good or bad thing as a I challenged a senior manager at the photocopier last year. Well I had no idea who he was, he could have been the cleaner or a mad murderer who had snuck into the building! No-one in this hotel was even slightly interested in what I was doing, I could be stealing the napkins and ash trays, who would notice? What a fantastic and stunning hotel but where was everyone??

Pondering this mystery, I rode back along the silent beach road passing by the spot where Linhs beauty salon used to be. Literally there was just a piece of uneven ground between two other shops, she really had taken everything. A couple of stray dogs were sniffing around on the rough piece of land where her former shop stood but apart from that all the other shops on the street were closed as well.

Arriving back at the hotel at lunchtime, I actually had a HOT shower, at last it was fixed. I then had to get ready for another outing with Anna, Eric and Sunny.

Sunny is another beautiful friend I made last year and I am looking forward to seeing her again.

Eric picked me up on his motorbike. Now I am not quite sure what the other guests thought when they saw me zoom off with my arms wrapped tightly around this young man, I certainly know what I would be thinking! Holding on tightly to Eric and slightly alarmed for my safety because he was a little bit more of a kamikaze rider that Greenie, we rode out deep into the paddy fields, where on earth were we going?

As it turns out some entrepreneur has built a coffee shop in the most divine spot overlooking the lush green rice fields which is now a favourite haunt of all the young and trendy Vietnamese. This place is in the middle of nowhere but was absolutely heaving, mainly with young women dressed in their best clothes and wearing full make up. I don't know how they do it - in that heat my make up just slides off my face. There are not many chairs but lots of trendy bean bags, cushions, chaise longs and what looks like wrought iron beds with mattresses. Eric and I sit on one of the double beds and chat whilst we wait for Anna and

Sunny to arrive. They arrive late in a bit of a fluster as La Vie had waited until this time to play up and would not settle for her afternoon nap.

Eric goes off to order the coffees whilst the girls snuggle up to me on the strange mattress/sofa. Anna is proudly showing off her new bag and earrings to Sunny who is holding up her own worn out bag. I feel a bit guilty but I didn't know that I would be seeing her or I would have brought her a bag as well.

Sunny looks like a stick insect, she has lost so much weight and she wasn't exactly fat to begin with. She is quite tall for a Vietnamese and I am quite worried by her skeletal look. It turns out that her boyfriend is in the police force and they cannot get married yet due to a member of her family having a criminal record. They have to wait another 4 years (she will be 30 then) until the record gets cleared and she worries everyday that he will meet someone else and waltz off into the sunset without her. She bursts into floods of tears and Anna and I comfort her. Blimey what is wrong with all of us weepy women?

Eric has given us emotional females a really wide berth and is gone for ages ordering the coffee's. He reappears about 20 minutes later, when he thinks it is safe to approach, with 4 coconut macchiato's. Yeah, I didn't know what is was either.

It's a lovely afternoon and the breeze is rustling through the rice and keeping the temperature down to a comfortable setting. We all sprawl around on our mattress and chat away about everything and nothing. Anna is convinced having a baby has made her go mad in the head and she thinks she is losing her marbles.

HaHa, wait until you are in the full flow of the menopause love, it will make the baby madness look like a day at the beach.

Half way through my coffee Anna asks me to come and have photos taken.

There then followed another mammoth photo session where we had to have a our photograph taken in every corner of the establishment. We literally had to queue up to stand in some of the most popular photogenic spots as everyone seemed to want their pics taken there. All the girls are posing and taking selfies in every conceivable space. We must have taken over 100 pictures. I find all that posing quite exhausting but they love it and I feel that I have to join in and we do end up with some lovely pictures.

These pictures then all appear on Instagram and the Vietnamese Facebook.

After about 2 hours with the 1 coffee each, we decide it is time to leave. This is very common, the Vietnamese will sit for hours in a coffee shop, only buy one coffee and make it last all day. Some of the businesses in the Old Town will not serve Viets, only tourists, as they do not make any money out of their own people! I offer to pay the bill but Eric has already beaten me to it.

Trying to get Eric's motorbike out of the car park was interesting as there was no organisation and bikes were parked everywhere. It probably didn't help his manoeuvrability with my hefty weight on the back. With big hugs and kisses to Anna and Sunny, after a 30 point turn on the bike, we rumble off through the paddy fields and he delivers me back to the hotel.

I never see Anna again.

I went into town on the shuttle bus again that evening and had an amazing prawn curry washed down with a couple of beers in a lovely restaurant overlooking the river. There seemed to be plenty of tourists around tonight but not anywhere as would be normal. After a walk along the river I get a taxi back with a trainee formula one driver who is on a mission to get back into town asap and drives like a lunatic on the empty roads. He was so bad a driver that I even put my seat belt on.

At 2am I am fully awake having a WhatsApp conversation with a my favourite Paramedic friend who doesn't realise the time difference. He had just retired and has been asked to help out the NHS with the Covid response. He advises me to stay in Vietnam and not go home as they are expecting things to get really bad if we follow the same pattern as Europe. What pattern? What is the Covid response? What is he talking about? I must admit I have not watched the news at all since I have been here and it is only Peter who has been giving me the latest. Boris Johnson is trying to play it down in the UK, talking about herd immunity and is off to the rugby on Saturday. So far the British are still functioning as normal. Everyone is still working, the children are still at school and everything else is open as usual. No-one at home seems to be panicking.

Honestly, the UK is not a third world country, how bad can it possibly get in the civilised world in the 21st century?
How bad indeed?

Friday 6th March

After that 2am disturbing online conversation I have an interrupted nights sleep. I toss and turn all night long and have hot flush after hot flush despite the arctic temperature blowing from the air con. It could be the beers before bedtime OR it could be that the Coronavirus is starting to register properly in my small fuzzy brain.

Friday 6th March turns out not to be the greatest day of my holiday.

When I eventually drag myself out of bed I feel decidedly out of sorts. There is nothing I can actually put my finger on, I feel a bit odd and woolly headed, like I am not there and am watching myself through a pane of glass. I know it sounds weird but this is a normal occurrence at this time of life, I have good days, bad days and terrible days and quite often feel like I am having an out of body experience.
 Maybe today I am just tired and the jet lag has finally caught up with me?

The morning begins with me not being able to open my safe. It just will not open, no matter how many times I tap in the code. This in turn makes me doubt my own memory. Am I putting in the correct number? Fortunately I know from last year that the hotels keep a pass key for all safes at reception. Yes I know, anyone could get hold of it, it's just their strange system. In the end I have to call Jimmy up to my room to sort it out for me. One of the batteries has moved in it's bracket so the digital code is not connecting. He resets it for me and I at last manage to retrieve my iPad and some cash.

At breakfast, there is surprisingly some food left this morning. Unfortunately there is a ten inch long black hair in mine which really puts me off eating anything, so apart from a cup of gnats pee tea, I go hungry yet again.

Even the weather is having a hissy fit today. It's cloudy but sunny at the same time and very hot, the hottest day so far. I cycle to Hidden beach and am dripping with sweat when I get there. After the cycle ride I find it very difficult to cool down, my blood is pumping fast around my body after the exertion and my skin is red hot to the touch. I sit under an umbrella all day but it doesn't make a lot of difference to my internal combustion: I am roasting.
There are still quite a few people at the beach which is reassuring that there still seems to be tourists around. I am wearing my favourite blue

bikini today which decides to disintegrate before my eyes in the strong sunshine and ends up going in the bin. If you have ever had that happen to you it is a weird sight, the fabric just starts to melt and come apart in the heat.

When I arrive back late afternoon to the hotel, Greenie and Eric are very pre-occupied and seem to be in a bad mood. I'm not sure what's going on with them but I get the feeling that something is definitely up. I don't get to speak to them as there appears to be a lot of people checking out and they are very busy.
I sort out a big bag of dirty washing and take it to the laundry next door. For £3 she will get it done by tomorrow morning. What a service.

After another hot shower I take a walk down the road. I am meeting Danny for a drink in the very friendly bar where I first met him last year.
I decided to walk down there in a new pair of sparkly flip flops. Stupidly I had forgotten how far the bar was from my hotel and by the time I get there the soles of my feet are on fire and I have enormous blisters coming up between my toes.
The landlady of the bar, who I know from last year, seems a bit frosty and appears to be in a miserable mood. I order a beer and wait for Danny whilst the normally welcoming landlady completely ignores me. The bar is entirely empty with the exception of two other female customers, I can't say it had a lively atmosphere. This place was always packed to the rafters and a really good laugh last year, now it seems dead and lifeless.

Danny suddenly appears as if by magic and the landlady makes some sarcastic comment about him. She ought to be careful she doesn't offend him, he is one of her regular customers and spends a lot of money in her bar. The other women, snigger amongst themselves and one of them makes a bitchy remark about Danny's reputation. I am very well aware that he's no angel but he has always been the perfect gentleman with me and we are just friends. We order something to eat but I don't like the atmosphere in here, Danny picks up on it and asks if I would prefer to go into town. After we have eaten our insipid and boring dinner we get a taxi into town and go in search of a new bar that he has heard about. This turns out to be a mistake as he drags me all over town looking for this place and I am beginning to feel a bit sick and lightheaded. When we find the bar, it is completely deserted with no customers and he doesn't want to go in. He then decides we will go to the Dive Bar.

This is more like it, it is heaving and full of young and trendy backpackers, most of them smoking weed. There is a live band playing loud rock music and it has a great vibe about it, just the sort of place I would normally love.

By now I have got a pain in my chest that won't go away and am feeling very nauseous. I pretend everything is fine, I want to enjoy myself as I don't get the opportunity to go to places like this very often. Peter would hate it in here.

We end up sitting with a group of very friendly Irish backpackers for the rest of the evening who don't stop to take a breath whilst talking. It's a good thing as I seem to have lost most of my conversational skills. After about an hour I disappear to the loo and lose half of my dinner as well. Being sick in a Unisex Vietnamese toilet that has been used by a load of drunk and stoned teenagers was not a pleasant experience. Twenty minutes later the rest of my meal makes a reappearance. I feel absolutely awful and just want to go to bed. I am so cross with myself, I am never sick on holiday, and in normal circumstances I would be having a lovely time. The band is really good and I would love to get up and dance, but any movement just makes me feel dizzy. Danny is laughing and joking with the Irish kids, giving it large with his loud personality, I try to join in but all I want to do is go to sleep. In the end I catch his eye and he asks me if I want to leave. He now appears to have the right hump and practically throws me into the back of a taxi and stomps off. I lay back in the taxi trying to fight off the feeling that I am going to vomit all over the back of the drivers head at any second.

Oh dear not a great day. Safely back at my hotel, I climb into bed and crash out completely.

Saturday 7th March

When I wake up I feel much better but still a bit nauseous. Eric takes it upon himself to make me some fresh ginger tea. I am not keen on the idea but it has an instantaneous effect and I don't feel so sick anymore. I get a message from an excited Peter to say he is just setting off for Heathrow, the flight is still going and he is all checked in.

Greenie informs me that she is organising a party for Peter and myself on Monday evening with all of my Vietnamese friends.

I am very excited and can't wait to see everyone all together again, it will be a lovely evening.

I get to the bottom of Greenie and Eric's pre-occupation. She tells me that there was a big staff meeting yesterday at the hotel. Apparently an extremely wealthy Vietnamese socialite who had been visiting the Milan fashion show had flown back to Vietnam via London last Monday. On arrival in Danang she had gone down with the Coronavirus as well as two of the flight crew and four passengers in her part of the aircraft. The authorities were now in the process of rounding up every passenger who was in the First Class cabin with her. Two of the passengers are staying at a luxury hotel just up the road and the Management have completely closed the hotel down and quarantined all the guests inside. I thought it looked very quiet when I cycled past yesterday. My hotel has also had quite a few cancellations for the next few weeks, this is peak season, they should be full and the management are very worried about business. Currently the hotel has 75% occupancy but the management are very concerned that if future guests continue to cancel, the hotel might have to lay off some of the staff. Obviously they are all worried for their jobs.

I mull all of this over on my cycle ride to the beach. Surely if they find all of these First Class passengers and quarantine them everything will be OK? Won't it? So far there had been no cases in Hoi An, these were the first and as it was only six people they can't spread it to everyone, can they? Because of the bureaucracy here I know the authorities will undoubtably find every single person who had contact with these people and isolate them. It will be OK I tell myself.
At this stage I had still not grasped the gravity of the worsening global situation. Was I being delusional or just in complete denial?

After another morning sunning myself on the beach I go to Linh's aunties salon for another massage which I had booked. When I get there it is completely closed which is very unusual. I sit on a chair outside and wait for 15 minutes but no-one turns up. I notice that the supermarket and laundry are also closed. That's funny, what is going on, where is everyone? It's certainly not like Linh to miss out on a bit of business.
I walk back to the hotel and find Greenie. She enlightens me to the answer - the Vietnamese are now scared to mix with Foreigners and nobody wants to do massages because they don't want to catch the virus from us!
As I now have nothing else to do, it's far too early for dinner, I take a walk along the deserted road to see if this is true. Sure enough, all of the massage and beauty parlours are indeed closed and fully locked up with the shutters down.

As I come around the corner I spot Danny sitting in a scruffy bar all on his own, he is the only customer. Normally there would be so many people around at this time of day that you would never notice a solitary person, this has happened twice now in a week which is exceedingly odd. He waves me over and orders me a drink but I can only face a tonic water. He has a bit of a moan at me for being totally miserable last night. Where on earth did that come from? When I explain what actually happened to me he apologises for his behaviour and the misunderstanding and we part on good terms. We promise to meet up again when our relatives have all gone home.

I never get to speak to him again.

That evening I go into town for another pizza. They still have no anchovies.

Sunday 8th March

At breakfast this morning I finally acknowledge to myself that I do not like this hotel, I want to move and fully intend to.
I now have a major dilemma. Greenie and Eric will be mortified if I tell them I don't like it here and think the service is awful. I need to think very carefully about how I handle this, but I've made up my mind that I am going to move.
I am unanimous in that.
They have also run out of bread at breakfast - again.

Peter messages me to say he is about to leave Singapore on his way to Danang, he should be here around lunchtime. The flight from London to Singapore was empty and he had a whole row to himself.
I lay on a sun bed by the swimming pool to wait for him. I haven't gone to the airport to meet him because Greenie and Eric weren't around when I booked the pick up car for him. Something got a bit lost in translation at reception, they wanted to charge me $20 on top of the $28 car price to travel to the airport with the driver which was a bit odd. I couldn't be bothered to argue with them over the strange price increase, so I didn't go. Peter has been here before, he's a big boy, he will be fine on his own.

I get a message from Peter a few hours later to say that he has landed in Danang but no car has turned up to pick him up. There is a flurry of calls from reception to find the driver who is asleep in the car park -

again. He runs off to find Peter who is still waiting outside the terminal. Even the drivers booked through this hotel give a bad service.

After a short wait the car finally pulls up at reception and Peter arrives, there is no welcoming committee for him as it is Eric and Greenies day off. I am pleased to see him and he is happy to see me. I unpack all of his luggage, which is mainly for me anyway, whilst he sits on the toilet catching up with all his Facebook messages and emails on his phone, the way men do.

He fills me in with all the local news and gossip back home. The virus is not causing any major problems in the UK and the Prime Minister seems quite blasé about what is happening in Europe. Nobody is unduly worried at the moment and it is business as usual. Somewhat comforted by that, we go down to the pool where Peter instantly crashes out on a sun bed and snores loudly all afternoon whilst I read my book, gnashing my teeth at the irritating noise.

For Peters first meal, we go to the restaurant next door. We have a lovely meal which costs £10, and consists of spring rolls, battered prawns and stir fried squid, all washed down with La Rue beer. Like me, Peter now knows he is truly in Vietnam after his first beer. The delicious meal is spoilt slightly by an enormous rat which appears underneath my chair and hurtles across the middle of the restaurant straight into the flower bed. I absolutely hate rats and am petrified of them and it sort of ruins the romantic atmosphere.

Back in our room I put a film on the TV, Peter nods off straight away even though it is only 8.30pm and sleeps like a baby all night long.

Monday 9th March

Unlike me, who does not get any sleep at all. Peter snores like a freight train and there is no escape from the horrendous noise in the tiny room. I end up with my pillow pulled over my head but that just keeps overheating me and sets off the hot flushes. I end up throwing off all the covers to cool down and then get freezing cold due to the temperature being the same as the North Pole in the room. I think only a pillow firmly placed over Peter's head would have stopped the noise! I have a thoroughly miserable night constantly shouting at him to shut up, he is in such a deep heavy sleep he doesn't even move let alone hear me. I get up in the morning more tired than when I went to bed.

This happens every time we go away, I don't know whether it is the stale air he has breathed in on the plane or if he has an allergy to going on holiday but it is really, really, annoying and I could kill him.

I had only been bitten twice so far, insects normally love me and I sometimes get eaten alive. I learnt a neat trick last year to take anti-histamine every day regardless, which really helps. I still get bitten but they don't generally itch or turn nasty. Unfortunately something has taken a culinary liking to me and I now have 8 bites on my legs and feet which must have occurred at the swimming pool yesterday, one of them is huge and has flared up into an angry red lump despite taking the tablets. I have to put anti histamine cream on it to stop it irritating. Even Peter has two tiny bites that he moans about constantly. Welcome to my normal holiday horror.

The usual service is resumed at breakfast. Peter asks for an omelette with no onion (he is allergic), when it arrives it is full of it and he has to pick all the bits out. I have completely given up with anything cooked and just have a slice of toast and a yoghurt.

We decide to cycle up to Hidden beach. It takes a while for Jimmy to find a bike that he can raise the seat of to Peters height, they don't make bikes for tall people in Vietnam! After trying out several cycles, he finds one that is sort of suitable and we set off along the deserted coast road. There are plenty of people at the beach and we stay there all day, Peter sleeps for most of the daylight hours. He does venture into the sea at one point but it is so rough that you can't really swim, he just bobs about in the waves.
I think he is just having a wee in the water.

I am really looking forward to the party this evening and seeing all of my Vietnamese friends. We leave the beach early so we have plenty of time to get ready. We are due to meet everyone at 5.30pm but because the beach Wi-fi is so sketchy I still don't know the exact arrangements.

When we get back to the hotel I receive a disturbing message from Greenie. The party has been cancelled as everyone is scared that they will catch something. Not necessarily from me as I have been there for 10 days and they know I do not have the virus. The crux of the matter is that they are all terrified that Peter has brought the Coronavirus in from Europe and do not want to risk seeing us. The local authorities are also now advising all Vietnamese not to socialise with each other and to stay indoors away from other people - especially foreign tourists.

They have also changed the visa entry system to the country overnight. Previously you only required a visa if entering Vietnam for over 14 days, it now transpires that you need a visa for any entry. Strangely enough all their airports and Vietnam embassies the world over have currently suspended issuing any visas to foreigners. So basically once the current tourists leave, no-one else will be arriving except the tourists who had already applied for their visa's in their home country and are still prepared to travel.

Peter looks up the virus rate for Vietnam, as of today there had only been 34 cases reported in the whole country. What on earth was everyone panicking about? They were hardly dropping like flies here.

I have a long phone conversation with Anna mainly about her baby and the virus. It sounds as if she has locked herself in her bedroom with La Vie and won't be coming out in the near future. She is sorry about cancelling the party but everyone is so worried about getting infected and they have to take their Governments advice.

This is one of only five Communist countries left in the world and the people will do as they are told. I am so sad, one of the main reasons for coming here was to spend time with her and La Vie and now I will not be seeing them again.

Feeling a bit dejected and very disappointed, Peter & I decide to go into town on the shuttle bus for dinner. By 8.30 the town was almost abandoned and I noticed that some of the restaurants and shops were already closed. The Old Town of Hoi An is not a late night sort of place at the best of times but it usually buzzes until around 10pm. We got a taxi back and lay in bed watching another film, but my mind was firmly on other things. This is getting completely out of hand, what are they all so petrified about, what will happen next?

Tuesday 10th March

I had an awful night with dark thoughts running through my head. The night sweats were off the scale and even Peter complained about the heat I was radiating in the small room. It was as if my high temperature was counteracting the cold air from the air con and neither of us could cool down. At least it gave him a taste of my nightly episodes.

As I said before, any sort of stress or worry seems to magnify the menopausal symptoms and tonight I was on fire. It felt like someone had lit a bonfire underneath me. I wasn't actually concerned about catching the virus; I had come here to spend time with my friends and now it looked like I would not be able to see some of them again. The whole trip would be ruined and I did not know when it would be possible to see them again in the near future.

Looking back now, that sounds really stupid in light of the seriousness of what was happening across Europe. At that exact moment in time I just could not understand what the panic was all about in a country that only had a tiny amount of cases amongst it's 90 million population.

After another crappy breakfast with bad service we decided we were going to check out of the hotel, but where to go? How was I going to tell Greenie without seriously offending her?

She didn't take it well.

Her first thought was that she had upset me in some way.

Her second thought was that I blamed her for getting me to stay in her hotel which I didn't like.

Her third thought was that I would not forgive her for cancelling the party.

In the end I managed to placate her by saying Peter and I just wanted to stay somewhere a little bit more romantic. Her hotel was fine and good value for money but it lacked a little bit of luxury, which she understood. At last. I think.

Looking online, all the hotels (with no exception) in this area had slashed their prices. Some hotels were only charging £10 per night and that was with breakfast and the use of a pool. All the luxury 5 star beach hotels had reduced their prices by at least half. We scrolled through the list and found a lovely looking hotel out in the middle of the paddy fields, about a mile away and tried to book it online. The Internet was really playing up today and wouldn't play ball, so we decided to try later on.

Cycling to the beach, it was really like a ghost town along the coast road, I wouldn't have been surprised if balls of tumbleweed had blown across the road. All the locals were hiding indoors away from us germ infested foreigners. The few restaurants that were staying open were empty, there was just no-one around. Fortunately there were still plenty of tourists at the beach and the bars were still open there.

It was another beautiful day. When I was here last year the weather was very changeable and humid most days. This year the weather has been almost perfect and I am dealing well with the heat and lower humidity. The warmth has done my knee good and apart from the odd twinge it is definitely much better. In fact my whole body looks and feels healthier and most of my constant joint pain has disappeared altogether. The tan is coming along nicely and the sun has lightened my hair to a more silvery look from the steely platinum colour that is my natural hair colour. Even my nails which never look good are long and unbroken. Well, at least I look half decent in spite of all the angst and worry. On the way back from the beach, we pass the luxury hotel that has all their guests in quarantine. It looks dead quiet, almost uninhabited and is coned and taped off along the front like a major police incident.

Back at the hotel Greenie wants to take Peter and I out for dinner as her treat. We agree to go out with her but we are adamant that she is not paying. Arm in arm we stroll along the road to the Blue Wave Restaurant which is still open and surprisingly full. There are a few tourists around on the street but I can see that a lot of the bars and most of the shops are closed, which is why they are all in here. We do end up having a lovely evening. Once Greenie has a few beers inside her she spills the beans about a lot of people I know. We end up talking about Toby Hot Boy. He was the Concierge at last years hotel and apparently he has a bit of a thing for Greenie. He sent her flowers on her birthday and is always messaging her. But he is not her mystery man, I wonder who it could be - she doesn't let on in front of Peter. She also tells me a lot of gossip about members of staff who were all carrying on with each other. It was just like anywhere else. If you spend too much time at work and not enough time at home you will end up making 'special' friends. She questions us expertly like the Spanish Inquisition as to why we want to move hotels. We go through the whole thing again, even Peter helps me out by saying he wants somewhere a bit more intimate as our hotel is a bit busy. I still don't think she completely believes us, but it is saving face with her and I think she at last accepts our decision. Phew! The food was very nice as always in here and I had three gin and tonics. I had decided to stop drinking the beer as I think it might be that which makes me feel a bit peculiar, exacerbates the hot flushes and keeps me awake during the night.

Back at the hotel we still cannot get the Wi-fi to connect, I am beginning to wonder if this is because a lot of the repair men around this area are not working and nothing is getting fixed?

Wednesday 11th March

Neither of us can be bothered with the crappy breakfast this morning. We set off on our bicycles on a mission to find another hotel. Deep down amongst the paddy fields is the little gem of a place which we had seen on the Internet. This hotel has 17 rooms which were laid out in two storey blocks set around a pretty lily pond surrounded by trees and flowers and is decorated with old motor bikes and other memorabilia. There are lots of ornamental pots and statues placed all around the property and there is a lovely swimming pool on the roof of the restaurant. It is stunningly beautiful with views of the rice fields from every side.

There is one small problem though: the owner can only fit us in for 5 days as she is fully booked after that. It turns out that they have two hotels and are closing one of them and moving the remaining guests here. We want a room here for ten days. After they make a lot of phone calls to their booking line, the manager says they have arranged for us to stay for the full amount of days that we want. I am presuming that they shunted one of the other guests off somewhere else so that they can get the money from us for 10 days rather than less money from a guest who might only be staying for a couple of days.

This place normally charges £75 per night but we get it for £45 which is double what we were paying in Greenies hotel. But there is a world of a difference between the two establishments. I haven't even seen my room yet but the beautiful decor and general feel of the place is definitely more up my street.

We cycle back to pack up our luggage and move. I am in a hurry to get back and get settled into our new place so I toss everything higgledy piggledy into the cases. Fortunately Greenie is being very gracious in defeat this morning and arranges for the hotel shuttle bus to take us to the new hotel. I think her geniality is down to the fact that her house literally overlooks the new hotel and she can still see me every day and will know what I am doing and where I am going. The other staff on reception are a bit shocked that we are leaving early as they know I am so friendly with her and Eric. But I am glad to leave this place - the hotel is bland, dull, in an ugly spot and the service is awful.

When we arrive back at our new temporary residence the staff are waiting for us, we get swiftly checked in and shown to our room. I am not disappointed - what a gorgeous bedroom. It is on the second floor with a large balcony overlooking the lily pond with chairs and a table decorated with colourful bowls of growing green rice. Inside there is a big airy space with a huge bed, sofa and desk complete with a laptop computer. The room has a unique bathroom lay out. On one side is a sink and arch through to the toilet, on the other side is another sink and arch through to the shower (with hot water). In the middle are double glass doors which lead to an outside bath and shower surrounded by plants and quirky stonework. I notice that everything is spotlessly clean and well maintained and the bed linen is proper cotton. There are toiletries galore and four glass bottles of drinking water which are refilled every day. Plastic waste is a huge problem in Vietnam and this hotel is trying to do it's bit by not having plastic bottles on the premises. The room is decorated in vibrant colours with dark wood furniture (very typical here) and lots of little knick knacks and nice decorative touches. It is quiet as a graveyard, there does not seem to be anyone around, but it is the early afternoon and I guess the other guests are probably out at the beach or off sightseeing.

Once unpacked we sprawl out by the swimming pool which again has had a lot of thought put into the design. There are double sun beds so you can sprawl together and huge fluffy towels are provided - not the tiny thin raggedy things I had been used to. I stand in the pool admiring the 360 degree view of the lush paddy fields, yes we made the right decision, I only wish I had done it last week.

The other overwhelmingly fantastic feature of this place was this it did not have a shuttle bus to the Old Town. No, but it did have fleet of genuine Willies jeeps left over from the Vietnam war (or American war as it is called here) that had been lovingly maintained and were now used to ferry guests back and forth to the town and beach. I love these robust little vehicles and would dearly like to own one, so this was a massive bonus for me.

Climbing aboard a jeep with a young Canadian couple we set off for the town. It was a bumpy old ride but such a novelty and I got to sit in the front. Good job really as it was a tight squeeze in the back. In town Peter and I decided to splash out and have dinner at the Hai Cafe. This charming restaurant is set in the courtyard of an original 16th century trading house and does amazing food. It is not particularly cheap but still costs less than going out for a pizza at home. We always go for dinner at least once when we are here and it is always packed. Tonight it is still fairly busy but there are a few spare tables dotted around. We have a lovely meal, the service is great and the ambience intimate and romantic.

The bill comes to just under £40.

Thursday 12th March

During the night we were both cold due to the fact that I had the air con on at freezing point and we only had a thin sheet to cover us. We kept waking up wrapped around each other trying to keep warm. Sometimes a hot flush does come in useful, but as we all know you can't just turn them on, they only arrive when you don't want them, at the most inconvenient time. I had noticed a duvet in the wardrobe which we will use tonight which means I can still have the room icy cold but can snuggle under it for warmth.

News from the UK government this morning is that they have had an almighty U-turn about the virus which they had previously been playing down. Now they appear to be taking it seriously and the British public are starting to panic buy. Toilet roll seems to be the thing that is flying off the shelves at an alarming rate. I didn't think Coronavirus gave you diarrhoea, why is that being bought up in such huge quantities?
I hope no-one burgles our house whilst we are away, we had an Amazon delivery of 90 rolls a few weeks ago and they are all stuffed in the airing cupboard.

In Vietnam they now have 39 cases which is nothing compared to the huge number in Spain and Italy. Remember there are 90 million people living here, 39 is a drop in the ocean but their Government here have taken it very seriously from the start which is probably why they don't have more cases. Any local who is out on the streets for any reason, serving in a restaurant or shop and working in a hotel are wearing face masks. The other thing here is that the people will do as they are told, if instructed to stay indoors they will and they do.

We go down to breakfast which is in the open air restaurant - again beautifully decorated. There is a huge choice to eat and the lovely staff bend over backwards to get anything you want. They even do Vietnamese iced coffees made with condensed milk. They are not to everyones taste but Peter and I love them. Peter gets his omelette with no onion and I stuff myself with loads and loads of fresh bread and butter.

After breakfast we realise we have left a copious amount of confectionary in the dressing table drawer at the other hotel. Peter hops on a hotel bike and cycles up there to retrieve them. Fortunately the inefficient cleaning staff haven't noticed that we have left 6 bags of wine gums behind! When he gets back, he is sweating like a pig and totally exhausted. He tries out the outdoor shower to cool down, the water is ice cold and he yells a lot until he gets used to the temperature. He states that the bike they gave him was a complete wreck and was very hard going. Yes, this hotels bikes are a bit old as I find out when we decide to cycle up to the beach later on. My bike had no gears or brakes that worked whatsoever but it did have a lovely bell.

On the way back from the beach we pop in to see Greenie. She looks very tired, a lot of the staff have decided to stay at home, even Eric, so she is working double shifts to cover reception. All their employees are worried about catching the virus and they have had so many cancellations that she thinks the hotel will have to close in April. Then what will she do for money for herself and the children? No such thing as Family Credit or the Dole here. Peter and I take advantage of there being no heavy traffic on the roads and ride the long route back to our hotel, cycling down the Cua Dai Road instead of going through the paddy fields. I am hurtling down the hill out of control as I have no brakes and can't slow down when someone steps out from behind a parked vehicle right front of me. Oh shit, it's Danny and I nearly run him down.
I can't physically stop to say hello as I whizz past him at the speed of sound.

It is the last time I ever see him.

That evening, taking advantage of the jeeps we head into town again to have another non anchovy decorated pizza and a glass of Dalat Red. Desperate measures are called for!
After dinner we went handbag shopping. They make fake designer bags here that are of extremely good quality leather and should cost around £20 each. The mainly female shop keepers really try it on and start the price at £100, in some places I can't even be bothered to haggle, we just walk out with them chasing us down the road. It is an exhausting feat, shopping here, they would sell their own grandmother to make a buck. In the end we find a shop keeper with some common sense and I get a black bag for me and a pink one for my sister at a decent price which we are all happy with. Peter works with leather in the shoe industry and he reckons the bags are worth every penny for the workmanship even if they are fake.
We end up drinking Merlot in the Marble wine bar, which is lovely but a bit pricey at £6 a glass, the same as home. There are quite a few people in there which does give it a bit of atmosphere. Peter says they have the best toilets in the whole town. He should know, he's tried

every one of them at some time. He could write his own book: 'Toilets I have used around the world'.
You could use the pages to wipe your arse. LOL!

Back in our lovely hotel room we play cards in bed and he beats me every time, he's far too sharp for my fuzzy hormonal brain to keep up with. He doesn't just beat me by a few points, he thrashes me and I end up getting a bit stroppy and throw all the cards across the bed. When we eventually go to sleep, he wakes me up at 2am with news of the horrendous Covid death figures for Italy and Spain. He then rolls over and goes straight back to sleep immediately whilst I lay awake mulling this terrible news over in my minuscule brain for hours on end.

Friday 13th March

We at least have a lovely cosy night underneath the duvet with the air con on full blast. When we go for breakfast, I can see Greenie on the balcony of her house waving frantically at me. She is definitely keeping tabs on us, I bet she has binoculars trained on our room. I wander over for a chat, her children are with her and ignore me completely. It's not that they don't make eye contact, it's more that they act like I am invisible and they can't actually see me, all very weird. She is working another double shift later today and is now doing the families laundry, her husband is still in bed. She says she has told him that he must go to the market to buy some food as they are running out. If he doesn't get up and go shopping today she will kill and eat all of his prize cockerels. This I find absolutely hilarious, that's one of the best ultimatums I've ever heard. Go Greenie go.

Anna is also running low on baby food and nappies for La Vie. She said the shelves were empty when she went shopping today.
Mind you there is still toilet roll available here so all is not lost!

After another sumptuous breakfast, attended by only 10 other guests, we set off on a long bike ride (well long for me) through the paddy fields and up onto the main beach road. It was very pleasant but eerily quiet, normally these tracks would be full of cyclists. Hidden out in the paddy fields are some Koi Carp fish farms which have tiny little bars and cafes attached to them, if you know where to look. We wanted to stop for a drink and a rest but they were all closed. We managed to cycle for 15 km in the searing heat until my dodgy knee finally gave out with all the effort on the dodgy bike and I struggled painfully to pedal back to the hotel.

Later that afternoon we tried several places to get some laundry done but they were all closed as well. There is a supermarket out on the main road and the lady who owns it is an amazing sales woman. She could give 'The Dragons' a run for their money. I never managed to get out of her shop without buying something whenever I entered her premises last year. I knew she would still be taking in laundry, nothing would ever close her business down, not even the Black Death. Peter was getting a bit desperate for some clean clothes as I had not packed him much as his case had been full of chocolates and sweets for the girls. We wandered out to her shop and sure enough she was open and still taking in laundry. We deposited a hefty bag of Peter's dirty clothes with her and left with purchases of a bottle of wine, some tiger balm and a bag of sweets!

We didn't go into town that evening. We walked back out to the main road (in the pitch dark) and found a new place that had just opened. It had a few customers and one table of absolutely paralytically drunk Australian dive instructors. I know they were dive instructors because they loudly announced it when we sat at the table next to them. They had drunk every cold La Rue beer in the house so Peter had to drink Saigon beer, which he said was OK. I was now firmly fixed on drinking gin and tonic only, they did not seem to keep me awake during the night so much. The divers were very chatty and launched into a very drunken foulmouthed tirade about the Vietnamese Government shutting down all the local dive sites which meant that they had no work for the foreseeable future.

When you start to think about it, it wasn't just the shops, bars and restaurants that were suffering. The authorities had shut down all of the tourist sights and anything of historical interest in the whole area. Peter and I had been planning to go up the coast to the city of Hue for two days by train but had already decided it would be safer not to as we might get stranded up there if the transport links were suddenly closed down. You wouldn't get much of a warning if they did, the authorities here would just do it with no consultation.

Whilst eating a delicious dinner of garlic prawns and squid cooked with ginger and lemongrass, we discussed the rapidly unfolding situation. Things were obviously starting to get out of hand in Europe and Covid19 was now beginning to spread throughout the UK. Flights were being cancelled all over the world. Peter checked both of our flights home, they were both still bookable and there was nothing on either of the websites to say they might be cancelled, so we were not unduly worried at that point. The weather was lovely, some of the restaurants and bars were still open, we were staying in a beautiful hotel and we had each other for company, so we decided to stick it out.

It was a very weird sensation once we got into our hotel room. It was so quiet and once the door was closed you were completely shut off from whatever was going on outside (which actually wasn't very much). Whenever Peter gets up during the night to use the loo he always takes his phone with him to check the news. It's obviously a man thing. When he gets back into bed at 2.00am he informs me that there were more grim death figures from Italy and the World Health Organisation (WHO) had declared that Europe was now considered the centre of the Pandemic. Spain had now declared a state of emergency and was in complete Lockdown. In the UK her Majesty the Queen had cancelled most of her engagements as a precaution. And it looked like the football season had come to an abrupt end, with all future games currently cancelled.

No wonder I can't sleep properly with all of that going around my head, it sounded like the end of the world as we know it. Peter also seemed much more restless than usual after his 2am bulletin, I know it's to do with Luton Towns football matches being cancelled. That will keep him awake and give him something to worry about for a change.

Saturday 14th March

In the morning we climbed aboard a jeep to go into town. Hoi An is lovely at night when it is all lit up but is also very picturesque in the daytime when the sunshine bathes the old houses in a completely different light. We had a good walk around the colourful shops and roamed around the narrow streets and alleys looking at the different goods for sale. Over the years I have bought so much stuff from here, my house is full of it, that I am now only looking for something I haven't seen before, something very different or unusual. I spot a black and cream lacquered half moon shape vase. It is spectacular and we both agree that we want to buy it. Fierce haggling starts, the shopkeeper wants £75, I offer her £10 and we are off, the game commences. I end up paying £22 but I do buy some other bits and pieces as well, so she does alright out of me.

It's very muggy today and we are both gagging for a drink after the shopping experience. I have a banging headache probably caused by the lack of water, it's got absolutely nothing to do with the current unfolding situation we find ourselves in - NOT. We sit in a tiny cafe in a

16th Century house underneath the original wooden beams drinking the excellent local coffee and watch the world go by. There are very few tourists around, it's mainly the Vietnamese going to the market which is still heaving and the bikes are causing pandemonium as usual. It's quite comforting to know that a tiny bit of this place is still functioning as per normal.

We sit by the pool all afternoon and do not see or hear another soul in the hotel or out in the paddy fields. Except for a few staff the hotel is deserted.

In the evening we went back into town by jeep to have dinner where we have a serious discussion during Happy Hour (not that happy tonight) about whether we should try to go home early or not. Travellers all over the world are being advised to get back to their own countries as soon as possible. It is very obvious that Vietnam is closing down along with the rest of the world, they don't want tourists here and we are certainly not feeling that welcome anymore. We were both beginning to worry about the very real problem of getting stuck here if our flights get cancelled. With everything closing would we be asked to leave the hotel and where else would we stay if it everything was shut down? What would we do for money? How long would we be here for? Peter runs his own business and needs to be in the UK, which is the reason why he only takes two weeks off at any time, and I have a job. All of these questions were running around our brains and if I were to admit it I felt an icy hand gripping my heart.

There had been 153,586 cases of Coronavirus across the world with 5789 deaths so far. It's still a minuscule amount of people on a planet of 7 billion people, how bad could it really get?

How bad indeed?

It's all make believe , isn't it? - Marilyn Monroe

3. Going Home

Sunday 15th March

We get a worrying message when we wake up from Peters mum. Her husband has been rushed into hospital suffering from pneumonia and sepsis. Peter manages to speak to Maureen but the line isn't very good, we lose a bit of the conversation but get the general gist: he is 83 and it doesn't look good. Oh dear, Maureen is on her own at home having to deal with this and there is nothing we can do from here. We feel totally helpless.

Flights from Asia into Central Europe are being cancelled at a rate of knots but all flights are still going to London. Peter is due to go home on 19th and I am due to leave on 22nd. All British travellers are officially being advised to return home from abroad as soon as possible by the Foreign Office. Anyone still arriving into Vietnam (tourists or returning locals) have to go straight into 14 days quarantine - no argument. Fortunately the authorities have taken over an empty 4 star hotel in Hoi An and it is being set up for isolating foreign visitors and returning residents. The original quarantine centre was an old soldiers barracks in Danang and was a bit rough by all accounts.

In the UK everyone over the age of 70 or with underlying medical conditions is being told to self-isolate and stay at home - that's my mother, sister and Maureen completely stuffed then. The virus is now causing problems in places like Iran and as far away as Australia. I don't feel slightly worried about catching Covid, as far as I can see Vietnam is a much safer place to be than Europe at the moment, but I am beginning to feel a bit nervous that we might get marooned here indefinitely. Peter and I don't know what to do for the best and have another big discussion about it over breakfast.

Up at the beach there are definitely fewer people around this morning. It's hot and sticky and we lounge around all day under our umbrella. It's another gorgeous day, the sand is white, the sea is blue but there is a weird sensation in the air, like a massive thunderstorm is coming. On the way back we call in to see Greenie. She has dark circles under her eyes and looks totally exhausted. Her hotel is practically empty of guests, she is the only member of staff around and says it will be closing on 20th March, much earlier than originally thought.

Back at our hotel we make the sensible decision to book me onto the same flight as Peter on 19th, so we can fly home together. He is not happy about leaving me here even though it is only three days behind him, we are just not prepared to take the risk of me getting stranded somewhere on my own. I am really upset about having to leave early, but even my airy fairy brain can see the logic in it. Fortunately the flight home is still fairly empty and I get booked easily. The downside is that it costs us an extra £550 that we hadn't budgeted for. We cancel my homeward flight on 22nd, I should get a small tax refund from them which can help pay towards this new flight.

Happier now that we have made the decision, we go out to eat at another local place. The hotel reception staff carefully question us as to where we are going when we leave our room, blimey they are at it now! There is a lovely restaurant out on the main road which I frequented last year, the staff actually remember me and make us very welcome. The food is delicious as always, they at least have not let their standards slip. There are quite a few tourists in here tonight, probably because most restaurants around here are closed. It's almost like a normal evening on holiday. Almost.

News from the UK tonight is that the Government are telling everyone to stay at home and only go out if necessary. Hmm, what about all of us who have jobs to go to? What about the schools and Universities? How is that going to work?
News from my office is that panic is setting in, we are starting to get a lot of cancellations.
Not good news.

Monday 16th March

Peter wakes me up at 2am with his latest news bulletin. The global death toll is now 7119. The British public have gone totally nuts and are panic buying everything. The supermarket shelves are empty and the world has gone completely mad.
I have only been away two and a half weeks and chaos has descended in the UK and the world has changed.

I break the news to Anna and Greenie on WhatsApp that I am going home three days early. They are very upset but let's face it, I haven't been able to spend much time with them, so it's all academic anyway. They are both besides themselves with worry about me going back to the UK as they think I will go down with the virus, the Vietnamese news is full of the Pandemic in Europe.

We end up talking to the young Canadian couple at breakfast who have also been advised to go home as soon as possible. Unfortunately their original flights had been cancelled and they had been up half of the night trying to book something else with not a lot of success. It doesn't help that the Internet is so dodgy at the moment. Whilst we are chatting the chap gets a message on his phone. They have managed to get on a flight from Danang to Tokyo with a 12 hour wait for a connecting flight to Vancouver tomorrow. It is the only available option and they have to go for it at huge expense otherwise they might not get home at all.

We head for the beach again as there isn't anything else to do - we can't visit anyone, or sit and socialise. It is very windy and the sea is rough but it's still sunny and warm. There are even fewer people around but the beach bars are still open and all the sun beds and umbrellas have been laid out which is a bit of a comfort.

I have a deep sense of foreboding that we are heading for a world meltdown. Is humanity being punished for ruining the planet and messing around with nature? Did this virus really come from a dead animal or was it manufactured in a laboratory and one of the test animals escaped and got into the food chain?
There are already reports that since the Italian lockdown, the canals in Venice have cleared of pollution and there are fish swimming in the water again.

We stay at the beach all day, right until the sun starts to go down, and then cycle back to our hotel. Strangely enough, all of the guests that were due to arrive have either cancelled, gone home early or not arrived at all. So currently there are only three rooms occupied and those guests are both leaving tomorrow morning, leaving just us on our lonesome to rattle around the empty hotel.

We get a jeep into town to go and have dinner. We end up talking to two older English couples in the restaurant who are here on holiday for another ten days. They don't understand the underlying panic in Europe and are determined to finish their trip and go home next week. So far they haven't checked their airlines website so see if the flight is still going : I hope they are still flying in seven days time. They don't seem at all bothered by the big hoo-ha, I wonder if they are in denial or are just going to take their chances. I suppose if you are retired and don't have to rush back to your job, this was a better and safer place than any to get stranded. Good Luck to them.

Peter and I ended up in a little bar we know well where we have an enormous piece of chocolate cake each and a glass of the local brew. Neither of us can then get off to sleep when we retire to bed as it lays festering in the bottom of our stomachs.

Tuesday 17th March

Peters piece of 2am news is that there have now been 71 deaths in the UK down to Covid 19, every one of them was someone with an underlying illness. So it's definitely arrived in England then. Another interesting snippet of information is that the UK population has spent £200 million extra this month in the supermarket on alcohol, far more than over any Christmas period.

Everyone is getting ready for something.

The Chancellor is putting together a financial package to try and keep businesses afloat as the Government announces that everything could go on hold for the next three months. The British airports are all up in arms as they are worried about staff losing their jobs as flights are cancelled across the entire globe. The football Euro's 2020 have been cancelled, that will upset fans.

Everyone is being told to do something called social distancing when they are around other people, keeping 2 metres apart. How is that going to work on buses and trains? It's really not looking as if the coming Spring months are going to be very enjoyable in any way, shape or form.

The only piece of good news is that Maureen's husband has picked up a little bit and is responding well in hospital but is still not quite out of danger yet. Maureen is being upbeat and very positive about it all, she never let's anything get her down, she is an amazing woman.

We cycle right into the centre of the Old Town today. This is not something I would normally even attempt to do as it's a bit dangerous with all the heavy vehicles ploughing up and down, but as there is so little traffic on the roads we decide to give it a go. It is a very pleasant ride and we go off the beaten track and end up in a suburb of the town which I have only ever been through in a taxi. We cycle right through the middle of a local food market which is busy and thriving with locals doing their shopping: I hope one of them is Greenies husband! We eventually meet the Thu Bon River and follow it to the town centre.

Along that part of the river there is no-one around and all the riverside hotels, bars and restaurants are closed.

Cycling back towards the coast, we eventually arrive at the almost empty beach and sit uncomfortably and thirsty for the rest of the afternoon. I say uncomfortably because all the sun loungers had mysteriously disappeared and the bars were shut. And my knee was killing me.

Whilst we are at the beach, Peter gets an alarming message on his phone that our flights on Thursday to Singapore have been cancelled. The Internet reception is not good at the beach at the best of times and he cannot find out any other information. We decide to go straight back to the hotel to find out what was going on. I have to say my heart was in my mouth and I was suppressing a rising panic. I'd gone all pale and shaky, Peter wasn't looking too happy either, he was frowning deeply - never a good sign on the face of the most laid back person in the world. Immediately all sorts of panicky visions and scenarios start racing through my head. We were just getting on the bikes when another email arrives to say we had been rebooked on an earlier flight. Golly, that was close, I cannot begin to describe the massive relief that overwhelmed us both.

Back in our room Peter fires up the lap top to get to the bottom of all of this. It is the short flight from Danang to Singapore that has been cancelled, the flight from Singapore to London is still going. The original flight was at 5pm but they have put us on an earlier flight at 11am, that's OK, it just means we will have to sit and wait at Singapore a bit longer.

He is scrolling through checking everything when he suddenly realises they have only rebooked him and not me. He double checks everything, yep I am not rebooked, I am not going anywhere.

That does it, my hormonal brain clicks into complete meltdown:

I can't go on this flight but cannot get back with my previous flight as we have cancelled it. Peter might have to go home without me and I will be stuck here for months on my own.

I will lose my job as I cannot imagine my company being very happy that I am on extended leave. I then won't ever get another job anyway as no-one wants a 55 year old menopausal woman working for them. Peter and I might not be able to weather the long separation and will split up, I won't be able to afford to live on my own so I will end up living in a caravan.

On and on my dopey brain went into overdrive which then resulted in having to rush to the toilet, this is my body's usual way of reacting to bad news.

With panic rising in both of us, we head down to reception to ring the local office of the Airline. We try explaining to the reception staff what we want to do and our concerns, they don't really understand our predicament. I end up having to ring Greenie to get her to translate to them what is happening so they can get us connected to the airline office.

When we eventually get to speak to someone, it is not great news. They are waiting for the computer system to transfer everyone over on to the earlier flight. It will be done in the order of date of booking. Peter booked in January, I only booked two days ago, I am at the bottom of the list. It may be that I get booked on to a different flight on another day, the lady said I could even be going tonight, we would get an email as soon as the computer clicked me over.

There then followed a very tense and strained four hours whilst we waited to find out what was happening. Erring on the side of caution and with nothing else to do, I decided to pack one of our suitcases incase I had to leave in a hurry. We walked along to the restaurant on the main road for some dinner where there were more unemployed drunken dive instructors. I couldn't eat a morsel but did manage to get three G&T's down my neck - in rapid succession.

Messages were coming in thick and fast from friends and family - COME HOME RIGHT NOW, THIS MINUTE, IMMEDIATELY. Not for want of trying I can tell you. How on earth did we end up in this weird and sticky situation? It had happened so quickly.

At last at 8.30pm we finally got the message we were waiting for - I was booked on both flights with Peter. Thank god for that!

We were both mightily relieved and I managed to get a couple of spring rolls down my neck to mix with the gin.

Good thing as my stomach was running on empty.

Wednesday 18th March

After a solitary breakfast, as we are the only remaining guests in the whole hotel, I get a jeep into town to do some shopping.

Not normal shopping mind you, I am on a mission to buy some drugs.

We have had an email from our local Doctors surgery stating that they were only going to be doing appointments over the phone and nothing in person for the near future. My fluffy brain has realised that if we go down with anything (chest/water/tooth infection etc) when we get home, we could have a real problem getting hold of any prescriptions for medication in a hurry. So I have hatched a plan to buy some antibiotics over the counter from a pharmacy I know in the Old Town. Sure enough, I get three sets of antibiotics (for three common conditions) and whilst I am at it I also manage to purchase two boxes of sleeping tablets. I don't use them regularly, more when I am desperate for a decent nights sleep and want total oblivion from the world. They are so addictive that my Dr will only give me twelve at a time and I have to make a personal visit to the surgery to get more as they won't give them out on a repeat prescription. The pharmacist hands over a little white bag, the total price for all of these illicit drugs - £8.

I take a last slow walk around the town trying to take in the sights and smells, to etch the vision onto my brain so I can recall it in the next few difficult months ahead. I am so sad that my time with my friends has been an almost complete disaster, I don't know when or if I will ever be coming back, it's too far in the distance to even contemplate it.
I receive reams of messages from Greenie, Anna & Eric. They are upset and distressed that I am leaving so soon and also terrified that I am going back to the centre of the Pandemic.
It's all too much for my fragile psyche and I end up sitting in a coffee shop in tears.
I don't feel very well, I get caught a bit short in town and have to rush to the nearest loo. Is it that I haven't drunk enough water or eaten something dodgy? No, I know exactly what it is - I am getting in a bit of a state about going home, if in fact we will actually get there and whether it is really a good idea to return anyway.

Back in our room, I stash all of the illicit drugs into Peters dirty socks and hide them at the bottom of the suitcase. There is a parcel in our room for me that has been left at reception by Anna's husband - Wow, he does exist after all. It is a framed photo of Anna and I with a little motto - 'Your little girl'. I instantly burst into tears.
I have such mixed emotions at this precise moment:
I know I must go home otherwise I could be stuck here for months but when will I see my darling girls again?
If I stayed when would I see Peter again? Whenever that might be, it could be months.
And what am I going to do here if I did stay? I can't work, I have no permit.

Where is the money going to come from to pay my way if I am not working?

On top of all of that, my visa was due to run out in a weeks time so I would probably get evicted from the country and heavily fined anyway.

I find Peter sprawled out by the swimming pool with his head in a book, I join him for a swim but feel a bit spaced out. I show him the photo frame and he can see that I am very upset and quite traumatised by the last few days.

After a short catnap I feel a little bit better so we get changed and go off in search of food - a sort of last supper. We eat at the same restaurant where we met the divers; tonight we are the only customers in there for the whole evening. There is no traffic at all on the main road and all the business and shops are locked up. There is no light from any of the houses, they go to bed early here. On the way back I am terrified that the rats are waiting to leap out on us. We see no rats but a large snake slithers across the road in front of us and disappears into the long grass. At the hotel all the lights are off except the one in reception and the one by our room, everything else is in eerie, silent darkness. We try to play cards in bed but I just cannot concentrate and keep losing again which then gives me the right hump.

I manage a group of volunteers who meet on Wednesday evenings. I speak to my friend, Lisa, who is running the unit in my absence. I suggest that maybe she should cancel the next few meetings as a safety precaution. On our WhatsApp group everyone sadly agrees that it is for the best, so the unit is temporarily closed down.

For how long we do not know.

Switching the light off I pray for a decent nights sleep, it is going to be a long tiring day tomorrow.

I just want it to be over now, it's been the strangest holiday ever, made up of three different parts:

1st week - OK but a bit weird
2nd week - Very weird
3rd week - Downright weird and I now want to go home.

Thursday 19th March

Peter's cheerful 2am news report is that Italy's death toll has overtaken that of China and the UK has 144 dead.
At home the department store Beales has closed all of it's stores. That's a favourite shop of mine wiped from the High Street.
Sadly, it is the first of many over the next few months.

The alarm goes off at 6.30am, rudely awakening me. I did manage to get some sleep despite the disturbing early hours briefing from my husband. After a shower we go down to the restaurant where the staff have laid out some bread, fruit and hot drinks for us. They have been very sweet and any other time we would have thoroughly enjoyed our stay at this beautiful hotel. Whilst we eat breakfast the staff are literally packing up the restaurant around us, they are going to lock the hotel up and all go home when we leave. Indefinitely.

Greenie, Eric and Sunny have broken the rules and turned up to see us off and were waiting for us in reception, Anna can't come because she is going into hospital today to have the operation on her dodgy hand. It's more than I can bear as I say goodbye to them, it is just too soon, we have not had enough time together. I give each of them a big hug, when I get to Greenie I lose it and break down completely, we hold onto each other really tight, I think my heart is going to break I am crying so much. I love that girl, she is the daughter I never had and at this point I do not know if I will ever see her again. It's a very emotional goodbye and even Peters eyes mist over when he sees how upset I am.
We get in the car and with a last wave to them, we set off for the long journey home, with me snivelling and drip drying all the way to the airport.

As we drive along the main coast road to Danang, which is the third largest city in Vietnam, there is no-one around, it is like an abandoned city. As we are approaching the outskirts we are pulled over by the Military and asked to get out of the car. I would say for dramatic effect that it was at gunpoint (it wasn't, but he did have a gun). At the side of the road are four people (couldn't say if they were male or female) wearing bio-hazard suits completely masked and gloved up and we are politely ushered towards them. We have to fill out a form with all our details of where we had been staying, where we had gone, when we arrived and the flight numbers we arrived on. They then took our temperatures and recorded it on the form. Phew, mine was only 36.3, no global warming emanating from me today. We were handed face masks, pink for me, blue for Peter, and informed that we would not be allowed into the city or the airport unless we wore them for the whole time - with no exceptions.

As we arrived at the International airport you could see that it was almost deserted too. On reading the departures board, every flight except 4 had been cancelled. There were 2 going to Taiwan, 1 to Japan and 1 to Singapore (ours) that were still flying. As you can imagine there were very few people queuing up to check in.

When we got to the desk there was a problem with the date between my visa and what had actually been stamped in my passport on my arrival. Peter was instructed to sit and wait whilst I was escorted by the check in girl to the Immigration hall where I was quizzed by a serious official as to the entry date on my passport. I had not noticed but when I arrived in Hanoi the officer who stamped my passport had recorded the date of expiry of my visa as 3-03-20. There then followed a bit of a kerfuffle between the check in staff and Immigration as to who was correct. If Immigration said that they were correct and wouldn't back down, it meant I had only three days left on my visa when I arrived and have illegally overstayed my welcome. In the end they decided it had been written down wrongly and actually said 30-3-20. This fortunately resulted in me not being arrested for having an out of date visa and heavily fined.

By now I was a little bit stressed to say the least and also getting very warm. The masks really make you hot and even Peter was suffering. They also make your glasses steam up so you have to wear them perched on the end of your nose to let the moisture out. Every passenger and member of staff was wearing them which gave the airport a slightly sinister feel as you could only see sets of eyes everywhere.

I had a bit of Vietnamese Dong left and wandered around the gift shops. I did buy a couple of key rings but could not muster up any enthusiasm for shopping, I wanted to get out of there.

Our flight was called and we made our way to the gate noticing that all the shops and restaurants looked like they were now getting ready to close. They were in fact waiting for us to leave so they could all go home - it was only 11am.

As our flight took off. Danang International airport closed down, (the Domestic terminal was still open) Central Vietnam shut it's doors and switched off all the lights to external visitors.

The short flight to Singapore was about half full, Peter and I had a row to ourselves. Everyone was quiet and subdued, well it is hard to have a conversation when you are mumbling underneath a mask with the engines of the old plane roaring in your ears.

I was so hot and uncomfortable that I thought I was going to combust, I never would have thought wearing a mask could make you produce so much heat. It was a mix of Western and Asian passengers aboard and we just did not know what to expect when we arrived in Singapore. As it turned out we were in for a big surprise.

Changi airport was heaving with what looked like the usual amount of passengers that pass through here every day. All the shops and restaurants were open and full of customers. Only around half of the people were wearing masks which was strange as I thought the Coronavirus was a problem here.

As it turned out, up to that date the Singaporeans had dealt with Covid-19 very well. Unfortunately after 19th March the disease got a real foot hold due to returning citizens who brought the virus back from all corners of the earth and the city had to go into full Lockdown. If we had returned home to the UK two days later we would have been quarantined in Singapore for another 14 days even though we were only passing through the airport. By then all flights to London could have been cancelled and we would have been stuck in Singapore indefinitely - not my favourite place. I spared a thought for the two older couples we had met a few days ago who were in Hoi An for another week yet. They would definitely get quarantined here, if in fact they could actually get out of Vietnam, and who knows if they would be able to fly to London in three weeks time.

We wandered around the terminal to try and kill some time and went to the orchid garden. Singapore is probably the only airport in the world that grows the most beautiful orchids in all of it's terminals. I love orchids but can't raise much enthusiasm for them today, but do manage to buy a box of cut flowers that you are allowed to take home with you which cost me £16.

They have some very upmarket designer shops here, way out of my price range. I did see an original of my new fake bag in the window of a very posh shop. It had a price tag of £2300.00!!! I declined the smart sales ladies offer to have a proper look at it.

We decided to splash out and pay to go into one of the airport lounges. Changi airport is so expensive to eat and drink that at £20 each the lounges are worth every penny. The downside is that we could only stay in there for three hours. But it was quiet and peaceful, away from the noisy concourse downstairs. There was plenty to eat and you could have whatever you wanted to drink. I had a plate of curry, some cake and three glasses of red wine, to dull the pain you understand. As there was no-one sitting anywhere near us we also removed our masks, well it is difficult to eat and drink whilst wearing one.

When our time was up in the lounge we still had four hours to kill before our flight. We walked around in circles but could not find anywhere to sit in the enormous terminal building, everywhere was packed out. Singapore is the gateway to the rest of the world and everyone was evidently trying to get home. We finally ended up sitting by the departure Gate for four hours, I read my book whilst Peter scrawled through his phone. At this point we had put our masks back on. We felt that they must be of some use, look at the Vietnamese, they wear them all the time and had managed to get away so far with very little spread of the disease.

By now time was getting on and we were beginning to feel tired, I hoped the plane was still empty as it had been at the time of booking, so we might get a bit of room to lay down and sleep. When we were eventually admitted to the departure gate, there were six flights all leaving around the same time and it was heaving with people. Everyone was nervously eyeing up everyone else, but very few passengers were masked up like us. At this point I would not have taken my mask off for any reason, who knew where all these thousands of people had travelled from and what they might be carrying.

The flight was eventually called and everyone did the usual airport thing and crammed into the queue straight away, no social distancing going on here at all. We held back a little, we did not want to stand with everyone else in the tunnel whilst we boarded. What was the point of going through everything we had and now throwing all precautions out of the window. When we got on board I was shocked to see it was rammed full. This was a A380 and it looked like all 441 seats were taken. There were English, French, Germans, Spanish, Scandinavians, Italians and Russians, all flying into London to try to get connecting flights back home. This airline had cancelled all flights into Central Europe and Russia and these passengers were taking their chances by going to the UK first, hoping to get a flight home out of London. So if they were carrying the virus they were taking it to London first, spreading it around and then taking it home to spread it around in their own country. How on earth was that being allowed?

At that time you could still fly into Europe from the UK. We were also a hub between USA and the rest of the world.

We appeared to be the only passengers wearing any sort of face covering, certainly in our part of the cabin. A huge Norwegian chap plonked himself down next to Peter, bang went my feeble hope of getting any sleep.

There then followed a 13 hour journey of pure purgatory where I was squashed into my seat, sitting bolt upright, with my knee causing me excruciating agony as I couldn't straighten it out, totally surrounded by different nationalities all coughing, sneezing, talking very loudly or snoring. I was so upset and stressed out at this point that I almost forgot to worry about the plane crashing on takeoff.

Peter and I wiped everything down, pulled up our hoodies and kept our masks on for the whole flight. I think we went through a whole bottle of hand gel, the other passengers seemed to be from a different planet, did they not know what was going on in Europe?

At that exact moment in time I felt if were we were going to catch any disease it would be on this flight.

The staff were lovely, the service was good, the alcohol free flowing and the meals were tasty - it was just all lost on me, I wanted to get home to the normality of my own home and bed. I did manage to watch the rest of 'Parasite' which I missed on the way to Hanoi, that felt like a million years ago. It's a strange film but I have definitely seen worse, I probably need to watch it again sometime. I dozed off several times but kept getting woken up by the pissed French bloke in front of me who was up and down like a yo-yo, knocking my seat every time he moved.

Friday 20th March

When we eventually landed into Heathrow it was still dark. Emerging from the plane onto another Continent was a surreal experience. It was like the whole Vietnamese episode had never happened, had it just been a bad dream? No-one was wearing masks, we seemed to be the only people in the whole of the terminal wearing face coverings. Everything was open and there was a huge crowd of people waiting at the arrivals gate when we came through.

Peter had an inspired idea to go to the M&S in the terminal to pick up some food and milk in case we couldn't get any in the supermarket at home. Most of the shelves were bare but he came out with a strange assortment of TV dinners, milk, iced buns and crisps. This was our first glimpse of the panic buying that had besieged Britain whilst we had been away.

We had to get on an airport parking bus to pick up Peters car which should have run every 20 minutes but the service had been reduced to hourly. Outside of the terminal there was very little sign of life, we had just missed a bus and had to wait another hour. It wasn't cold but it felt like Siberia having come from the heat and humidity of Vietnam.

It wasn't a bad dream then, it was real.

We eventually got to our car, we were the only passengers on the bus. On the way home the M25 still had plenty of traffic but it was all moving, not the biggest car park in the world today.

We had arranged to pick our dog up from my sisters house en route. We had strict instructions that we would not be allowed in the house and the dog exchange had to take place on the doorstep. She was totally paranoid about catching this virus as she has asthma and was high risk. I stayed in the car, waving at her and my nephew who were watching from the upstairs window whilst Peter and my sisters husband did the dog swap on the drive. My poor brother in law later got the biggest bollocking off my sister for speaking to Peter for so long!

When we got back home, we dumped all the luggage and the dog. She always ignores us for a few days every time we come home from holiday, she already had the right hump and retired to her bed. We then ventured out to our local supermarket. We had no food in the house and thought it might be a bit of a marathon if we had to go to several shops to get any food.

It's the last thing you want to do after a 29 hour journey but needs must. In the end the shop was open as usual, we just walked in, there were no queues. There was also not a lot of stock. There was a complete lack of meat, eggs, rice, pasta, toilet roll, cleaning products and soap. We managed to get some food, including quite a lot of frozen stuff which I don't usually buy, to fill up the fridge and freezer. It was an odd shopping experience though, there was a very strange atmosphere and it was so unusual to see so many empty shelves. We are so used to the shops hardly ever running out of anything. Talking to the lady on the till, she said that three pallets of toilet roll had been put out this morning and was gone within 5 minutes. She also said some customers had been pinching it out of other peoples trolleys and Security had been called to the aisle. What on earth is that all about? Fighting over toilet rolls - what a bunch of morons.

Back home we put the shopping away and I set about unpacking our cases. I always wash every piece of clothing we take, even if it hasn't been worn as I find it all has that certain holiday smell. Lifting out one of Peters shoes, a handful of sand sprayed out and went all over the bed and carpet. Standing in the bedroom clutching a dirty T shirt to my face with sand all over my feet, I shut my eyes, breathed in the smell and transported myself back to Hoi An. I could see the girls, hear the motorcycles, feel the heat and smell the food. I felt a sort of blackness starting to descend, I could see an invisible small black dog out of the corner of my eye, so I quickly set about making myself busy to beat the misery off.

I arranged my beautiful purple orchids in a glass vase and put them on the kitchen table, a reminder that I had in fact been on holiday even if it didn't feel like it.

Maureen's husband was improving slowly but she says he is still very weak and his dementia has really kicked in. He can't do anything for himself and has no idea where he is part of the time. She is worried that he will catch the virus and in his fragile state it will definitely finish him off.

The latest news in our village was that all the schools were closing down until possibly September. What! That was complete madness. It was also bad news for me, the boy next door drove me mad kicking his football against the fence. I don't care what other noise the kids next door make, inside or out, but the sound of him whacking his leather football around a garden the size of a postage stamp was really irritating. It had been difficult enough last year to sit in the garden and get some peace but at least they went out now and again. If he was at home for 5 months I would never get a moments silence in my own back garden for the whole Summer.

Later on that evening Peter whipped up one of the TV dinners each as if he were a Michelin star chef and we opened a bottle of wine. We managed to stay awake until 9pm when we gave in to the jet lag and retired to bed.

It is always lovely to get into your own bed isn't it?

What would the next few months have in store for us all?

Saturday 21st March

This morning we get a bit of an idea, rumours were beginning to circulate in the media that the UK might go into total Lockdown next week. We hatched a plan and set off to visit the DIY store. It seemed like everyone else had the same idea, as the shop was very busy and a lot of the shelves were already empty. We bought paint, brushes and rollers. None of this was for Peter's use you understand, it was all for me. We have a three storey house (which I decorate) and there is a lot of wall to paint. Last time I did it it nearly killed me and I was younger then, the menopause hadn't got it's vicious grip on me at that time. Now it was looking like I might have a lot of free time on my hands so I might as well just get on with it, there wouldn't be anything else to do at weekends. I could do it slowly floor by floor and try to ignore the upheaval it would cause. At least it would take my mind off of everything else.

When we got home from the shops Peter spent all afternoon on his laptop, talking to his 'Virtual' friends as I call them, completely oblivious to me doing all the holiday washing and ironing. I wasn't even due to come home until tomorrow and Peter had previously said he would do the housework before he picked me up from Heathrow. That obviously hadn't happened, the house hadn't been touched since I cleaned it three weeks ago, so I had to do that as well. The dog was still sulking on her bed and hadn't moved since she got home.

What a homecoming. I had really thought when I first set off on my three week holiday that I would come home happy and healed and it would set me up to get me through the Summer months. A bit of R&R after the crappy six months I had gone through was supposed to be the tonic to uplift and empower me. Well, there had been fat chance of any of that happening after the strange few weeks I had just had, which my middle aged hormonal brain was still trying to process.
Now I was home my night sweats had gone into complete overdrive, I was a soaking wet boiling hot mess in the bedroom. I felt deflated and flat, a sure sign of being a bit stressed out. I looked up the figures for Vietnam, they now had over 100 cases but no deaths. The UK currently had 4094 cases and 180 poor people had died.

Should I have taken my paramedic friends advice and just stayed there and sat it out?
The jury was still out at this point.

Sunday 22nd March

It was Mothers Day today and what did Maureen get as a present? Her still very ill husband sent home by ambulance for her to care for on her own. She is 82.

She has been told that as from tomorrow there will be a care package arranged, so she should get some help with getting him up, washed and dressed. As for her own mental wellbeing, being locked in for weeks with a sick, frail person with dementia for sole company was not going to be easy. Knowing Maureen, she will just take it on the chin and get on with it - she never moans. We can't go to see them as we have been abroad and have been advised not to visit them as they are classed as vulnerable. It's a sad situation, we can't do anything except be at the end of the phone.

I receive a call from my boss informing me that I must work from home for the next week. I point out that Vietnam is much safer than here and I do not have the virus or any symptoms but it falls on deaf ears. The company says I must self isolate for 7 days as I have just come in from abroad, even though that is not what the Foreign office advocates for people coming in from Vietnam. Due to the way I am feeling at the moment this is not what I want to hear. I need to go back to work and see my colleagues, not sit at home vegetating on my arse for another week.

Oh well at least I will be able to get over the jet lag properly before I have to return to the daily work routine.

I receive lots of frantic messages from Greenie and Anna, they are almost hysterical (hard for a Viet to do) that I am going to die. The Vietnamese news is really emphasising the high death rate in Europe and they are frantic for me. I play it down and this placates them a little bit.

Anna tells me that the police have been checking up on all the locals to ensure they are not going out and are abiding by the rules. Her husbands coffee shop has been raided by the police, fortunately he had no customers in there at the time. She is out of hospital but has to have physiotherapy daily at the hospital and she can't get anyone to look after La Vie whilst she attends her sessions. I tell her that her husband will just have to pull his finger out - she doesn't really understand what I mean.

Peter spends most of the day fiddling around on his lap top again. He says he is working, well that's a new name for it. The weather is nice so

I venture out to the garden, the grass has got really long and needs cutting. I lug the Fly-mo out of the shed and set about mowing the lawn. I am just finishing the last corner of the garden when a tiny stone flies up into the air. There then follows a noise that will be forever etched on my brain, it sounded like a bullet being fired from a gun. Turning around I can see that a tiny stone has hit the (expensive) patio bi-fold doors and has smashed one of the glass panels. Completely smashed it to smithereens like a shattered windscreen. I stand there, frozen to the spot totally horrified, Peter looks like he is about to have a coronary. On examination there is a tiny hole in the glass, the stone must have been going very fast to cause such wreckage. It has not gone all the way through the double glazed panels, only one side. Fortunately we can both acknowledge that it is just an unfortunate accident, there are far more important things going on in the world to make too much fuss over it. It's just another thing gone wrong. The worry is that with the current situation unfolding, when will it ever get fixed? Peters goes off in the car to purchase something to secure the broken pane with and I finish the lawn off with the garden shears on my hands and knees.
I am terrified to use the hover mower ever again.

Later in the afternoon we went out to pick up my new car which we had ordered two weeks before I went on holiday. If we had known then what we know now we would never have ordered it and I would have kept the old one. But the deal had been done, the deposit paid, the paperwork signed and it was now ready for collection.
The car was lovely. It was such a shame, as it turned out I didn't really get to drive it anywhere except to work and the supermarket for the next few months.

Every moment wasted looking back, keeps us moving forward - Hilary Clinton

4. First Lockdown

Monday 23rd March

So today was the first day of a week working from home for me. It was a novel experience, one I hope never to repeat. I know some of my friends absolutely love it, I didn't enjoy it at all and felt very isolated and a bit excluded from what was going on in the office. After the three strange weeks I had just experienced, I needed to be with people and this was not a healthy scenario for me. All the office staff kept in touch by WhatsApp, some of them were also working from home, but I hated every second, it wasn't for me at all.

It probably wasn't helped by the chaos that unfolded within the company. We were instructed to cancel everything up until the end of June which we had just spent months sorting out. From what I understood from what was going on in the office, total panic and pandemonium had set in and everyone was running around like chickens with their heads cut off. We had been told the week before to only follow the online guidance on our website but different sets of management were making decisions left right and centre and no-one knew what the hell was going on.

I sat in front of my computer for 8 solid hours letting our customers know what was happening, making calls and dealing with the 400 emails that were waiting for me after my holiday.

Peter had been trying all day to get hold of the insurance company and the glazier regarding the broken glass for the patio door, but couldn't get through to anyone. It was like everything had already shut down.

When Peter came home from work we watched the evening news together: it was all confirmed.

As from today the UK would be in total Lockdown for three weeks and the police had the power to fine you if you broke the rules. There were only four reasons you could leave your house :

To go to work if you couldn't work from home
To go shopping only for food or medicine
To attend to any medical need
To take one form of exercise per day for 1 hour

And that was it.

In the 21st century, a 1st world country ranked as having the sixth largest economy on the planet was shut down due to a virus that had emanated (allegedly) from a meat market in China.

Tuesday 24th March

Peter now had a major dilemma. He runs his own business with a partner out of a factory in Leicester. They had a big machinery installation booked in Somerset for today which was worth quite a lot of money to the business. They were going to need that injection of cash to get them through this period. It had all been arranged with the shop keeper and they had to decide whether to do the job or not. In the end Peter got up at 2am and went off to do it, fortunately they did not get stopped by the police. Afterwards they went into their own factory, shut it down and sent all the staff home on furlough, including Peter and his business partner.

Peter was now going to be at home for the foreseeable future. He set about looking at what the Government was going to do to financially help out small businesses. He worked out that his business probably had enough money in the bank along with help from the furlough scheme to last until August. All of his customers were now closed, you cannot repair and install machinery from home, so he was temporarily out of work.

OMG, would we end up killing each other, stuck at home together with no outside interests?? Most couples only spend significant amounts of time together during holidays and Christmas, how would we cope for three weeks locked up in the house?

Poor Maureen was at her wits end, no carers had turned up to help her and she could not get through to anyone on the phone who could offer any helpful solution. I know there was an unprecedented crisis on, but who leaves an 82 year old woman to care for a very sick, elderly, senile man on her own at home without ensuring that help was in place before they sent him home from hospital? At this rate the two of them would end up in hospital and we could lose them both.

I set up a family WhatsApp group so that we could all keep in touch as it was evident we would not be seeing each other for some time. Everyday throughout this weird period, someone posted a funny picture or video which at least made you smile or grimace whichever way you looked at it. I hadn't seen my mother since the middle of February and who knows when we would meet again. This was a real technological challenge for her, but two days later she popped up on the WhatsApp chat. She even mastered sending a sticker with her comments, something that I still hadn't fathomed out how to do. I included Maureen in the family group, she said the daily chat and funny video's kept her sane.

In my home office I was still tapping away on the computer. I am not very good with technology and needed somehow to log onto Microsoft TEAMS for a meeting. Fortunately Peter was in a benevolent mood, he normally gets arsey with me when I ask him for help with the computer. He moved everything around, set up TEAMS for me, arranged my work and voluntary stuff into a better system and even set up Classic FM so I could listen to it whilst I was working. At least it helped to drown out the sound of the banging football next door. Mind you they were now in a bit of a home schooling regime and the football only came out at break times today which was fair enough.

From the sound of it, it might be that being at home was better than being in the office. Apparently there were all sorts of people wandering around the building setting up new emergency systems to deal with the business side of things, there was no self distancing and some of the staff were getting very nervous and upset about catching the virus with the vast amount of new people coming in and out all the time.

I spent the evening ringing around my volunteers who I had not spoken to for 4 weeks, making sure they were all OK. We already had a WhatsApp group set up and I encouraged everyone to keep in touch, it might be a while until we saw each other again. About 60% of my members were still working full time, around 20% were furloughed and the rest either had medical conditions or were living with family who did. One of my ladies was laid up in bed along with her husband, they both had chest infections and were really unwell; that didn't sound good.
The Coronavirus symptoms were a bad cough, a very high temperature and loss of smell and taste: yep, they had all of those.

Big news from the sporting world was that the 2020 Olympics had been postponed until next year. The Summer Olympics have only ever been cancelled three times in its history, once in 1916 during WW1 and twice during WW2. This was extraordinary and worryingly the start of all large sporting and outdoor events being cancelled, including Wimbledon and the London Marathon.

Wednesday 25th March

Today all restaurants, pubs, shops, gyms, garden centres, parks, museums, cinemas, in fact anywhere you might enjoy going for leisure, were closed leaving the British public with nowhere to go, even if you could you couldn't. If you get my drift.

The news today is that Spain officially has now had more deaths than China, with 3434 fatalities. Prince Charles has been confirmed as suffering from the Coronavirus, but so far the queen has not succumbed. Good old girl, she would just keep on going anyway.
An interesting fact was that India had now gone into Lockdown. How on earth were the Government going to keep 1.3 billion people indoors? Apparently the answer is armed police out on the streets.
Another interesting piece of information was that Wuhan, where the virus originated, had hardly any new cases and the town was beginning to return to some normality. Rub it in why don't you! You cause a world meltdown and then calmly mention your town is nearly free of it! From a British national volunteering perspective, 17,000 amazing people had come forward to assist the NHS in any way they can.

Peter decided today was the day (after 15 years) to prune a Leylandii tree at the bottom of our garden. So he spent all day sawing, swinging from a ladder covered in tree sap and generally making a complete mess of the garden. He was as happy as a pig in shit. The weather was lovely and what was there not to enjoy out in the fresh air. Unfortunately there was no way of getting rid of the tree debris as all the tidy tips were closed and the green bin collection had been suspended, so he had to pile it all up in a heap in front of the shed. This resulted in me not being able to get my deck chair out, so whenever I wanted to sit in the garden I had to sit on a hard metal bench.

A carer had finally turned up this morning to assist Maureen with her husband, at last a light at the end of the tunnel for her. She says they were marvellous with him - thank the lord for that.

I sat at my desk all day long and tapped out email after email to our customers, cancelling all of their organised events which they had worked hard on. It was particularly poignant that all of the special VE Day celebrations would have to be cancelled. A lot of them were rebooking for next year which was great but that wouldn't help with our current cash flow.

For the first time in 30 years as a volunteer, I had the whole Summer off, completely unheard of. This is something I had secretly wished for over the last few years, now it was a glaring reality. I could actually attend fetes, galas, concerts, garden shows, open air cinema's, horse racing and air shows as a visitor instead of working, what a lovely thought. But then the truth of our situation would come crashing down on me that I would have to stay indoors like everyone else, it was starting to look as if there would be no events to attend countrywide. And oh shit, Peter who is actually a bit of a workaholic would be at home ALL THE TIME.

I had already worked out that the murder, birth and divorce rate was going to go through the roof during this time. Oh dear would we become one of the statistics? I might kill him or divorce him but I realised at least I wouldn't get pregnant, it was much too late at 55 for that to happen to me.

Thursday 26th March

I wake up to a barrage of messages from Greenie and Anna, they are still besides themselves with worry about me. The big news each day in Vietnam is all about the increasing death toll in Europe and they are panicking for me. I don't know what else to tell them apart from that I am OK and have no signs and symptoms.
They have now had 141 cases now in Vietnam but no deaths, our figures must look horrendous compared to theirs and they obviously think Armageddon has arrived in the UK.

I get messages and videos sent to me throughout the day. This is an unparalleled time in history and at the moment being at home is a novelty for everyone. It's all a bit of a lark having three weeks of paid leave. It appears most of my friends and family are decorating, gardening or catching up with jobs around the house. Everyone is keeping busy, let's face it it's only for three weeks.
Yeah really?

Peter has at last managed to get hold of the glazier regarding our broken door, he never did get any answer from the insurance company. The company has ordered the glass but we have no idea when it will get fixed as they have shut down as well. We were also supposed to be having a brand new front door installed today which we ordered before the holiday but that has been cancelled as well due to obvious reasons.

So we have two doors in waiting.

As part of my working day today I have been asked to do an online Loggist course so that I will be able to help out in a Call Centre that is being set up at work. This had to be the least exciting course I have ever done and I'm not really sure how it will help much with answering the phone.
It was two hours of my life that I will never get back.

Whilst I was busy dying of boredom online, the British people came out onto their doorsteps for a huge round of applause for the NHS which I completely missed. Peter didn't do it either as he was on a work call. I was told it was a very special moment.

I feel that at last I am now properly back on UK time and the jet lag has gone, but I am not sleeping well at all. I keep re-running my holiday through my head, and it disturbs me so much the way it had all unfolded. My brain is still trying to process how it happened so fast, there was so little signal of the world melt down. Yes we had heard of Covid 19 but there was no warning that it would take off globally the way it did. One week it was OK and the next.......
We were so lucky to get home but I am not sure if I have done the right thing (for me) in coming home, and it is giving me sleepless nights. The sweats are particularly vicious at the moment and I awake several times during the night soaking wet. The bed clothes are sticking to me and I literally have sweat running down my chest between my boobs. It is not a pleasant sensation. I then have to lay on top of the duvet to cool down where the sweat dries on my body and I end up freezing cold.
My brain doesn't stop churning, mad thoughts are whizzing through my head - meanwhile Peter drops off the minute his head hits the pillow.

Friday 27th March

I don't usually work on Fridays but due to the current situation I thought it might be prudent to check my work emails throughout the day in case one of our customers is waiting for an answer from me. So all day long I was up and down the stairs to the computer.

I did receive one important email, not from a customer though. Peter and I were about to celebrate our 20th wedding anniversary and had booked a cruise for the end of April. At this point we had no expectations that we would be going and suspected that it would get cancelled. I have to say the cruise company were more than fair. We could have our money back or we could book another cruise up to March 2022 at 125% of what we had paid. Which meant that even though we had only paid £1700, we could book another cruise for £2100 and not pay any extra.We decided to leave the money with them for the mean time and would look at it later on in the year or early 2021, I am sure the cruise company had enough to do at the moment.

I emptied our second bedroom and ensuite, piling everything into the box room one floor up. My plan for today was to start painting. Peter helped move the furniture out, leaving the double mattress leaning against the bannister on the landing and then went back to staring all day at his laptop. He had been asked to assist in arranging some voluntary assistance for some workers who were setting up an enormous temporary mortuary not far from our house to take the bodies from the overcrowded hospital morgues.
I think it was exactly at that point that I finally realised the novelty week off we had just had was becoming a very real and deadly serious situation.

So whilst Peter was occupied with sorting out people for that, I got my brushes and rollers out and commenced the mammoth task of decorating most of the house. My plan was to do the bedroom, ensuite, downstairs toilet, three floors of the hall and then the little box room. Not all at once, obviously.
I hadn't decorated for five years and back then I found it an exhausting task. I am menopausal, five years older with creaky joints, it would probably finish me off this time. But it needed doing desperately and might cheer me up if the house looked fresh and clean.

<u>Saturday 28th March</u>

I was up bright and early to get on with the decorating. The bedroom was painted cornflower white, which is really pale blue, and I wanted it pure white. Unfortunately it soon became evident that it would need at least two coats of paint if not three, as the blue was still showing through. I thought that was the point of buying one coat paint? I might as well buy the cheaper stuff if it is going to need several coats, three coats of one coat was blooming expensive, if you understand where I am coming from.
All day I laboured on whilst Peter sat at the breakfast bar organising his mortuary cover. He ought to be very careful, he might end up in there himself if he doesn't at least bring me a cup of tea and a sandwich.

The ensuite was already white and only needed one coat which dried very quickly. I then decided to give it a really good clean. I only need glasses for close up work so don't usually wear them when I am cleaning but for some reason I kept them on. That's another thing that is on the downwards slide, my eyesight. I used to have fantastic vision and it is only in the last five years that I have needed glasses. I cannot read anything printed without them. Each time I have an eye test the prescription gets stronger.

OMG I could not believe how dirty the bathroom was. It always looks clean but with my close up glasses on I could see that the tiles and sink pedestal were filthy. I felt quite embarrassed that I hadn't noticed before, don't know why. Peter obviously hasn't noticed what a skanky cleaner I am. By the time I was finished you needed to wear your sunglasses in there, it was pristine and a job well done.

I was just finishing off when the phone rang. I heard Peter pick it up and get heavily involved in a conversation - this is unusual for him, sometimes he doesn't even speak, he just passes the handset over to me. I caught bits and pieces of it and got the gist that someone we knew had died.

'Who is it?' I whispered.

'Julie' Peter said.

An icy grip clutched my heart, my best friend Julie was dead? I had only spoken to her a few days ago, she wasn't even ill then.

He handed the phone over, Julie was speaking on the other end. Phew what a relief! But it was not good news, her 85 year old dad died yesterday morning from what sounded like a sudden heart attack. We had a long chat, it was so sudden, apart from a bit of dementia he was in generally good health. What happens now? Can they have a funeral? All unanswered questions. She had a phone appointment to register the death on Monday once she received the death certificate by email.

As I was completely covered from head to toe in white emulsion I had a bath to soak it all off. I was tired and ached all over, much more than usual, I am just not used to all of that stretching and bending. My joints ache constantly anyway and this massive task had put extra pressure on them. My knee was absolute agony where I had been kneeling on it to paint the skirting boards.

After dinner I drank two goldfish bowl size gin and tonics and passed out on the sofa.

Sunday 29th March

Peter and I had an awful night. The chemical smell of the gloss paint had made its way throughout the house and we were both awake half of the night with dodgy breathing and itchy eyes. The enormous G&T's I had drunk before bedtime didn't help with my night sweats either. They were completely off the scale again and I woke up time after time, laying in a big wet patch in the bed. So elegant, refined and romantic!

This mornings news is that over 10,000 people have now died in Italy and the UK death figure is up to 1228. New York City has announced that they will run out of critical medical supplies by 5th April, which sounds odd as their President has been boasting of being able to provide PPE to the rest of the world.

I manage to do the last coat of paint in the bedroom and also get the downstairs loo painted. That was also filthy on closer inspection, by the time I was finished it literally sparkled. It was so lovely to be able to put everything back in the bedroom and get the mattress off the landing. I hate living in a mess, I am a very tidy and organised person, Peter calls me Mrs Neat. I put away a lot of ornaments and discarded some pictures, so the room looked fresh and new.
I was very pleased with my handiwork but oooh, I ached in some funny places, I had used muscles that I had forgotten existed. Another bath was called for and I lay in there for ages letting the paint soak off of my skin and the hot water ease my discomfort.
Peter in the meantime had miraculously rubbed down and painted the garage door to match the colour of the new door we were waiting for. The garage was used to keep his precious motorbikes in which was the only reason he got involved with any painting at all.

The only other thing that happened today was that our washing machine started to make a funny noise and was doing the 'Lambada' around the kitchen when it was on the spin cycle. All the electrical appliances in our kitchen had been brand new when we moved in 15 years ago. The cooker had died at Christmas and it was only time before everything else followed it to the kitchen graveyard. I just hope it doesn't go now.

Monday 30th March

This morning I am allowed to go in to the office - Hurrah. For the first time in four weeks I put on smart clothes, stiletto shoes and a trowel full of makeup. The A1, which is normally a car park on Monday mornings, has hardly any traffic and I get to work in record time. When I walk into the office they all whistle at me. I refuse to let my standards slip even during this crisis. One of the younger girls says that she would faint if I came to work wearing jeans and trainers!

Oh it's good to see everyone, I am so pleased to see all my colleagues, but one of them is missing. Our friend Tracey has some medical conditions and is working from home temporarily, no-one knows when we will see her in the office again. After filling them all in on my holiday nightmare, they filled me in with what had been happening at work.

Everything had been cancelled until the end of June, it was now all about how much money we were going to lose. Fortunately the NHS had requested some assistance which could bring in some much needed income.

Tempers had been very frayed the previous week and some personnel seemed to be on a mission to conquer the world. Shit had been flying around at a rate of knots and staff had been pulled left, right & centre. And there was still no self distancing. A Call Centre had been set up with 7 desks all lined up next to each other and the room seemed to be crammed with people all the time, Peter was in there today helping out in a voluntary capacity. Volunteers were calling in thick and fast from all over the region to see where they could help, and it was general pandemonium. But I am informed that it was much better organised than the previous week.

I don't do chaos very well, thank heavens I had stayed at home.

I rang my friend Julie at lunchtime to see what progress she had made with her dads funeral arrangements. The death certificate said her fathers death was caused by the Coronavirus, which seemed very odd to us. Even the Doctor at the hospital had said it was probably a heart attack. This is all probably due to them not having the time or staff to carry out a postmortem. I suppose it doesn't make any difference, he's gone, it won't change anything for anybody whether it was Coronavirus or heart attack. My friend had an online appointment later in the week to discuss the funeral which would only allow a maximum of 10 mourners.

The drive home from work that evening was a very strange experience. I probably only passed a dozen cars during the normal rush hour at 5pm. The A1 had hardly any traffic at all. It was like an apocalypse had occurred and I felt very alone on that drive home with no other vehicles around.

When I got in, we opened a bottle of wine and slouched in front of the TV, a terrible habit that we got into over the next few weeks.

Tuesday 31st March

Back in the office, we are working either a late or early shift now to cover the phones in the Call Centre between 8am and 8pm. It was evident that social distancing is not being taken seriously in our building. There are signs up everywhere but no-one takes a blind bit of notice, people are wandering in and out, willy nilly. Some of the girls in my office are really scared of catching the virus, let's face it the media is full of it and some people are actually terrified. I am starting to get a bit cross about the lack of concern for some of my colleagues. I feel my anger beginning to come to the fore and know I am not going to be able to keep my big mouth shut for much longer.

The UN has stated that this Pandemic is the worlds biggest crisis since the 2nd World War. I had to look that word up as I don't understand the difference between an Epidemic and a Pandemic:
Epidemic is a disease that affects a large number of the population within a community, population or region
Pandemic is an Epidemic that is spread over multiple countries or continents.
So the Coronavirus is a world Pandemic.The way to remember it is that the 'P' in Pandemic means it has got a 'passport' and will travel.
Well, I learnt something new today.

It has not been a great day when I arrive home at 20.45 pm. I can't be bothered to start cooking at this time of night so we have a bag of crisps each, open another bottle of wine in front of the TV and roll into bed around 11.30pm, which is really late for us.

Wednesday 1st April

I am on late shift which means I get another lay in. I am really not a morning person and have offered to do all of the late shifts which are not so popular with the other girls in the office. Peter and I don't wake up until 8.30. Normally he would be out of the house by 5am and I

would get up at 7am. When he eventually gets up he makes me a cup of tea and comes back to bed where I am still snuggled under the duvet. We try to have a lunchtime meal before I leave for work at 1pm which serves as breakfast as well for me. As you can already tell, the normal dietary routine has gone right down the tubes and I am already starting to notice a bit of extra weight here and there.
This then becomes the normal pattern of our days.

Everyone is on a mission in the office to wind everyone else up and there are a lot of ego's on display. There are certainly a lot of peacocks strutting around. As there are so many people in and out of the Call Centre, we girls have elected to stay isolated in our office until needed, getting on with what little work we have left. The young Call Centre manager on shift has other ideas, he taps his fingers on the table and demands we sit in there with the rest of them.
We just ignore him. Someone should warn him that he should never argue with three menopausal women, he won't EVER win.

The Office Manager and myself put up signs asking people not to come upstairs unless absolutely necessary, everyone ignores them. We try locking the office door but that doesn't work either; when there is a knock on the door we open it and someone saunters in with a set of keys that could have been left on reception. Two of my colleagues are nearly in tears, they are terrified of catching the virus and passing it on to their elderly relatives. I myself am not even slightly worried about catching it but I do not like to see them upset. I march in to see the boss and explain that we are not happy about the lack of social distancing in the building, he prints out more notices and signs them to make them look more official. We stick them up all around the building, you can hardly see through the glass front door it is covered in so many signs. Nobody takes the slightest bit of notice, they don't think it applies to them and still they wander in to our office. As a last resort we put some screens across the stairs, surely they can't miss them.

Oh yes they can. Two people, come waltzing into our office looking for someone on a social call. Where was the hygiene in that? They have obviously moved the screens aside to get up the stairs. Are they blind, did they not read the signs?
This the last straw and I tell them that they really should not be upstairs. They start giving me a mouthful and I hold up my hand to challenge them as to why they have ignored all the signs. If it was that important one of them could have come to convey a message, it doesn't need both of them. An almighty argument then erupts which the boss has to get

involved in. They say they are being excluded from upstairs and it's not right, even though they have their own work room set up downstairs (which we are not allowed entry to). They seem to think as they are working for us they are perfectly entitled to go wherever they want in the building. The boss says he is between a rock and a hard place. No he isn't, his job is to protect the staff who are still working and obey the Governments advice about self distancing.

In the end I walk away, I've only been back at work three days and am worn out with it all already. No-one in our office has an ego and I can't be doing with the ego's of men with small penises.

I go home, there is a packet of crisps and a very large glass of wine waiting for me.

Thursday 2nd April

This morning I got up early and ventured out to the supermarket, as we haven't been shopping since 20th March and needed more food. One thing I have noticed is that I am not throwing anything away. Any old veg out of the fridge, I just cut the black bits off and cook it, I scrape any green mould off the cheese, fortunately Peter doesn't notice the difference.

Shopping was a weird experience. The car park was empty, normally it would be full of shoppers going into town as well as into the supermarket. The queue went around the back of the store and out into the car park. It was only that long because we were all trying to stay 2 metres apart, it did move fairly quickly and I was inside within 15 minutes. Most of the shelves were fairly well stocked apart from a complete absence of toilet roll and soap. The luxury of browsing had gone out of the window and I literally zoomed around the shop just buying what was on my list. At the checkout there was a huge perspex screen between me and the very chatty cashier who wanted to discuss the merits of every item on the conveyor belt. Why do they always want to natter when you want to get in and out in a hurry?

The washing machine is definitely on the blink, it has been dancing around the kitchen again, this time I swear it was doing a Cha Cha Cha. How much longer can it keep going? It would be a nightmare if it breaks down now, how soon could we get another one? I always said if I was on a desert island the two items I would take with me are my washing machine and my kitchen scissors, they are the two most useful things on the planet in my book. Oh well, I will have plenty of time to

hand wash all of Peters dirty pants and socks in the coming weeks if it dies on us.
Oh the joy of it all.

I manage to speak to my friend Mary who I met in Hoi An last year. She lives in Dublin and has a holiday home in the South of France, I had a lovely few days with her there in October. I had been planning to go to see her in Dublin this Summer but that was obviously off the cards now. She was OK, hating the Lockdown, she is a very friendly and sociable person. Normal lively Dublin had completely shut down and was like a ghost town, all very depressing.

After a quick snack for lunch I went to the office. The atmosphere is awful and no-one seems very happy. The phones are quiet and so far we had only been asked to help out at one hospital and the makeshift mortuary, so some of our volunteers were going nuts because there is so little to do at the moment. A lot of normally very busy people had had the brakes applied full on in their lives and now did not know what to do with themselves.
I might be in the minority but actually thought this was a good thing as it meant the NHS was coping well with the situation and was not overrun.

I get a very alarming text message halfway through my shift from one of the sons of my friend and her husband who had chest infections. They were being transferred to hospital with suspected Covid -19 and were both very ill. I immediately rang him, he could hardly speak he was crying so much, they were actually loading his parents into the ambulances as we spoke. He didn't know when he would see them again as he would not be allowed anywhere near the hospital to visit and he was beside himself. He is a really big lad and to hear him sobbing his heart out like that was truly awful and gut wrenching. I hung up the phone and broke down in tears myself.

The virus had now entered my own circle of friends and was becoming very real and very dangerous.

When I got home at 20.30 pm (I missed the clap for NHS again), Peter had brought me a massive bunch of red roses to cheer me up and a glass of red wine was waiting for me before I even got in the door.
Who says romance is dead?
(I later discovered that the roses had been reduced to £1.25 at the petrol station. But it's the thought that counts).

Friday 3rd April

This morning the Excel Centre in London was opened by Prince Charles by video link as the Nightingale Hospital. This hospital had the capacity for 4000 beds, should they be needed and there were plans for 6 other Nightingale hospitals to be built around the country. It also came to light that Boris Johnson had got signs of the virus, indeed looking at the news footage of him on the doorstep of No.10 last night for the NHS clap, he looked bloody terrible.

Peter has been asked if he would assist with management of the night shift volunteers working at the Nightingale starting next week. As he has nothing else to do, he has agreed. I'm not sure if I am completely happy about this, but he says he will get changed before he leaves the hospital, will put all his clothes straight in the washing machine and have a shower as soon as he gets in. Ha, that's if the machine is still working after it exhausted itself doing the Hokey Cokey this morning across the kitchen.

The only saving grace for most people stuck at home at the moment is that it is fairly warm and sunny. Those people who have gardens can at least get outside and the kids can run off some pent up energy. I really feel for people living in flats with no outside space, it must be very difficult. We have an ex colleague who has 5 children under the age of 7 living with her and her husband in a two bedroom flat; she must be crawling the walls.

The latest figures hot off the press are grim. 1,094,000 infected people worldwide, with 58,000 deaths. The UK had its deadliest day so far with another 684 deaths bringing the total to 3605. The virus has now claimed victims as far apart as Egypt and the Falkland Islands.
President Trump has not really helped matters by refusing to follow his own Administrations guidelines for the public to cover their faces when outside. His wife is advocating the opposite and is imploring Americans to take the pandemic seriously. They obviously don't talk to each other over the breakfast table.
The debate about face masks is all over the news. In Britain Scientists and boffins are saying that wearing a mask doesn't make any difference. But look at Vietnam, they wear masks all the time and it had not spread there. Surely if you sneeze and your mouth is covered, you are not releasing germs into the air and vice versa you can't breathe in anyone

else's germs? It makes utter sense to me. But I am not a highly educated person, what the hell do I know?

Peter is volunteering in the call centre and he comes home later to find me half cut, sprawled out on the sofa clutching another goldfish bowl of gin.

Saturday 4th April

News from Luton hospital is that my friend and her husband are so ill they are totally unaware of what is going on around them. The younger son has rung to let me know the situation as the older son is in such an emotional state. I really feel for them, they are such a close family, it must be ghastly not to be able to see each other. My friend has been diagnosed with Pneumonia, de-hydration and a possible kidney infection and is being pumped full of antibiotics, she doesn't have the Coronavirus and has been moved to a 'clean' ward. We do not really know what is happening with her husband except he is having continuous problems with his breathing.

It is a very warm and sunny Spring day and 3000 people have descended on a park in Lewisham and have to be dispersed by the police.
What is wrong with everyone? Why are you not listening to the advice? This is not a game, we are not on holiday, people are dying out there, listen to the advice:
DO NOT GO OUT.

Looking in the mirror, I desperately need a haircut, eyebrow wax, eyelash tint and my gel toenails need re-doing. I had my hair cut the week before I went to Vietnam, I wear it in a very short cropped style and it needs to be cut every 6 weeks to keep it looking funky. All hairdressers are currently closed so I decide to give myself a bit of a trim with a pair of £1 scissors. When I have finished it looks OK, a bit lumpy in places as it needs thinning out properly. I will just have to stop looking in the mirror as with the slightly longer hair I am starting to resemble my mother, which makes Peter snigger. A lot. Not that I do spend a lot of time staring at my reflection in the looking glass, it's Peter who tends to hog the bathroom. I can't do anything about the eyelashes, but I pluck my eyebrows and try to ignore the toenails altogether.

Peter spends all of day making a video of our dog singing ' *Patience*' by Take That.
Not very useful or productive (but hilarious).

Sunday 5th April

It was really hot today and I sat out on my decking in my bikini trying to top up my holiday suntan. I am nearly 56 years old and know that I do not have the figure of a supermodel but I am passed caring what the neighbours or anyones else thinks. It is just unfortunate that I cannot get my comfy deck chair out of the shed because of all the tree cuttings that are still in the way.

The police are called out again today, this time to Hove beach where there are large groups of people socialising and having BBQ's. What is wrong with the British mentality? Why can't we do as advised? I hope the NHS and the rest of the population do not have to pay in the long run for this blatant un-cooperation and breaking of the restrictions.

Peter has got all industrious today and is painting the black bollards out the front of the house. He is currently tied by several bungee cords to a ladder and is hanging perilously off the top of a lamppost waving a paint brush around covered in black gloopy paint. I leave him to it, it's too hot to supervise.

Her Majesty the Queen gives an address to the nation this evening from Windsor Castle. It is only the fifth time that she has ever done a special address during her whole reign. It is a rallying cry to the NHS and key workers, with a message to everyone else to please follow the guidelines. Apparently we will all meet again, don't know where, don't know when.
After her speech it was confirmed that Boris Johnson had been taken to hospital with breathing difficulties.

Monday 6th April

I cannot find any motivation to get out of bed this morning, probably not helped by the two bottles of wine we drank last night. I was awake half the night with hot flushes and palpitations, and ended up pacing the landing at 3am feeling very lightheaded and nauseous. If you have ever had palpitations, they are not a pleasant sensation. It feels like your heart is going to erupt out of your chest and the sound of it beating is really loud in your ears. I wonder if this is what the start of a heart attack feels like?

It has now been two weeks of the Lockdown and the novelty has worn off for most people. We all want to get back to our normal lives and routine.

Unfortunately normal seems like a long way off.

A lot of my friends are still working, some of them are doing much longer hours than usual. A lot of them have been furloughed and are stuck at home scratching around for things to do. Some of them are starting to get a little bit fed up, the good weather at least is helping a bit, we are not cooped up indoors whilst it pours with rain outside like a usual English Spring. Everyone now has very clean houses and our gardens look immaculate. The allotments across the road from our house, which quite often look abandoned, are beginning to look very organised and tidy, with no weeds, and there seems to be people working on them each day.

When I get into work later that afternoon, the office is in uproar. We have been told to provide cover 7 days per week in the Call Centre. Some of the staff actually want to be furloughed but we are now being asked to provide cover every day. It is Easter this weekend and everyone was looking forward to having 4 days off in a row but now it looks like we will all be working for part of it. I don't mind working weekends, but a bit of prior consultation would have been nice. Mind you, it's not like any of us had a lot of plans for the Bank Holiday, what are we going to be able to do? Nothing is open and we can't see our relatives or friends.

There's a lovely piece on the news about a 99 year old ex British army officer, Captain Tom Moore, who is walking laps of his garden on his walking frame to try and raise £1000 for the NHS before his 100th birthday on 30th April.

Go for it Captain Tom, it brings tears to your eyes to watch him.

When I get home, after the weirdest journey where I saw hardly any vehicles or people, I manage to get through the evening without the aid of an alcoholic drink or a piece of chocolate.

This I feel is a real achievement and I should get a gold star and a big fat red tick.

Tuesday 7th April

My brain is completely overloaded with what is happening (or not) at work and I do not sleep very well at all, maybe it is because I didn't have a drink. We are not working as flat out as usual but I find being in the office very stressful and my mind will not shut down even though I feel exhausted each evening. I have never been a person to bring work home with them, I can always leave it behind me at the front door. But now it is on my mind all the time and the constant changing of the goal posts within the organisation is doing my head in. I am wondering what the hell will happen next.

I am a very cut and dried person: either it is or it isn't, there is no room in my head for possibly maybe. If you make a decision stick with it, don't try changing things when something doesn't work immediately, take some time and at least give it a chance. If it doesn't work out, accept it as a learning curve and then try something different. DO NOT then try to blame someone else for your idea that has gone wrong. And for Gods sake don't change something that works really well just because you can.
More importantly, DO NOT ASK ME FOR MY OPINION if you don't really want to hear it.

I've had Greenie and Anna on at me again this morning wishing I was back with them. It's always lovely to hear from them but it's upsetting and unsettling as well, I miss them so much but there is nothing I can do about it.
The world death toll currently stands at 78,000 with 1,381,000 infected. The UK has now lost 4943 people to the virus and 55,000 have tested positive. The virus has now hit Africa and they have declared that 10,000 people are infected, but the thinking is that we will probably never know the true figures to come out of that continent.
More importantly the death figure is at last showing signs of slowing down in Italy, Spain and France, hopefully we will follow their pattern
Even more depressing is the economic news that 195,000,000 jobs worldwide will be affected by this global crisis. Well, mine is definitely one of them. I will become a statistic.

Peter nips out to buy some eggs and milk and comes back £115 lighter. As well as a couple of bags of goodies and a case of beer, he has brought me a new lawnmower.
It is our 20th wedding anniversary tomorrow and this is my present. Not any old lawn mower you understand, a manual one that I have to push

so I avoid breaking any more windows. Very thoughtful and so charmingly sentimental.

Other mysterious parcels have been arriving over the last few days from Amazon, I soon discover that they are not romantic gifts for me but Airfix models to keep him amused over the next few weeks.

The news from Luton hospital is that they have now decided that my friend does have Coronavirus and have moved her back down to the Covid ward, she is responding well to drugs and is a lot more with it. Her husband is still struggling with his breathing and his SATS are all over the place but he is holding his own. The information from the hospital is sketchy in places and the boys are home alone struggling to find out what is going on. I imagine it is complete chaos in the hospital, but the good news is that they are both responding to treatment. It is all positive.

I manage another evening without a drink but do eat a copious amount of chocolate. I haven't had a proper cooked dinner for three days now and we have eaten a lot of rubbish containing sugar. I spend half of the night wide awake, pacing the landing, feeling very sick and very hot. The sugar is rushing through my body and I know it is partially responsible for the dreaded menopausal symptoms tonight, but I cannot seem to put a lid on my bad diet at the moment, I am not in the right frame of mind.

Wednesday 8th April

Today is my 20th wedding anniversary. It is an achievement in this day and age to be married that long. Unfortunately we don't get to have much of a celebration. We had planned a family party for Easter weekend and we were then going on our cruise at the end of the month. It's all been cancelled, so we won't get to see any family and who knows when we will. We receive a lot of cards in the post and Peter produces a strange little card he brought at the petrol station. There was nothing really to get excited about especially when he spent most of our 'special' day making a plastic model of a Willys Jeep, I was actually glad to be going to work.

Todays headlines are that Boris Johnson is in intensive care on a ventilator.
 I get the dreadful news that my friend who is in hospital has just lost both of her parents to Covid in the last two days, they had been in a care home in Luton. How can one family have so much bad luck? I ring the

boys but am totally lost for words, they are both stunned, I don't know what to say to give them any sort of comfort. They are both self isolating and following the rules, having no contact with their parents and now they have lost both of their grandparents.
Sometimes life is really shit.

When I get home, I warm up a quiche and open a tin of baked beans, we have that washed down with a bottle of Tattinger champagne.
Pure class.
It's a wedding anniversary not to remember.

Thursday 9th April

So it's been 3 weeks since we got home from Vietnam and we are stuck in Groundhog day.
We wake up late and have a cup of tea in bed.
We get up and have a sort of Brunch.
Peter sits on his arse all day, taking a few phone calls, logging on to Teams meetings whilst spending the rest of his time making Air-fix models. The Willys jeep is finished and he is now making a Spitfire.
We take the dog for a very long walk. (She's never been out so much and is completely knackered).
I do the cleaning, washing, ironing, gardening, cooking and then go to work on the late shift, get home at 8.45pm, eat a packet of crisps for tea and usually have a glass of wine.
We fall into bed very late after watching TV all evening.

Then repeat.

There is one upside to all of this, I have discovered toast and fruit yoghurt again. I stopped eating yoghurt five years ago and rarely eat toast. Toast with butter and marmalade is delicious. Now I am having it for breakfast everyday.

Fortunately I now have two days off, I am working on Saturday this week, so spend all day doing the household chores. As an added treat I also have plans to start the enormous job of painting our hall - all three floors of it.

We do get to do the doorstep clap for the NHS this evening. Peter isn't keen but stands there to show willing. It is an odd thing to do, stand at your front door clapping like Flipper into the air at no-one, but all the neighbours are out and for a brief few seconds you get to speak to another person.

The shocking news from the High Street is that my favourite shop, Debenhams, has gone into Administration. Oh no, this is a catastrophe for me, it is the only place apart from M&S that really caters for my age group at a reasonable price. Where will I buy my clothes in the future?

Tonight we have ordered an Indian takeaway, this is our special anniversary meal, and we wash it down decadently with another bottle of champagne.
I eat every single thing on my plate.

Friday 10th April

I spend all day painting the first floor of the hall. I can see it is already a vast improvement and looks much cleaner and modern. In the meantime I clean all the tiles in our main bathroom with neat bleach. Oh dear another thing I have missed, they are filthy too.

One good piece of news is that Peter is no longer required to go to the Nightingale Hospital as they haven't had many patients in, so they do not need as many volunteers as originally thought. Again I think this must be a good thing, as it means that the NHS is coping and managing brilliantly.
The bad news is that bodies are now being brought into the makeshift mortuary down the road from the surrounding hospitals, apparently both of my friends parents are in there.

The washing machine is doing the salsa today and Peter has had enough. On to the lap top he goes to see how quickly we can possibly get a new one. This is where he excels on the Internet, comparing prices and delivery dates, flicking backwards and forwards between websites. As we are not currently going out or buying anything, we have plenty of money in the bank, so he decides it's time to get a new fridge/freezer (that was making a funny noise as well) and we might as well get a microwave to match, so we order all three in black to match the cooker. We get them at an extremely reasonable price from an online company who give us a 20% discount for having a Blue Light Card. For a small fee of £15 they will also take away the old ones. What a bargain.

The glass in the patio door has now started falling out chunk by chunk and the tiny hole is now about 2 inches across. Every time we close the door another bit of glass falls out.

I have to have another bath to soak all of the paint off of me. I do not know how I manage to get so much of it on me and not on the wall. Once clean, I attempt to sit in the garden for a few hours as the weather is so nice. I really think the boy next door has an irritation radar built in, he seems to know exactly when I go out in the garden as within seconds of sitting down he is out there whacking a football at the fence just by my head. I already have a banging headache caused by the smell of the paint, I also think I am slightly dehydrated as my vision goes a bit funny. I know I am not drinking as much water as usual and feel a bit dizzy, the vicious night sweats aren't helping with my daily hydration at all. The amount of booze I am consuming isn't helping either.
In the end I can't stand the noise any longer and retire indoors, I'll try again later.

Saturday 11th April

Peter gets up early this morning to go and do a shift in the call centre, so I get a nice lay in until I have to join him at 10am. There is a particularly annoying person in the building today who I am trying to avoid, they are such a know it all, they wind me up and make me spit feathers. I don't have an awful lot of patience at the best of times, the menopause makes you extremely intolerant, so I am laying low, keeping out of their way.
This is the first time Peter and I have worked together on this project and for some strange reason he thinks he is my boss! It shows how little he knows. The phones are very quiet this afternoon and we are all stuck in the office on a beautiful sunny day staring at three screens willing the silent phones to ring to give us something to do.

There is some good news today, my friend has been released from hospital and allowed to go home. The bad news is that her husband is still having issues with his breathing and is not quite out of the woods yet, they now think he has a series of blood clots on his lungs.

There is a disturbing fact on the news tonight that gives me pause for thought. Domestic abuse cases (that we are aware of) have risen by 69% in the last three weeks. I am not surprised by that, some families cannot even get through two weeks at Christmas or a fortnights Summer holiday without a blazing row. Being locked up together with no visitors to break the tension must be some peoples idea of Hell and I am sure there will be some horror stories to come out at the end of all of this.

Sunday 12th April

The gruesome facts today are that there are now 1,844,400 reported cases worldwide with 113,00 global deaths, and the figures show that the horrendous death toll in the UK has gone over the 10,000 mark. The UK Government has been criticised for not having enough PPE for the NHS. This I find odd as we have had no trouble at all getting hold of PPE for work. It always turns up a few days after the order has gone in. An advisor has said that the UK could end up with the highest death toll in Europe, well we are certainly on the way to that figure. The virus is now affecting countries like Jordan and the Sudan. Nowhere is untouched apart from Greenland and surprise, surprise North Korea - as if they would tell us anyway.

One of the Duchess of Cambridges favourite shops, LK Bennett, has been brought out and saved from closure but they are still going to have to shut 15 retail stores. Even the golden touch of HRH has failed to safeguard this chain.

It was a lovely morning and I decided to eat my breakfast sitting out on the decking. Within 10 seconds of sitting down a football has whacked against the fence. Sod this, I am not in the mood today. I go back indoors and ferociously start painting the first floor of the hall. I find painting quite therapeutic and soon get into the swing of it and forget about my irritation. We have all the back doors open, I put Classic FM on really loud; if you hate classical music there is nothing worse. Whilst I am slaving my guts out, sweating like a little piglet, Peter sits at the breakfast bar lovingly painting his model Spitfire.

In the afternoon Peter roars off on his motorbike for a stint in the Call Centre and I apply the second coat of paint to the hall. I have to say it looks like a different house. The pale grey colour makes it look a lot more modern and with the sparkling white doors it looks really nice and clean.
After a hot bath I catch up with a my lovely friend Tracey who is isolated on her own and working from home. We have a really long chat, not sure what we find to talk about for so long as neither of us has done anything lately. She normally looks after her mum and it has been difficult staying apart.

I also speak to Maureen, she is cheerful and praising to high heaven the lovely carers who are helping her out. She is managing OK but dying to see us, it's been a long time.

After dinner I decide for a change to sit in the lounge upstairs to watch TV. Our TV is so confusing and there are so many remote controls to press, I cannot even manage to get the picture to come on. I give up and sit in silence all evening playing on my iPad. When Peter comes home he points several remotes at the TV and miraculously it comes to life. Smart arse.

Monday 13th April

The weather has changed for the first time in weeks, it is cold and windy and actually rained for a short time. The garden could really do with some heavy rain, after the dry and warm spell the grass is starting to go brown and the plants are a bit limp.
I spend my day painting, I get halfway up the second flight of stairs when I run out of paint. Peter instantly jumps online and orders me two more tins, the downside is that there is a ten day wait. I think he wants to keep me occupied otherwise I might start questioning him about his Spitfire or Jeep. I clear up the mess and put away the equipment, Mrs Neat does not want it cluttering up the hall for the next 10 days.

I talk to my sick friend, she is feeling much better now she is home - there is nothing like your own bed when you are ill. She is still very breathless and has a dry cough but is obviously on the mend. She hasn't even begun to deal with the death of her parents yet, her brother is sorting out the details. Her husband isn't doing quite as well, they obviously can't go to see him, his breathing is so bad the Doctors have had to put him on Oxygen whilst laying on his stomach. Apparently that way the lungs fill up and absorb the gas better.
Finger crossed that he will pick up and soon be home with his family.

I also speak to my friend Lisa, it's a bit of a depressing conversation. She is in the middle of having an extension to her house and the builders have stopped working, so they are living on a building site. Her first grandchild is due in May and it is beginning to look as if they might not get to see the baby. Her daughter, who is an A&E nurse, is self isolating at home after showing signs of Covid. Lisa's 50th Birthday celebrations in August are looking like they might have to be cancelled as well.

I don't bring much to the conversation, I am full of doom and gloom; I have done nothing, been nowhere and am going nowhere in the near future.

Peters is in the call centre again on the late shift and when he gets in we have a big row. That's not bad going as we have now been together practically everyday since 8th March and it is the first time we have cross words. We both say some things that we shouldn't and I end up sleeping in the spare bedroom which I secretly enjoy as I have the bed to myself and I do not have to listen to him snoring. Every time I have a hot flush I roll over to the cold side of the bed, it is pure bliss.

Tuesday 14th April

I have trouble getting up this morning as I can hardly move and I am still very cross with Peter. I ask him to help me put some pictures back up in the hall, but he makes such a fuss about leaving his unfinished Spitfire, that I lose my rag and scream like a banshee at him. I burst into tears and storm out of the house, slamming the door behind me. I walk for miles and miles ranting and raving in my head about what an arsehole he is.
I am totally exhausted, I have practically painted the whole house single handed and he has sat in front of his lap top talking to his virtual friends, making stupid videos of the dog and sticking cheap plastic airplanes together.
When I get home he immediately apologises. This is a very difficult thing for any man to do. It is all I need to hear and the matter is forgotten instantly.

Boris is out of hospital and advocating the amazing NHS treatment that he received. He says he got no special treatment, yeah like I believe that, most people don't have armed police outside their ward.
Take note Boris, the NHS should be the pride of this country, the envy of the whole world. Stop closing hospitals, invest more money and give the staff a decent pay rise.

I am not going to do anything else today, I am having a day off from the world. The weather is distinctly chilly compared to what we have had, a bit like my current frame of mind.
We open another bottle of wine, our garage resembles a bottle bank but we cannot get rid of any of the glass as all the recycling bins are full and overflowing.
Everyone in the UK is on the sauce.

Wednesday 15th April

It is my 56th birthday today and it's another damp squib. Peter produces another strange little card he brought at the petrol station and gives me a parcel wrapped in an Amazon bag. Inside is a note book and a small box containing some foot cream, hand cream, and a lip salve. It's not exactly a diamond necklace, I've thrown more exciting things in the bin. But it is the only present and card that I receive so I should be more grateful. He apologises for the crappy gift, I know it is the COVID situation, he promises that he will get me something nice for my birthday and anniversary when the shops re-open.

Anna remembers it is my birthday and sends me a little video of her and La Vie, but I don't hear a word from Greenie which upsets me a tad. I was in Vietnam for my birthday last year and they made a huge fuss of me. I also went out to lunch at a gorgeous restaurant with Danny and out to dinner with a randy old chap called Den, that's another story entirely, but it crosses my mind several times during the day.

I don't hear from my best friend Julie, she has more important things on her mind today. It is her dads funeral in Liverpool. They have decided to keep it small with just herself, her husband, brother and sister in law attending at the local crematorium. He was a proper Liverpudlian character, her dad, and it's very sad. They are taking the opportunity as they are up there to close down his house, turn off the water, empty the fridge etc, as who knows when they will be able get back to clear it out and put it on the housing market.

The weather is beautiful again and we take the dog out for a long walk over the fields and around the lakes before I have to go to work on the late shift. The allotments are really coming on and there appears to be lots of people working on them. Usually there is only one man and his dog over there.

My boss messages me to say to come in half an hour later as a special treat for my birthday. When I get into the office there are balloons all over the place and a present on my desk, at least my work colleagues have remembered. I go into the Call Centre for my shift, the room is full of people and social distancing is not being observed. I suppose we have all been working together for 4 weeks, if anyone had the virus we would surely have been showing the symptoms by now. There is suddenly an influx of people into the room and the big boss comes in bearing a huge red velvet cake, there is a chorus of Happy Birthday and we all tuck in.

They really are a lovely bunch of people that I work with, we all get on so well, even though tempers have been a bit frayed lately, we are a great TEAM.

When I get home the postman has been and delivered cards from all of my friends. The cards are of varying quality. You can tell that they are cards that people have found in the bottom of their drawers and cupboards, having not been able to get to the shops. But I am pleased as punch that everyone has remembered. Peter pours me a large G&T and I throw my ever growing backside onto the sofa for the rest of the evening.

Thursday 16th April

After the G&T's from the night before I wake up really, really late, we are definitely getting into a dangerous pattern here. Going to bed late and getting up late, how we will ever attune to the sound of an early alarm clock again, I do not know.

I mooch around all morning, the thermometer reads 25C. I get out my new lawn mower and give it a try. It is really easy to use and the lawn is done in 10 minutes flat. I pull out a few weeds but there is nothing else to be done in the garden until I can get some new plants for my pots. At the moment all the garden centres and nurseries are closed so there is nowhere local to buy anything.

It's deathly silent in the garden today. I stand and listen, there are no planes soaring overhead, no cars on the bypass, no children voices and I cannot hear any trains in the distance either. All I can hear is birdsong. It is a bit dreamlike and a bit odd.

I am on lates again today, it is eerily quiet in the Call Centre as well, whenever the phone rings it makes us jump and we all fight with each other to answer it.

Peter has spent all day making a model of a Sherman Tank, well that is going to be very useful if he doesn't get any work, maybe he can sell these models as works of art. He did do some washing today which is laying drying over every conceivable surface in the kitchen. I don't know why he just didn't put it in the tumble dryer.

The latest Coronavirus news is awful. There are now over 2,000,000 cases worldwide with 142,735 deaths. The USA has the largest number of infected people followed by Spain. What else comes as a big shock is that over 5,000,000 people in the USA have now registered as unemployed. Singapore has had a massive leap in cases due to their returning migrant workforce and they have gone into full Lockdown. I wonder if those two couples we met in Hoi An are still there?

When I get home we watch the Governments press conference together. It doesn't come as any surprise but it is depressing news. The Lockdown has been extended for another three weeks.

It seems that when you get to a certain age you almost give yourself permission to misbehave and say what you think - Julie Walters

5. Extended Lockdown

Friday 17th April

As if things are not bad enough this morning, it is grey and overcast to match the general mood of the nation. The upside is that it does rain for most of the day which is much needed in the garden and farmers fields.

I am in trouble today. I can feel that my mental health is on a bit of a slide and for the first real time since the Covid crisis began I am starting to feel depressed. I really do not want to end up in the situation I was in last Summer, I was in a very dark place back then, mainly due to the fluctuating symptoms caused by the menopause. This black feeling that I have today is more of a nagging worry at the moment rather than any sort of impending breakdown.
I have so many emotions and thought whooshing around in my menopausal head. When will all of this end? What will be left of our jobs? If we have a job. What will be left of the High Street? Will we ever be able to leave the country again? How many more people are going to lose their lives? Will any of my family or friends catch it? Will I ever see my Vietnamese friends ever again? What if the virus comes back again next Winter? - the world may never recover, the economy certainly won't.
I tell Peter that I am a bit worried about my state of mind, he needs to understand what I am feeling in case I go downhill. The trouble with my husband is that he does not worry about anything - absolutely nothing bothers him. Even the fact that his 20 year old business could go tits up in August doesn't seem to be preoccupying him. The only real concern he has at the moment is that Luton Town FC might get relegated from the Championship.
He does at least listen to me, whether it registers with him is anyones guess.

When I get to work there is a strange Email from a senior Manager up North. It would appear some of the staff are scratching around for things to do and have hit upon part of my job and are questioning me about my work. I am on the lowest pay grade within the company and now two much higher paid staff are trying to do some of my job. I know there is not much to do at the moment, surely these staff could be furloughed if they have no work? And if my job actually warrants the type of salary that these staff are on, why am I at the bottom of the pay scale?

When I get home there is a belated Birthday parcel waiting for me. Julie has sent me a gorgeous Yankee Candle and a lovely card, it cheers me up no end.

Saturday 18th April

I am working 10-4 today. I actually have a busy morning as I have been tasked with co-ordinating a daily report with regards to how many jobs our people are going to. As the weeks go by this turns into an almost full time job as it changes on an hourly basis and needs to be kept as updated as possible.
Peter turns up at 2pm for his shift along with a female I have not yet had any dealings with. She is pleasant enough but does not stop talking the whole time, yak, yak, yak in my ear. Please give it a rest love! I am glad when I go home and my eardrums get a rest. I leave Peter alone to listen to her for the remainder of the afternoon.

I decide to pick up some shopping on the way home. I notice two major things:
Firstly, there were a lot of people in the shop in family groups which surprised me. Surely it would be safer for one person from the household to do the weekly shop? The supermarket is well set up with social distancing tape on the floor, perspex screens at the checkouts and a one way system around the aisles, there is also a very cheerful lady outside squirting everyone with hand gel. The store is fairly well stocked apart from the fresh fruit and veg. I am a bit late in the day and there is very little left.
Secondly, wow the prices of everything has gone up. Except the gin, which is on special offer and I buy another litre, just in case of an emergency in our house you understand.
I had thought that I might be able to purchase a tin of gloss paint but there wasn't any. I loaded all the shopping into the car and suddenly had a light bulb moment. Would Wilkinsons be open in the precinct? I walked around the corner, it was an almost spooky experience with all the shops closed and as it was 17.00 on a Saturday there was no-one around. Sure enough though Wilko was open and fully stocked with all cleaning products, soap, hand gel, anti-bacterial wipes, in fact everything that was in short supply in the bigger stores. More importantly, I also managed to get a tin of paint.

On the way home I get a call from my nephew who has been volunteering at the mortuary. It is the last day today, the build is finished and they no longer require our services. He needs to bring some stuff back to my house and wants to know where I am. I tell him to dump it all in front of the garage, I will be home 20 minutes. He decides to sit it out and when I get home he is still waiting outside the house. It is lovely to see him and I know we shouldn't, but he comes in for a drink and a chat. We sit at opposite ends of the kitchen table. He has serious mental health issues but at the moment seems to be coping very well. He explains that Lockdown is how people with Mental health issues feel most of the time. Anxious, fearful, worried, stressed, panicked, frightened, ill - not something most of us feel on a day to day basis. These are all emotions I know only too well and most menopausal women experience some or all of these feelings at some time during the change of life. Fortunately he is currently in a good place despite being furloughed, he also works for my company and is worried about his job that he loves.

I lay on the sofa all evening with a big glass of gin and an enormous bar of chocolate watching ' Spectre' on the TV. Pierce Brosnan was my favourite James Bond, in fact he is my perfect man, I have gorgeous photos of him hidden on my phone. I think I am secretly in with a chance with him, his wife is quite a big lady, he must like the more buxom woman with a fat arse. I like Daniel Craig as well - I would definitely put my slippers under his bed (if he ever asked me to of course. I wouldn't just break into his house and put them there, he would have to ask me nicely).

When Peter gets in he is utterly exhausted. The girl I left him with in the Call Centre has worn him out with her incessant chatter. Peter rarely says anything negative about anyone but he states that she was damn hard work, his ears hurt and he needs a cold beer.

Sunday 19th April

I get a panicky message from Greenie this morning, she has realised she forgot my Birthday. She is full of apologies, I understand she has a lot on her mind at the moment with no work, no wages and the kids at home all day long, like a lot of people in the UK. I also get a photo from Anna of La Vie wearing another one of the outfits I gave her. Anna looks much better now after her operation, I didn't like the look of her in a photo she sent me a few weeks ago, she looked a funny colour. They are still in full Lockdown in Vietnam despite only having 268 cases and still no fatalities across the whole country.

The brilliant news is that my friends husband has been released from hospital and is on his way home. As well as recovering from Covid he now needs a course of drugs to deal with the blood clots, but it's all looking good and I am so pleased that they will all be back together this evening. The messages flood in from all of our friends on WhatsApp and we get a lovely message of thanks from the family.

As I now have three days off in a row, I spend the day painting the second and top floor of the hall with my new tin of paint. Somehow I end up covered in it and the carpet gets a coat as well which I have to clean off with white spirit. But at last all of the gloss work is done, I am just waiting for the emulsion to arrive so I can get it finished. I am totally worn out by 14.30 pm after I have cleaned up the carpet and myself and have to retire to the comfort of the sofa for the rest of the day.

I at least manage to cook a proper dinner for when Peter comes in, we have chicken and fresh vegetables. It taste fabulous after all the rubbish we have been eating lately.

Monday 20th April

I spend part of the day doing chores around the house whilst Peter lovingly paints his Sherman tank. After we walked the dog I lay on the sofa wrapped in a blanket for the rest of the afternoon. I am tired, feel sad and very low. If you can't live your life doing the things you enjoy, what is the point ?

Peter spends the rest of the afternoon and evening making a video of the dog singing a song from '*the Greatest Showman*'. It is a special request from myself and goes down a storm on our family WhatsApp group.

Tuesday 21st April

Because I have nothing to do this morning I decide to tackle the weeds and piles of dead leaves in our road. No-one else ever does anything about them and it makes the area look a bit scruffy and unkempt. It looks so much better when I have finished and I am pleased I made the effort even if nobody else in the road gives a stuff. I end up talking to the old girl who lives around the corner. She makes a comment about how much she likes my hair style. Is she blind, I look like Cruella De Vil.

I notice as we watch TV from the comfort of our much used sofa, that there are lots more advertisements to do with gambling. Different lotteries, bingo, sports betting and other types of prize winning games are all being aimed at the bored person sitting at home. On one advert break during a film, there were three different companies trying to entice you to spend your money with promises of big cash prizes. Honestly is this really a caring and sensible thing to push at present? How is this being allowed on prime time TV during this difficult time? Some people will end up in debt which is not going to help their families if they lose their jobs.

My beautiful orchids that I brought at Singapore airport are still going, every time I look at them it brings a lump to my throat. They were worth every penny.

The terrible death toll in the UK is not yet showing any sign of slowing down. It is slowing down in Europe though but now Mexico and South America are reporting an increase in the infection and mortality rate. New York City alone had 481 deaths yesterday, it seems totally out of control there.
One interesting piece of information is that the thick smog that envelops the city of Delhi has disappeared during the Indian Lockdown. I have been to Delhi and there is a constant haze that hangs over the place even on the sunniest of days. The skies have cleared above the city and the air is clean once again because there is no traffic or air pollution.
A shocking fact that has come out is that the fatalities in care homes in the UK and Wales has quadrupled in a week. This could be due to a shortage of staff but probably more likely that as they are all confined together, someone has brought the disease in and it's gone rampant.

Another favourite High street shop has closed its doors today. Cath Kidston has shut all of its High Street stores but is keeping the online part of the business going.

Wednesday 22nd April

There is misleading article in the tabloid press this morning about a shortage of staff at the Nightingale Hospital. The claim is that the hospital is operating at only 1% of its capacity due to a lack of staff. This may well be true that they are running at 1% but the truth of the matter is that the NHS are managing so well that they have not had the need to move many patients there. The amount of volunteers originally required has been reduced as they are not needed either. The other Nightingale hospitals have admitted no patients apart from the Manchester site.

Surely this is a really good sign that the Pandemic hasn't got as bad as originally thought? What is it with the British press that they can't see that this is a positive sign?

The most exciting thing that happened today was that the bin men resumed the green waste and glass collection in our village. I managed to get rid of a lot of the Leylandii tree that Peter cut down and now at least I can get in the shed.

Peter managed to get rid of our empty glass bottles. I am glad I wasn't with him, it was embarrassing to see how many we had got through in 4 weeks.

A bottle of gin now seems to be on our current weekly shopping list as a food staple.

It's another quiet day in the office. 50% of the paid staff in our building have been furloughed, we are lucky or not whichever way you decide to look at it, that we are still working. We have a big discussion between ourselves that surely the organisation will have to make some redundancies going forward. With our main sources of income currently cancelled, we look like we could be the prime targets. This just gives everyone something else to worry about.

My anxiety ramps up a notch and I am awake half the night with fiendish night sweats, drenching my clothes and the duvet.

Please don't take my job and my independence as well as my sanity.

Thursday 23rd April

All the bars and restaurants are starting to reopen in Hoi An. Currently they have only had 268 cases across the country with 244 recovered and no fatalities. Only Hanoi City was still in Lockdown. How come this third world country has had such a success rate at keeping this pandemic out? Surely we can all learn something from this? Wearing masks, keeping to the Lockdown, observing social distancing and obeying the rules maybe?

It's strange what snippets of news I pick up on which actually register in my brain, when other things just pass through my vortex and I cannot recall them at all. Richard Gere has become a father at 70 years of age. At a time when most men of that age would be tending to the garden, watching cricket and playing with their grandchildren, he has impregnated someone. Totally amazing!

As I left for work I thought I was hallucinating; there were three fully grown peacocks on the grass verge at the end of my street strutting their stuff. It was a very weird sight on a housing estate, where on earth have they come from?

In the office there is a sombre atmosphere. We are concerned about our jobs, despite a business as usual strategy from the 1st July. I think we are living in Fairyland. There is no way business is going to suddenly burst into life in July. There is a lot of talk about the 'Exit Strategy', come on let's be realistic, maybe in September things will pick up, let's honestly acknowledge that the Summer season is completely cancelled. Even if we are allowed out in June or July, money is going to be the big concern for everyone and there might not be much left to spend on other projects.

On the way home, driving up the A1, tears run down my face and I cry all the way home. A black cloud is descending. I cannot envisage anything ever being the same again. The economy is shot to pieces, apparently we have only just finished paying off our debt from the second world war. This is going to cost trillions and the country will still be paying for it when I am long dead. Unemployment is going to go through the roof, taxes will go up, NI will increase, food will be more expensive, in fact everything will cost more. What will happen to my old age pension? Undoubtably that will be ultimately be used to pay for some of this. No-one has any idea what will happen with the housing market, up or down, who knows? As for going on a holiday - well that is anybody's guess when that will be allowed or even possible.

I'd like to say that when I got in my husband noticed that I was a bit upset and ran round fussing after me, but he was very busy painting the plastic ambulance he had just made.
Oh and we had missed the clap for the NHS again.

Friday 24th April

There is a complete flap on at work this morning. It seems we have been giving the wrong data to Head Office. The problem is that there are so many people with their fingers in so many pies trying to keep busy that the left hand doesn't know what the right is doing. The other issue is that personnel are changing on a daily basis and it is not being updated regularly. The Office Manager and myself take the job on and tell everyone else to butt out and leave well alone. We spend all day checking, rechecking and treble checking the numbers. At last we have some sort of system in place and are 99% sure that we have the correct figures to send to HQ.

One of our volunteers comes into the office today, in his day job he works for the traffic police. He tells us that the number of road accidents are down at the moment but the few accidents that are occurring are spectacular crashes. Some drivers are taking advantage of the lack of other vehicles on the roads and are hoofing it down the motorways at lightening speed causing horrendous crashes and injuries. What is the matter with these idiots?

When I got home, I spent the evening catching up with some friends and family. It was obvious that some were run ragged with work and some were bored stiff. My nephew was getting a bit bored, which doesn't help his mental health, so I found him a little job cleaning cars for a couple of days. At least it got him out of the house and the vehicles have never been so spotless.
My friend who had been in hospital was on good form and apart from a little bit of breathlessness was pretty much over the virus. My volunteers hadn't seen each other for 5 weeks and I hadn't seen any of them for 8 weeks so I hatched a plan to hold a TEAMS meeting for next week that Peter helped me set up on the computer.

My husband was really getting on my nerves this evening. He hadn't done anything all day except glue together a plastic airplane, make a video of the dog singing 'Careless Whisper' and drink beer, he hasn't lifted a finger around the place. I had a busy day and my patience with everything was running very thin. When we went to bed he snored like a train due to the amount of beer he had consumed. I totally lost my rag with him and ended up decamping to the spare bedroom at 2AM because I could not stand the noise any longer.

Saturday 25th April

I wake up freezing cold in the spare bed, but at least I got some sleep despite the freight train rumbling upstairs. I could still hear him one floor down!

I get a message from Greenie telling me that at last her children are going back to school on 4th May. She says she misses me and loves me. What else can I say, I feel the same.

I also speak to Mary in Dublin, she is desperate to go to her Summer place in France, but has no idea when that will be. There are still no flights to Europe.

The skies are still deathly quiet over our house too. We are in Stansteds flightpath and there is nothing up there.

Peter is in a favourable mood this morning and helps me to move all of the heavy plant pots and furniture off the decking. He then proceeds to give it all a good clean with the pressure washer. He enjoys doing this because he is using a gadget; it is definitely a man thing. We had been debating about replacing the decking but I think a good clean and a coat of teak oil will make it look better, and really we might need to save the money. We leave it to dry out overnight.

At 4pm we open our first bottle of wine - Well it's 5 o'clock somewhere.

At the daily Government press conference it is confirmed we have now passed the 20,000 death figure here in Britain, and that doesn't include the number of deaths in care homes.

There are now 2.84 million infected worldwide with 199,874 deaths. Some other news from Pakistan is that some Doctors and nurses are going on hunger strike as a protest at the lack of PPE for themselves and their colleagues. Well, that's really going to help the situation there isn't it?

The only good thing that happened today was that Saudi Arabia has extended its ceasefire in the battle against Yemen.

The maddest thing that happened was Donald trump has suggested that if we all injected ourselves with neat Dettol it might kill the virus.

Please tell me he was only joking.

Sunday 26th April

I got up early and set about oiling the decking whilst Peter supervised me from the comfort of the sofa. He lent me a pair of knee protectors that he uses for work. I must say they were very useful as I was on my knees for the best part of the morning. The decking looked really good but the smell of the oil would take a few days to die down.

I spend the afternoon on the phone to friends and family. Maureen is doing OK, the care package is working well except the carers don't come at the same time each day and sometimes her husband isn't washed and dressed until before lunch. I remember that problem only too well with my dad. I catch up with my mother, she's fine. Julie and I have a long chat, she has good days and bad days, she acknowledges that at least her dad didn't end up in a care home, he was happy in his own house right up to the end and never got ill or frail. My sister is fine, keeping busy with all her hobbies and allotment.

I suddenly realise that I haven't heard from Danny for four weeks. He usually sends me a funny picture or joke every couple of weeks but not lately. I drop him a message but he doesn't reply, I hope he is alright. It turned out that he had teamed up with a couple of young female stranded Irish back packers and was out getting drunk with them every night. So he's obviously died and gone to heaven.

Monday 27th April

A large parcel arrives for me which I am not expecting. When I eventually get all the gaffer tape off and open it, it contains a brightly painted bird box. There is a note - ' Happy Birthday and Happy Anniversary' but no name, I have no idea where it has come from. Looking at the wrapping there is no name or address only a postcode. Aha, looking at the postcode I work out it has come from my friend Carlos. I am very touched that he has remembered and ask Peter to hang it on the fence for me.

When I get home from work that evening after another secret cry in the car whilst driving up the empty A1, the sink is full of dirty breakfast crockery, the tumble dryer is full of dry screwed up clothing and Peter has not had any dinner.

When I complain, he points to the fence; at least he had put up the bird box.

Tuesday 28th April

There was a funny sound which awakened me during the early hours. I couldn't quite figure it out at first, then I realised what it was: torrential rain. It rained all night and on and off all the following day. Thank goodness the ground was dusty and bone dry and my lawn was reduced to brown straw.

When I get home from work our lovely new washing machine and fridge freezer are both installed. Peter looks pleased as punch with himself - he had finished his plastic airplane and also had time to plumb the new machine in **and** he has cleaned the floor.

I have two G&T's this evening, well it has been three days since the last one.

Wednesday 29th April

It is dreary, overcast and wet, whatever happened to the sunshine?

In the news today Boris Johnson's girlfriend has given birth to a baby boy and they have called him Wilfred. What a bloody awful name.

I trial my first TEAMS meeting tonight. It is the first time I have run anything like this and have no action plan and no expectations of how it will go. Everyone is thrilled to bits to see each other. It is lovely to be able to speak and see them all but it turns into a bit of a free for all. It is obvious that there are people who do not understand the concept of a conference call and it is complete chaos with people interrupting each other and all trying to talk at the same time.
One of my friends who does this sort of thing all the time, rang me afterwards to give me some advice, I now have a better idea of how to run it next week.

Whilst I am on my call, Peter is on his. They are talking about 'the end of the beginning'.
What a load of crap, we are not over this yet by a long shot.

Thursday 30th April

Peter gets an email this morning regarding the paint he ordered weeks ago. It states that they do not have any in stock and have refunded his money. I have a real problem now as the top floor of the hall is still not finished, what if we can't get any more of that particular colour? Please God that I don't have to start all over again - it will kill me. Peter alleviates my worries, fires up his laptop and logs onto Wickes, they have the paint in stock and he can pick it up tomorrow!

The highlight of the day is another fortnightly visit to the supermarket. I decide to go early which is probably a bit of a mistake. There is a huge

queue already waiting which winds around the building, but it does move fairly fast and I only end up waiting for 20 minutes before I am allowed inside. It is well stocked and I manage to get everything that we need for another two weeks. I must admit there was a fair amount of chocolate, wine, sweets and beer in my trolley. Would these be considered as essential food items?
Definitely in our house.

It is another miserable wet day so I am stuck indoors on my day off. The rain does have one fantastic overwhelming factor, the kid next door cannot play football so I don't get the constant thump, thump, whack that I hear every single day. As I sit in my study tapping away on the computer, silence reigns in our soggy back garden.
Peace at last.
That evening I indulge myself by watching the new series of 'The Real Marigold hotel'. It is a sign of things to come - that will be me in 20 years time.
Maybe without the dodgy facelifts and botox.

The fantastic news today is that Captain Tom, who set out on 6th April to raise £1000 for the NHS before his 100th birthday today has now raised £32,790,000, which is utterly staggering. Watching this old boy shuffle around his garden on his walking frame has hit a note with the public and money is flooding in from around the globe.
What a fantastic inspiration to us all - Happy Birthday Sir.

It is the last day of April, we have been in this turmoil for 8 weeks and locked indoors for 5. The crime rate has gone down. Domestic abuse has gone up.
Nature has come back to life in the strangest of places due to a lack of pollution.
Billions of people have been affected by this virus, whether that be with their health, mental health or the worldwide recession which is now likely to hit most of the population on planet earth in one way or another. The USA alone now has 30 million people claiming unemployment benefit.

228,908 people have lost their lives globally, shockingly the bulk of the fatalities are not in 3rd world countries:
USA - 62,200 deaths
Italy - 27,682 deaths
UK - 26,097 deaths
Spain - 24,543 deaths

How on earth did this happen in Europe? Peter thinks it is because we have no travel restrictions and people can cross the European borders easily and London is the hub between Europe and the USA.

The high rate in the USA is sort of understandable, their President did not take it seriously from the start, a bit like our own Prime Minister. In Hong Kong where 7 million people live on top of each other, personal space is not something the Chinese are known for, they have only had 4 deaths from Covid. Surely that cannot be correct? How is that even possible?

An interesting fact has come out this week, more people have died in the USA in the last 8 weeks of Coronavirus than died in the Vietnam war during a 10 year period.

Friday 1st May

When I awake this morning I had a bit of a panic attack. It was a strange sensation like someone was sitting heavily on my chest, my heart was beating very fast and I could hear it pounding in my ears. I don't know what caused it but later on my sister rang me, it was 10 years today since my dad died. He's reminding me.

Peter picked up the tins of paint and I spent all day painting and managed at last to finish the hall. I did get five minutes of help from Peter but the rest was all my own work. I am a devil for punishment, against my better judgement I then started on the little box room. Half way through the afternoon, I had had enough and we took the dog for a long walk over the lakes behind Henlow Grange. On the way back my back seized up and I hobbled the rest of the way home in great pain.

It's the start of Ramadan today, I imagine there will be a huge problem with family gatherings. According to my friend Jagdish, there is an Asian area in Luton which has been functioning almost as normal throughout this crisis. All the shops were open and everyone was still out on the streets. My friend and his wife have stopped going shopping there as he thinks it is unsafe. I don't think he is wrong.

I receive a gorgeous picture of Greenie and her daughter today wearing matching outfits which gives me a real lift. I am also contacted on Instagram by friends of friends in Vietnam who now want to follow me. I do actually know them all, I am not just making contact with strangers!

That evening as a change from watching TV, we play Scrabble. It is one thing that I am better at than Peter and I beat him twice, much to his annoyance.

Saturday 2nd May

My orchids are dead and sadly I have to throw them in the bin. They were worth every penny of the £16 and lasted 6 weeks. I know it's weird but I almost feel like they were a lifeline to my girls.
Yes I know, complete and utter nonsense.

Peter is in the Call Centre, so I finish the painting, clear up the mess, rehang the curtains, put away the decorating materials and arrange everything back in its place. All very satisfying and the hall looks fabulous, even if I say so myself.

Our neighbours have brought their children a puppy which has arrived today. Neither of them have any experience of owning a dog, they say it is to give the children some responsibility. All dog owners know that it's nearly always mum who eventually ends up doing the dog duties and picking up the poo. I tell them that it will be like having another child, I'm sure they don't believe me. Peter and I chuckle to ourselves. Sure enough the puppy yaps for two hours from 3am until 5am and the following day they are all red eyed and exhausted. Unfortunately the constant yapping and crying has spooked our weird little dog and when we wake up in the morning she is snuggled between us. She must be a stealth dog as we never felt her get up on the bed.

Sunday 3rd May

I feel like I am pulling lead weights around and it is difficult to get out of bed. My knees in particular don't want to work this morning and it is difficult to get down the stairs. I am like a geriatric taking the steps one at a time. I acknowledge that at this time of life I am no Spring chicken but the constant aches and pains get on my bloody nerves. I used to be very sporty: hockey, running, athletic, aerobics, and I do wonder if you actually pay for all that exercise as you age. Your joints were worn out too early by all the sport you did when you were younger and you pay for it in later life.

It is a National holiday in Vietnam this weekend and the Old Town in Hoi An is heaving with people. Everything has re-opened and the locals are out having a lovely time in their home town without zillions of tourists getting in their way. I receive some lovely photos from the girls. Anna has taken La Vie for her first haircut. I don't know what planet she was on but she lets them shave all her hair off leaving the baby with what looks like a small Brillo pad on her head. Poor child! If it was a boy it would probably be very fashionable but not on a little girl. Greenie is actually working. The hotel is full of Vietnamese holiday makers so she has gone into work for three days. I also get some pictures of the town from Danny, he is sitting in a bar watching the Vietnamese partying whilst drinking half price beer. All the bars and restaurants have reduced their prices to entice customers in and to get rid of some of their stock, I presume before it goes out of date. Even the big five star hotels have opened up their elite bars and are selling off their drinks at a bargain price.

God I wish I was there. I would give my right arm to be allowed to go to a restaurant lit up by pretty colourful lanterns for dinner and sit drinking (cheap) wine overlooking the river that is covered with floating candles.

This afternoon we are working together again. Peter still doesn't get it that he is not my boss! I somehow, through a misunderstanding, manage to upset one of our volunteers. He complains to my manager, who rings his manager, who rings Peter, who then speaks to me. Why he didn't just come up one flight of stairs to speak to me directly I will never know. I asked him not to do something, he translated that as I went into the room screaming at him.

Talk about a conversation getting something lost in translation.

My friend Elaine rings me, it's been a while since we spoke. She is still working from home and has successfully managed to get her elderly sister moved from her bungalow to a luxury care home. That was a real achievement to get that done at this time and she is worn out with it all. We have a good old natter as it is very quiet in the Call Centre again. Is this a good thing I ask myself, is the virus starting to abate?

When we get home I thrash Peter at Scrabble again. He can't understand this and is totally baffled. I am usually so woolly headed and can never remember a thing, how can my fluffy brain suddenly produce a seven letter word on a triple word score?

It is a very satisfying moment and I relish every second of it.

Monday 4th May

I awake at 4am feeling sick and am very hot to the touch. I spend a lovely half hour bent over the toilet trying to throw up with my fingers down the back of my throat. I have no idea what has caused this. I manage to go back to sleep and when I get up at 7.30am, I feel fine and think I dreamed the whole episode.
I am up early as our shifts have changed again. I am now back on four days in a row leaving me with my normal three days off over the weekend.

News from London today is that the Nightingale hospital at the Excel centre is closing down next week. It must have cost a fortune to set up but they have only treated 54 patients over the whole time it was open. It is going into hibernation and will be used again if we have a second spike once this Lockdown is eased.
Heaven forbid that happens.

The global rate of infections stands at 3.5 million, with over 250,000 deaths. The UK Government announces that we have had the smallest daily increase since the end of March. Unfortunately our death figure is still going up and we have now lost 28,734 people.
Germany is looking at easing its restrictions and 4.4 million Italians are going back to work. Travel restrictions from any EU country to France are being lifted and those visitors will be exempt from 2 weeks quarantine. Not the UK citizens though, that's one of the prices to pay for coming out of the EU.

I recall that the number of people killed in Asia on Boxing Day 2004 by the Tsunami was 225,000. In one day.

When I get home Peter has heated up a pizza for tea, bless him.
I do feel a bit nauseous when I eat it, maybe last night wasn't a dream.

Tuesday 5th May

It was hard work getting up early again this morning. I have an odd message from Anna on my phone, she has had a weird dream. She dreamt that I said I was coming to live in Vietnam and was renting a house from her husband. All a bit odd in that he runs a coffee shop and does a bit if teaching. Not weird in that it is something I think about constantly.

In the last 9 weeks I have been piling on the pounds to such a degree that a lot of my clothes are very tight and I am getting a bit limited as to what I can wear that is suitable for the office. I feel fat and bloated but cannot find any motivation to stop the unhealthy eating and drinking. I could blame it all on the menopause, everyone knows that it is responsible for the pounds piling on, but we all know my problem is my current terrible diet. I just do not have the self control or will power at the moment to do anything about it, so I look like Mrs Blobby.

The good news is that as I have had a bit more time recently to spend on my facial beauty routine, my skin is in good condition and feels like silk.

My hair on the other hand is another matter altogether. It is growing at a rate of knots and really starting to look a mess. I give it another trim with my £1 scissors but it needs a professional cut, fat chance of that happening in the near future. Mind you if it grows any longer I can always put it in a pony tail.

Oddest thing today was the multi millionaire Elon Musk and his partner 'C' (also known as the pop star Grimes) were delivered of a son that they have oddly named XAE A-12.

Can't wait for his name to be called out in the register at school.

There is a bit of positivity today, some good news at last, the UK death rate has started to drop.

The devastating bit of news is that phone calls to 'Refuge' which is the UK's biggest domestic abuse charity are up by 700% a day.

That figure is mind blowing and deeply disturbing.

The least interesting bit of news is that 3 McDonalds takeaways are going to re-open next week in Luton. Some people are rejoicing in the street, saddo's.

The sickliest bit of new is that a book has been released today called 'Finding Freedom'. I like the Royal Family and these two entitled and privileged people think they are more special than a 1200 year old monarchy and I hate the way they have treated the Queen. I hope the book bombs.

Wednesday 6th May

I am in late again today, we do not receive one phone call in a whole six hour period. Fortunately I have my admin paperwork to do and manage to keep myself occupied.

I hold my weekly TEAMS meeting with my voluntary unit when I get in. There is an interesting piece of information from two of the members who work for the NHS ; it seems that all the ambulance calls in their town are down. This could possibly be due to the fact that there are more ambulances on every shift, they have some which are being driven by firemen or is it that the virus is indeed slowing down? Because all operations, appointments, procedures etc have been cancelled at the hospital, the wards are half empty again, surely this is a good sign?

Sadly we are now officially the first country in Europe to pass the 30,000 mark for deaths from Covid19.

The other bad news is that jobs are starting to go in the UK. British Airways have announced that they are going to have to release 12,000 of their staff. Virgin Airways are going to have to shed 3,000 staff and are also pulling out of Gatwick Airport. It won't just be 15,000 people who lose their jobs, there will be all the cleaning, catering & maintenance staff that go with it.

It's started then, redundancies across the country.

Thursday 7th May

All everyone can talk about at work is are they going to lose their job ? It's a depressing thought, but being realistic the company cannot keep all of their staff on furlough forever, the scheme will eventually have to come to an end. It could take six to nine months for our business to pick up and the management will need to make some tough decisions.
As far as I can see the UK economy has been totally blasted out of the water and will take years to recover. As I said earlier, we will be paying for it for years, certainly long after I am buried six foot underground.

The Government has said that the Lockdown will persist at the moment and there will be no easing of the rules. There is a lot of talk about 'the Exit Strategy' and the restrictions that will have to be put in place as Lockdown eases. They have declared that there will now be a 14 day quarantine period for anyone arriving in the UK. This is a bit like closing the gate after the horse has bolted and should have been brought in 2 months ago.

A lot of people I know, especially ones who have stayed indoors and haven't been out for weeks, are still very scared of catching the virus and think we should stay locked down for a lot longer. As I have been going into work each day and my routine hasn't changed much, I no longer even really think about catching Covid anymore. But I do think some businesses should now be allowed to start running as long as they take the necessary precautions, certainly dentists, builders, manufacturing & small companies. A lot of these firms do not have huge financial backing and will go bust if they don't start up again very soon.

The Bank of England has cheerfully said the UK economy will shrink by 14% this year creating the deepest recession on record.

I rest my case M'Lord.

Friday 8th May

Today is the anniversary of VE day and an extraordinarily sunny and gorgeous day for a British Bank Holiday. We are celebrating 75 years since Germany's surrender which ended the second world war after 6 long hard years. It is such a shame that all the festivities have had to be cancelled across the world. In our street and across the country the Union Jacks are hanging out of the windows and the bunting is up. We haven't forgotten and we all celebrate in the best way possible.

We can't find our Union Jack anywhere in the garage. So we end up hanging one of Peters red, white & blue cycling shirts out of the first floor window. We did find a pair of Union Jack boxer shorts but didn't think the neighbours would appreciate seeing Peters smalls on display, but he did wear them in honour of the day.

At 5pm everyone in our road set up deck chairs and picnic tables on their drives, at least 2M apart, obviously. We sat out there until 11pm chatting, talking, eating, drinking and listening to the Queens speech. It actually turned into a very nice evening and we talked to people we hadn't seen for months.

Strangely enough we haven't spoken to or seen any of them since.

Saturday 9th May

It is blisteringly hot today, Peter has gone into the Call Centre and I just want to lay relaxing in the garden and read my book. I spend all day going in and out of the house like a yoyo trying to avoid the football noise. I count 14 different times HE comes out into the garden and hoofs the ball around. I lose count of how many times he whacks the fence by my head. At 4pm I can stand it no longer and retreat indoors for the rest of the day.

Classic FM is then played very loudly for the rest of the evening.

Sunday 10th May

This morning we do a naughty thing. Maureen has broken her mobile phone which she desperately needs to keep in touch with everyone. Peter ordered her a new one which was delivered yesterday, so we are off to her house to set it up. It's only a 45 minute journey and surely it counts as looking after elderly relatives?
When we arrive we go through the gate and straight into the back garden. We sit on the patio whilst she and her husband sit in the lounge with the door slightly ajar. They are thrilled to see us, it's been a long time. I know she really wants a big hug, but we do the sensible thing and keep apart from each other.
I sit on the patio sunbathing whilst Maureen and Peter set up the new phone. Delicious morsels keep appearing through the doors. Maureen's husband falls asleep for the rest of the time we are there. She talks non stop, it's obvious she needed to let off some steam, so we sit and listen. When we go to leave, her husband wakes up and thinks we have just arrived. It has given her a bit of a break at least.

When we get home we lay on the sofa for the rest of the afternoon, waiting for the Governments press conference to see if we can have any freedom.

There is a conditional 3 step plan to start to release the Lockdown made up of five sections that must happen if we don't all go mad and rush out partying into the streets:

1. Protect the NHS
2. There needs to be a sustained fall in deaths
3. There needs to be a sustained fall in the infection rate
4. There needs to be more testing and more PPE needs to be available
5. There is no spike in infections

We are still at Covid alert level 4 (5 being the highest) and the Government now has changed its slogan to "Stay Alert'.

There is an interesting set of new rules from No.10 depending on which way you interpret them. This is what they are basically saying in a very round about way:

Step 1
From Monday you can go back to work if you can't work from home but we would prefer that you don't go out at all.
Go to work by car, bike or walk but we would prefer that you don't use public transport.
You can take unlimited exercise with members of your household or one person outside of your household but we would prefer you didn't.
You must ensure 2 metres social distancing so we would rather you don't mix with anyone.

Step2
Some schools and small shops may reopen on 1st June along with outdoor markets and car showrooms.

Step3
 Bigger shops can open later in the month on this conditional plan. If we all behave ourselves some restaurants, catering outlets and other public places may be able to open from 4th July.

Basically Boris is saying be sensible, don't all rush out, but it doesn't go down well with some of the public. They want clearcut instructions of where they can go, who with and for how long etc,etc.
I have a friend who works in a Government office and she told me that they were getting phone calls asking for actual specifics, one example was:
' If I live in a caravan, does the household consist of only the people living in my caravan or everyone who lives on the caravan site?"
I think she told them to go get a life and stop wasting time asking stupid questions!
She is menopausal too, no surprise there then, eh?

For Gods sake everyone, take some personal responsibility and just be careful.

Stay strong. make them wonder why you are still smiling - Anon

6. Staying Alert

Monday 11th May

There is another Government press conference this evening to try and clarify some of the points raised yesterday. The great British Public are confused and need it explaining in more detail. Again Boris urges everyone to be cautious but the reporters are having none of it. I listen to three of them and two members of the public asking their questions. All five questions are pretty much the same in a round about way and Boris gives the same answer to each of them in the political round about way. No-one is appeased and they ask even more daft questions. I end up shouting at the TV ' use your common sense people' and switch it off, it's really getting on my wick.

Donald Trump has ordered all White House staff to wear face masks after one of his valet's tested positive on 7th May.
Trump isn't doing it himself, just his staff, it might ruin his hair style.

Tuesday 12th May

It's Anna's 1st wedding anniversary and she sent me a picture of her husband and LaVie with a huge cake. The cake is nearly as big as the baby. At least I know the husband is still around. I asked her what they were doing to celebrate. She says they went out for dinner last night, to a restaurant in Danang. I ask if it was a romantic evening. The answer back was a big fat NO. Not sure what to make of that but she seems happy enough at the moment. Considering that she lives with a huge extended family, she doesn't seem to get an awful lot of help with LaVie, she says all her time is consumed with the baby. Vietnamese men obviously have nothing to do with childcare.
Greenie is currently working weekends in the hotel's registration centre, hopefully taking bookings for the Summer. I can't see anyone from Europe being able to go as there are still very strict (now 21 day) quarantine rules in place for any arriving visitors and you can't get a visa anyway. I am presuming the bulk of their tourists for this year will come from within Vietnam itself. At least Greenie is working and earning some money for herself.

The confusion caused by the Governments latest announcement rages on again today, the press are having a field day with it. Some people just cannot decide for themselves what constitutes being sensible and are still rambling on about specifics.

I have got more important things to worry about. I have put on so much weight that most of my clothes are too tight and I have nothing to wear. I have always carried any extra weight on my bum but now I have a proper spare tyre and my arse is the size of a small country.

Unfortunately due to Peter being at home all the time, our normally sensible diet has gone right out of the window. He keeps nipping out to M&S or Tesco and coming home with an assortment of delicious titbits. My weekly diet currently seems to be made up of Microwave dinners, cheesy Wotsits, Percy Pigs, Magnum ice-creams, iced buns or chocolate eclairs, wine gums, gin and wine. I do cook at the weekend but the rest of the time we are out of control food wise. I know it's the boredom, we can't go out or see our friends, so we sit on the sofa each evening eating & drinking.

During the menopause most women put on a bit of weight, it's all part and parcel of the hormonal changes but the extra heft I am now carrying around will take ages to shift and I am hardly motivated to do any exercise. I can hardly get off of the sofa let alone run around the block. It gets so much harder to lose weight the older you get, I know I should stop eating right now but things are so depressing at the moment, a massive bag of wine gums and a G&T are the only thing to look forward to.

For some reason, which completely flummoxes Peter, I put the empty milk bottles out on the doorstep before I go to bed. The milkman is not due until Friday.

Wednesday 13th May

I didn't get up until 10.30 am. Apart from going to work at 1pm, I had nothing else to do. The garden is immaculate, the house is sparkling clean, the laundry and ironing baskets are all empty and there is plenty of food in the fridge.

Peter spends all day trying to make a complicated video of the dog in four sections singing' *Bohemian Rhapsody*'. His mother declares it a masterpiece.

Tui has sadly announced 8,000 redundancies across Europe. Let's be honest, I can't see anyone being able to go on a package holiday for some time so it's not really a big surprise. You could go to Spain for a fortnight, spend the whole time in their quarantine system and then return home to spend another two weeks in UK quarantine. Unless you are retired and time is not an issue, who is even going to bother? Even holidays in the UK are not achievable at the moment. Holidays parks and hotels are still closed and cannot open until given the green light which will probably be in July - all of this is dependent on whether we have a spike in infections or not. We must stay alert!

This morning the tube, buses and trains were packed with people trying to return to work as per the Governments confusing instructions. Commuters were crammed in, most of them not wearing masks or gloves.

It has been decided that house moves and viewings can resume again, I know my friend Julie and her husband are desperate to sell up so that they can buy a yacht to retire on. Hopefully now they can get on with their amazing plan.

The USA unemployment rate has gone up 14.7% meaning that there are more Americans out of work now than since the Great Depression in the 1930's. 20 million people lost their jobs in the USA in April alone.
The good news in the UK is that the furlough scheme has been extended to October, hopefully that way more people here will keep their jobs.
And Peter at least will be bringing in some income.

The city of Wuhan, where this all of this started has had a small flurry of new infections over the weekend and the Chinese are set to test the 11 million population of the entire city.
The Russians say they have only had 10,000 cases in the whole country and much less deaths than countries in Europe. Reading between the lines, I don't think anyone believes them.
Spain's figures have gone up slightly as they release the Lockdown but even so there are now plans to relax the EU border controls in the coming weeks.

It's eerily quiet in the office this afternoon. Honestly if you believed the news every day, you would lock yourself in the house and never come out.

When I get home I hold my unit TEAMS meeting. Some interesting information comes out of it via members who work for the ambulance service. They say calls are down again this week, what they are attending are more to do with the public having silly accidents now they have been allowed a bit more freedom than picking up any more Covid Cases. This indeed is good news.

My friend Jagdish relates a hilarious story of his delight and glee at being able to go to the tidy tip, after emptying out his loft and shed. He lives one mile from the tip and the journey in and out took him just over three hours.

Thursday 14th May

I got up really early this morning and went out on a mission. Garden centres re-opened this morning, whoopee. Off I went full of optimism, I would have something to do over the weekend if I could get some bedding plants.
Unfortunately no-one had informed our local centre that they could re-open and it was still closed. I drove back home with the right hump and tackled a pile of ironing instead.

The lovely news is that my friend Lisa is now a grandmother. Her daughter in law gave birth early this morning and she has a beautiful granddaughter. The downside is that no-one can go to visit and Lisa can't cuddle her newborn grandchild.
I really feel for her, she was so excited about becoming a grandparent.

When Peter and I get into the Call Centre this afternoon, there are new social distancing posters up everywhere and red and white taped boxes on the floor of all the offices for staff to stand in if they want to speak to anyone. We have to take our temperature every morning before we go up the stairs. If it is over 37.5, we have to go home again for a week. It's all a bit late if you ask me. If any of us had it we would have passed it on to each other by now.

There is an announcement today which we had all been expecting. It is official, the company are going to make 255 staff redundant with the bulk of that number coming from the training department. We all knew it had to happen but it's still a shock when you hear it from the top and we are demoralised and unsettled by the news.

When we get home we open another bottle of wine which keeps me awake half the night and pacing the landing at 2am with palpitations. I know I should stop drinking before I go to bed it's not doing me any good. Unlike most people, alcohol usually knocks you out; not me at the moment, it just keeps me alert.

Friday 15th May

A tiny miracle has occurred today, Peter has gone to Liverpool to visit a customer with a problem. It is not a job, he is not working just giving some advice. As it is my day off I was going to go with him but would just have to sit in the car, I can't exactly go and look around the shops, so I opt to stay home alone. I am pleased he has gone off on his own for the day with a purpose. He is the most laid back person in the world but I have detected a shift in his mood and am beginning to get the feeling that this situation might actually be starting to get to him.

I went off to the supermarket again. I have never enjoyed doing the food shop but at least before all of this Covid stuff you could have a browse around. Now I just want to get in and out as fast as I can, which isn't possible because I have to queue for 20 minutes before they let me in. Because I am classed as a key worker I could show my Blue Light card and go to the front of the queue but that would make me feel like a fraud. As I am not in a hurry I wait with everyone else. We all shuffle along looking at our mobiles trying to keep within the taped 2metre boxes. It's not a pleasant experience and I am glad to finally get out of there. I literally wash myself down with hand sanitiser when I get back to the car.

I have an email from the office, there will be a meeting on Tuesday to discuss jobs and redundancies. That's really something to look forward to isn't it? It doesn't just affect me, my nephew could be at risk too, something that my sister is dreading.

I feel a bit flat and fed up today, not surprising really with the announcement yesterday. I see nothing on the horizon to look forward to and now the cherry on the cake is that I could lose my job. It's not the best job in the world, the pay is rubbish, the office is hardly elegant or beautifully decorated but I wouldn't go back to my last job for all the tea in China. We have such a good team, no ego's, no bitchiness, just friendly helpful people, all very good at what they do. Everyone brings something to the table.
Please don't break us up.

My normally well groomed hair looks a complete mess, it is so long I have to tuck it behind my ears. And I am definitely beginning to resemble Billy Bunter (Anna was right), I daren't look in the mirror, especially side on, especially naked.

All the incoming phone calls and funny videos are starting to slow down as everyone gets used to being at home. Everyone was quite cheerful to begin with but now the Lockdown is getting to us all and we are bored and cheesed off. Even Peter hasn't made a video of our singing dog for a few days. He redeems himself by doing '*Hello*' by Adele, which I think is the best one yet and gets my nomination for an Oscar for 'best leading role of a dog singing an Adele song'.

I speak to my mother, who I am sure is away with the fairies, much to my amazement she asks me if I have been working through the Covid crisis? ERR YES.

The Nightingale hospital closed today. It has to be a really good sign that it wasn't needed. Doesn't it?

We end up drinking two bottles of red wine this evening and I am awake half the night again feeling sick, thirsty and fuzzy headed. Every time I drink a swig of water or even move position in bed it sets off a hot flush. I can't win.

Saturday 16th May

I get up really early to go to B&Q this morning to get some plants. When I arrive there at 9.10am the queue to get in goes halfway across the car park. I really can't be bothered with it so drive back home. Along the bypass I remember that there is a small plant nursery near the roundabout, I am in luck, it is open and has everything that I want. I probably end up paying about £10 more than I usually would but there is no queue and the plants look very large and healthy.

When I arrive home silence reigns so I step out onto my patio. The kid next door definitely has an annoyance radar and immediately appears in his garden armed with a football the second my foot touches the stone slabs. I try very hard to ignore him, I love my garden and want it to look nice, so I persevere with my planting, quietly cursing every time his ball whacks against the fence.

Eventually he goes in and I get some peace. After 20 minutes inside he is obviously bored and comes out banging around again. I am kneeling down by a tub when he whacks a ball against the fence right by my head, I lose my patience and shout at him. His mother hears and at least tells him to stop for a while. Finally I am finished and apart from the parched brown grass, the garden looks really nice.

I get a worrying message from my sister that my nephew has shingles. I instantly ring her, she says he is not in a good way. As I have said he suffers from Mental health issues and is already struggling with the Lockdown and possible losing his job. Oh dear, my sister is in tears she feels so sorry for him. It never rains but pours in their house. There's not much I can do except let her talk and leave my nephew a message, I know he won't answer the phone at the moment.

There is a big protest in Central London today. The crowds are protesting about the Lockdown as they say it is unlawful and suppressing their civil rights. Jeremy Corbin's brother is one of the activists. That's setting a really good example to the public.
I do not know what makes some people tick. The latest UK figures are grim, 277,985 infections with 34,466 deaths. And they are the official figures, what about people who have probably had it but not needed any medical care. Which bit of that isn't so serious that it needs exceptional restrictions to stop it spreading?
As far away as the Himalayas, Nepal has had their first fatality and Brazil now has officially the 4th highest number of confirmed cases across the globe.
USA is 1st, Russia 2nd and UK 3rd. Not something we can be proud of.

Meanwhile back in Vietnam, domestic tourism has gone through the roof. The Viets are taking full advantage of having their beautiful country to themselves and are all on holiday.

Due to my increasing girth I have worked out a small fitness regime to try and do every day. Along with ensuring I go with Peter to walk the dog, I am going to make a real effort to at least tone up. I only have the one G&T tonight and retire to bed early.

Sunday 17th May

My sister sends me a hilarious video that explains the difference between men and women's thinking patterns:
Apparently women's brains are a massive ball of electric wire that never stops moving and is connected to everything by something called emotion.
Mens brains are made up of individual little boxes. There is a box for the wife, the kids, one for the job, hobby, money, motorbike, car, mother, etc,etc. All of these boxes are contained inside his brain but they never touch each other.
All men have a secret box in his brain that contains nothing, this is his favourite box. This is the box he would use everyday if he could, it is called 'The Nothing Box' and is completely empty.

This is obviously the box Peter spends most of his time using.

I do at least pin him down to clear out our DVD cupboard. With Smart TV's you can watch anything you want more or less and we hardly use them anymore. We have a bit of a tug of war over a few films but we do end up clearing out at least half. They go up to the box room with all the other stuff accumulating for when I can do a car boot sale.

I cook an enormous chilli just for me which I freeze in batches to take to work for my tea when I am on late shifts. I love very spicy food and you could strip the wallpaper with it, it is so hot, but delicious.
I send my manager, a picture of my G&T at 4pm. This becomes a recurring theme between us over the next few weekends, it's definitely 5 o'clock somewhere.

When Peter gets in later he is full of himself as he has had three battles with bureaucracy this evening which he declares he won 3-0.

Monday 18th May

It is evident on the A1 this morning that some drivers have not driven a car on a motorway for some time. It is total carnage with people cutting you up, braking suddenly and trying to pull on to the motorway at 25 miles an hour.
The slow return to work has begun.

Speculation is rife in the office today, we are all guessing as to what will be said at tomorrows meeting and everyone is a bit tense. 60% of me says that we will be OK, we are the only events team still working and also assisting with the Call Centre. Logic tells me that they will want that to continue. 40% of me says that sometimes the most logical thing is the least popular and they could close us down and move the office to somewhere like Outer Mongolia. No-one will want to relocate so we could all be out of work. Who knows, it is anyones guess?
I am trying very hard not to let it get to me. Peter always says why stress yourself about something that may not happen and even if it does you have no control over it, so stop fretting about it.
Easy for him to say.

At lunch time my boss and myself decide to resume our lunch time walks and saunter off into the sunshine. We haven't done this since February and it's good to get out of the office and get a bit of fresh air and exercise.

On my way home, I pass our local garden centre, it is now fully open for business, wouldn't you just know it!

My friend Hilary rings me and we have a long chat. We speak on the TEAMS meeting on Wednesdays but it is nice to have a proper catch up. She has neighbours from hell who have two small children who fight constantly in the garden and she cannot wait for them to go back to school. I know how she feels.

Peter and I have both forgotten about the microwave we ordered and suddenly realise it has not turned up yet. Peter is on it like a rat up a drain pipe, I never knew he could move that fast.

Tuesday 19th May

The lovely news this morning is that Captain Tom has been knighted by the Queen. The rest of the Queens birthday honours have been postponed until later in the year. I expect there will be a lot of deserving people who have done amazing things through this Covid period on that list. And a lot who haven't.

It is confirmed that the restaurant chain Bella Italia and its associates are in financial difficulties, that's along with Chiquita's, Carluccios and Pizza Express who are already in trouble.

Peter drove to Somerset this morning to do another engineering favour for a customer, so that's him occupied for a few hours.

There is a lot more traffic and people around this morning. Mind you the weather is phenomenal, the best May we have had for years. Every one is out walking, running, cycling and exercising their exhausted dogs.

We all shuffle into the meeting with our Manager about the job losses. I was still on 60/40 when I went in. When I came out I was still none the wiser. Basically we were told we might be at risk but no decisions had been made as to who was going. 255 staff would be made redundant within the company and 35 of that number would come out of our side of the business. We all asked a few questions and raised a few points but it was evident that our boss didn't know any of the answers, so we all shuffled out again slightly baffled.

We were all greatly cheered up by some hilarious photo's that Peter sent me during the afternoon . He has only tried to cut his own hair! I had said I would do it when I got home but he couldn't wait and has tackled it himself with a razor. It looks simply awful, he certainly gave the '*Peaky Blinders*' a run for their money. So when I got in I used his electric shaver to tidy it up and gave the top a trim. It looked really good when it was finished, but I did decline his most generous offer for him to give me a trim and tidy up my messy barnet.

Wednesday 20th May

It's blisteringly hot today and we take the dog out early. When we get back she retires to her favourite spot in the garden and we have to spray her with Factor 50 suncream as she keeps burning her belly.

My hair is now completely out of control and I just don't know what to do with it. It normally takes about three minutes to finger dry, it's now taking 15 minutes using a styling brush!! I usually get up with my hair looking the same as when I went to bed, some days I even forget to brush it and no-one notices. Today I have tried using a hot brush to give it a bit of a lift but it just ends up looking like a huge bouffant. I looked like Mrs Slocombe from '*Are you being served*' but without the blue rinse. Or I could be Cruella De Vil's little sister, whichever way you look at it, it looks bloody awful.

So now I am trying to dry it flat and tuck it seductively behind my ears. I am even using hair spray to try and keep it in place, something I never use. I haven't had hair this long for about 15 years and find it so difficult to manage. I know women who have long curly hair which they wash and straighten every single day, how much time does that take? Life is just too short to spend hours messing around with hair every day, I just want to get up and go.

Some women suffer bit of hair loss during the menopause but not me, it is like a lions mane and really thick.

The back which is normally very short against my neck is now so long that it is curling up against my collar. I look a bit like Fusspot out of the '*Beano*'. Against all of my best instincts I ask Peter to cut the wispy bits off. It actually looks OK when he had finished, but is now so thick at the back I have a bit of a wedgie going on.

Don't even get me started on the rest of the body where there is a definite wedgie going on around my waistline.

When I get in to work everyone is a bit tetchy, we are all a bit uptight. We want to stay working together, we don't want to lose anyone. We also don't want anyone else brought in to what is a very successful mix of people to upset the apple cart.

It is brought to my attention by one of my colleagues that another member of staff in another office, far, far away, is about to start meddling with another part of my job that I have been doing for two years. This is without any consultation with myself or my line manager, in fact they have not even asked me where I am with the task. As far as I can see there is team of high level people desperate to stay working who are poking their noses into aspects of other jobs that they normally wouldn't touch with a barge pole, it's far below their pay grade. This is the second time that this has happened to me during this crisis. I take extreme exception to it, if someone doing my job warrants that sort of salary, why wasn't I on that pay scale in the first place? I write a formal letter of complaint to my senior manager. He knows nothing about what is going on behind our backs and stamps on it immediately.

This will all probably backfire on me somewhere along the line.

I have learnt over the years that it doesn't really pay to complain at work, it never gets you anywhere. You always need to be positive and never say anything negative, even if everything is falling apart in front of your eyes. You cannot be truthful and state the 'bleedin' obvious, no-one wants to hear it. Look what happens to Whistle Blowers, they always end up getting sacked and unless they can afford a big court case, they end up with nothing except a reputation for being a troublemaker. Raising any sort of grievance always comes back and bites you on the bum .
Do not ask for my opinion if you genuinely do not want to hear my answer. I still have not fathomed out how to do corporate speak and I would rather die than lick someones boots if I did not agree with their point of view. There are a LOT of arse lickers and brown nosers around at the moment, I notice.

All of this is probably why I have never really progressed in any company I have worked for. Yes I know; it is my own fault for being so pigheaded and gobby.

It's that time of week for my TEAMS meeting. We have a good old chin wag and a bit of a laugh. My friend Lisa proudly holds up photo's of her gorgeous granddaughter. One of the girls is having problems with the Internet and sounds like a strangled duck which is hilarious. Peter has set up a background for me and it causes much hilarity that I look like I am sitting in 'Ab Fabs' kitchen with three fridges full of Bolly behind me. (It's actually not that far from the truth).

One thing which does come out of the chat is that my friends who work for the NHS have dealt with Covid after Covid case this week. This is not what the government is telling us. Maybe Bedfordshire is a hot spot at the moment.

Thursday 21st May

I am rudely woken by the sound of aircraft above the house around 1am. The noise is so loud that it even wakes Peter out of his slumber, and he could sleep through an earthquake (and has whilst on holiday in Bali!). At one point we are convinced that something is about to crash into the house. The whole house is vibrating but we cannot see anything out of the window, the sound is awesome in the stillness of the night. The deafening noise is bouncing around and echoing off the houses, in the distance I spot something moving in the moonlight. Three Chinook helicopters, with no lights on, are dipping towards the ground and then shooting back up into the air, we watch them circling over the house and then zooming in again. It looks like it is going on at the airfield, two miles away, Peter thinks it could be a training exercise.
It is either that or something bad is going on.

After the disturbed night, it's difficult to wake up in the morning. Peter got up at 5am and has gone off to help another customer out in Wilmslow, he was bleary eyed when he left. I do not know how we will ever get back into a normal working pattern of getting up early every day.

Whilst I am in work a group of volunteers from an Indian temple in Luton pop in with some donations of food and drinks for the staff and volunteers working out of the building. A few of us have our photo take with them, they are very kind and lovely people - thank you.

It's very hot again and the parks and beaches are rammed with families having a day out. I don't think that was what Boris had in mind when he said 'I will give you some freedom but you must stay alert'. I know the kids are all bored, we are all bored, but most of us are still trying to protect each other and the NHS, some people don't give a fig about the rest of the population.

I miss the clap yet again for the NHS, I see all the flashing blue lights at the Hospital as I pass at 8pm and there are lots of people out on their front lawns chatting to their neighbours, it's almost a festive atmosphere.

For only the second time during this Lockdown we order an Indian takeaway. Peter says they have a good safe system in there and everyone has to queue outside, it's all very organised and very busy. I eat every delicious morsel on my plate.

It's been 9 weeks today since we left Vietnam, it seems like a lifetime ago. To date they have had 324 cases of the Coronavirus there and no deaths. They currently have an airline pilot seriously ill in hospital and they are fighting around the clock to save his life to keep their zero death figure against the awful figures from the rest of the world. Especially the USA.

Figures across the world now stand at over 5 million infected cases, with the true number probably significantly higher, with 328,471 deaths. In the UK we have lost 36,042 souls. Worryingly just today there have been 106,000 new cases globally, which is the highest number of new infections in a single day since this began.
Despite these figures, across Europe the Lockdown is beginning to ease, still with some restrictions in place, and shops and businesses are starting to open. St Pauls Basilica in Rome has re-opened to visitors, all worshippers fervently praying for this to end I suspect.
The weather has been glorious and there has been a surge of visitors to the beaches in France, Holland and the UK. All of this despite warnings in Europe that there is possibly a second wave of the virus on the way.
Figures show that the amount of people that died in April in Belgium was the worst death toll there since the Nazi Occupation in the 1940's. Russia has now owned up and admitted they have had 3,000 deaths. Afghanistan has also admitted that they have run out of hospital beds and there are dead bodies on the streets on the eve of Eid.
There is a super cyclone on its way to the coast of Eastern India and Bangladesh, the authorities there say that the restrictions are making any evacuations very difficult.
That is stating the bleedin' obvious.

The only good news is that the emissions of Carbon Monoxide fell 17% at the peak of the Lockdown. Nature is coming back to life.

Back in China in the city of Wuhan, where there have been no new cases, there is now a complete ban on eating wild animals.
You don't say.

Friday 22nd May

I arise from my slumber at 9am after having had an argument with our dog at 5am. I think the new puppy next door has definitely upset her equilibrium and our little mutt has gone a bit needy during the early hours. What she really wants to do is get on the bed and snuggle up with Peter, I won't let her and tell her to go downstairs. She goes off with her tail between her legs, if she could stick her two paws up at me she would.

When I get downstairs I lay out my pilates mat to do my daily exercises.Whilst I am doing a roll down, the dog nonchalantly wanders over and pukes up all over my foot.

Peter finds this hilarious and nearly falls off of his chair laughing.

I am sure the dog winked at him.

I spend all morning doing the housework, giving everything a good clean. Because we have had such good weather and have had the doors and windows open, everything is covered in a fine layer of dust.

Peter goes off to the bottle bank to empty what looks like an entire Off Licence from the garage. He really needed an articulated lorry to convey the empties.

When he gets back we decide to clear out the loft, another job we hadn't got around to for donkeys years. We are accompanied by music from Peters pop icon - Toyah. He suddenly realises that he hasn't done a video of the dog singing one of her songs and promptly gets distracted from the task at hand. We spend the rest of the day emptying boxes of photo's, birthday cards and lots of other accumulated rubbish that we don't really need to keep. We managed to condense it down to three boxes which went back in the loft, the rest of it went in the bin or my growing pile of crap for a car boot sale. We also found Larry the Lamb. Larry is the most flea-bitten beloved toy you could possibly imagine, but Peter will not part with him. I had to immediately wash my hands after just touching it.

It's still very warm but today the wind has picked up and there is a very strong breeze, at least it blows the cobwebs away when we walk Vomit the dog.

As we cross the allotments, we can see that they are in really good shape, tidy and well tended. A few months ago most of these were overgrown and a dumping ground for rubbish. There has been a lot of hard work done over the last few weeks and they look amazing with lots of rows of neat veg. There are lots of families over there getting stuck in together and there is a nice atmosphere. Everyone speaks to us as we pass by which is unusual, normally everyones ignores each other around here.

Saturday 23rd May

Two more businesses have gone bust today — Shearings the coach holiday company and Hertz rental cars worldwide.

On the journey to the office we are driving down the A1 when all the traffic starts to slow up on both sides of the motorway. There does not appear to have been an accident but then we spot the reason, there is a black Labrador running amok between the cars. Some poor bloke who has parked up on the hard shoulder is running up and down with a lead in his hand. It is obviously his dog, but on earth how did it get out of the car? The dog is having a lovely time playing chase, causing absolute chaos as he zig zags across all of the traffic lanes. We wind the window down to try and attract his attention but he is having such a good time, he thinks it is all a great game. Fortunately someone behind us manages to grab him and hands him over to his owner. As we drive off there is a woman parked up on the hard shoulder crying and white as a sheet, we wonder if she nearly hit him.
After all of that excitement the Call Centre is quiet as a graveyard for the whole shift.

Sunday 24th May

There is a report on the news that half of the UK are struggling to sleep during this Lockdown. Not in our house, we are having no such difficulty at the moment (makes a change for me), our big problem is getting up in the mornings. We are so zonked out, that for the second night in a row we find the dog has joined us at some point and we didn't even notice.

 I am going to wash my car, I have had it 9 weeks and it hasn't been cleaned once. Mind you it's only dusty, it's hardly been anywhere to get properly dirty. I normally take it to the local carwash run by excellent Polish cleaners but they are closed so I am going to have to do it myself. I run the hose round the side of the house and set about wetting the car before I add the soap. The minute I press the trigger, the hose explodes and water goes everywhere except on the car. I am soaked to the skin. The hose has split and is now useless. So I have to do it the old fashioned way with a bucket and sponge which takes ages.

Because it is so hot the neighbours are staying indoors so I take full advantage and sit out on the decking in my bikini looking like Jabba the Hut on holiday. The weather has been amazing and today is no exception, for a few hours at least there is peace in our garden. I spend half an hour brushing teak oil onto some wooden statues that have faded in the sun to spruce them up. See what I mean about everything looking immaculate, would I normally even bother with such a task? My boss sends me a message at 2pm; 'It's five o'clock somewhere' with a photo of a glass of wine. Blimey she's starting early today.

I speak to my friend Mary in Ireland, she is desperate to go to her place in the South of France, but there are still no flights available until July from Dublin. At least she won't have to go into 14 days of quarantine when she eventually gets there. She extends her warm invitation for me to come over at any time when it's possible.
Not for want of trying Mary, I can assure you.

It's the end of Mental Health Awareness week. It's been especially poignant during this difficult time. People who would not be the 'type' you would think to suffer mentally are really struggling with being locked in. Loneliness and isolation are common symptoms of mental health issues and sufferers feel these all the time. But for anyone not accustomed to these feelings, it's a very strange sensation to feel the sort of panic and anxiety which they go through every day, sometimes even hourly.
Fortunately my nephew is a bit more up beat today and feeling better, his shingles have gone. Tomorrow is a whole new day though and who know's how he will feel?
Considering what I went through last year, I think I am coping really well with the current situation and don't feel too bad, I have good days and then not so good days, but I soldier on. I think still being able to go to work and mix with my colleagues has definitely helped. I shudder to think how I would have coped if this incident had happened last year, I am not sure if I would have got through it. Even Peter acknowledges that I am managing well, I am keeping an eye on him though, he seems a bit lost at the moment. I asked him this evening what he misses most, his answer was totally predictable: work, football and cricket.

Monday 25th May

There is an uproar in the press this morning regarding the fact that there are no lifeguards on duty at any of the UK's beaches. Unfortunately two swimmers have died in Cornwall and everyone is up in arms about it. Excuse me people are you not listening? You are not supposed to be swarming to the beaches, it has not been allowed yet and all the lifeguards are on furlough.

I sit in the garden again on this scorching hot Bank Holiday Monday; I look like I have been to the Bahamas I am so brown. Unfortunately the kid next door is also out there - I wish he was in the Bahamas. Today he bangs his ball around on 9 separate occasions and I give up at 3pm and go inside for a bath. I know he is bored with being stuck indoors but we are all fed up and I think it would be courtesy to at least let the neighbours have a bit of peace at the weekends, he has all week to play football when I am at work.

When Peter gets in at 3pm, I have cooked a proper dinner with vegetables and everything. We wash it all down with a bottle of champagne, very decadent - well it's five o'clock. Somewhere. Again.

We put the news on to watch the press briefing. Alan Cummings, the PM's side kick has been caught breaking the Lockdown by going up North to see his parents with a side visit to Barnard Castle. The public are calling for his resignation but he is not having any of it. I listen to his argument, it was all about child care apparently and I can see his point of view. On the other side of the coin, every other parent in the country who has had childcare issues did not break the Lockdown. The Public are furious that the Government are telling us one thing and doing something different themselves. In the end I switch it off, it is making me cringe listening to a senior government minister giving details of where he stopped to have a pee.

Tuesday 26th May

Saudi Arabia is revising their curfew rules and praying at a mosques will now be allowed. Only the City of Mecca is to remain on curfew due to the millions who gather there. That would definitely be a huge breeding ground for the virus.
Iceland is another country who has released Lockdown and all their pubs and clubs are re-opening. They have had a meticulous test and trace strategy in place during Lockdown and have only had 1804

infections and 10 deaths. How come other countries have been so successful at keeping the virus at bay and we have such awful statistics? Australia has refused to open its borders to foreigners as they do not want an influx of the virus and will remain closed for the near future. Spain is now open for business to Europe, except how will anyone from the UK get there? Our airlines are still not flying.

Trump has told the world that he is taking an anti-malaria (I can't spell it or even pronounce it) drug to avoid Covid. Prescriptions of this medication have gone through the roof in the USA. The WHO has suspended their trials of this particular drug due to the side effects. But Donald remains adamant that they are working.

Overnight an unarmed black man has been killed by four police officers in Minneapolis when they arrested him for allegedly passing counterfeit notes in a shop. They knelt on his neck for 9 minutes and didn't notice that he had stopped breathing. What, didn't they notice that he wasn't struggling anymore? Didn't they notice he had gone a funny colour? I think you would instinctively know if someone underneath you stopped moving, one of the officers must have noticed.
There is going to be big trouble over this, to add to the rest of America's current problems, you mark my words.

The debate rages on over Alan Cummings. Peter is adamant that he should resign but it is evident Mr Cummings really doesn't think he's done anything wrong. The Government has been asked outright if they now intend to refund fines to anyone who broke the Lockdown if they can prove it was to do with childcare. No-one gets a definitive answer, as usual.

On the way to work there are more out of the habit drivers on the motorway, pulling out without signalling, driving at a snails pace and causing motoring mayhem. I narrowly miss getting pushed on to the hard shoulder by some blind woman who evidently did not see a bright red Mini next to her as she haphazardly swapped lanes.

It is very hot again and tempers are a bit frayed in the office. It is such a strange atmosphere. We all know nothing much is going ahead within the next few months but there is still a team of senior people hanging in there saying that business will be as usual from July. It is really getting on everyones nerves, I wish someone higher up the food chain would just be honest and admit that it isn't going to happen.

It is affecting us in the office in different ways. The Office Manager hasn't seen her new grandson or daughter since January and is a bit emotional and weepy. One of my colleagues has had enough of the business as usual routine. I am sick to the teeth with other people trying to take away bits of my job. One of the lads is being stabbed in the back constantly and the others are worried and confused about their jobs. The swearing is off the scale.

When I get home I do get a nice surprise. Our new front door has been fitted which looks really lovely. The down side is that Peter has gone all technical and fitted it with digital locks which you have on your phone or a fob. I am very worried with my forgetful menopausal brain that I will go out without both items and have no way of getting back into the house. (We used to be able to tap in a code on the last door). Peter thinks about this (realising the true reality of me locking myself out) and proceeds to fit a new lock to the garage and another to the internal door. He puts the key in an outside security box with a code that I have to memorise. What happened to just having a front door key?
I will never remember any of this.

Wednesday 27th May

Just for a change of scenery I accompany Peter to Screwfix, he has to pick up some more bits for the new door. At the store there is a long queue trailing around the car park of bored looking men wearing strange concoctions of shorts, socks and sandals. It's a weird but thrilling feeling to actually be out somewhere different.
Oh dear how far we have fallen to get excited by a trip to Screwfix!

When we get home peace reigns in the garden so I sit out for a couple of hours before I go to work. The Alan Cummings saga still fills the news, I am bored and so over it now. It is apparent that he is not going to resign, he thinks he is right and that is final.
The Government is also warning that if there are flares ups of infections they will initiate local Lockdowns. I make a conscious decision that I am not going to watch the news anymore, it just winds me up and scares people.
The good news is that dentists can re-open next week. I do feel for the poor people who have had dental problems during this time. They have been in pain for weeks with no help. I know my mother was due to have a plate fitted just before the Lockdown after she had to have a front tooth removed. She has had to spend the whole time at home with a big

gap in her mouth, I suppose it was better being at home than having to go out looking like that.

When I get home (after fighting to get in the new front door with my fob) I hold my weekly TEAMS meeting. It turns out that I am not the only person desperate for the kids to go back to school. One of my volunteers has had to listen to two children fighting in the garden for nine weeks and another has listened to a mother screaming at the top of her voice at her kids every single day.

Thursday 28th May

I have another panic attack when I awake. I literally cannot breathe properly for a few minutes and my heart is beating so fast and loud, I am sure they can hear it across the road. I hope this is not a flare up of my Graves Disease. It has been laying dormant for two years and I am currently not on any medication. But I was warned that it could be set off again by stress, the Dr reckoned it was all caused by the trauma of the menopause in the first place. We are living in unusual times and even though I am generally coping well, life is a bit uncertain and I do worry that it might trigger it off again.

Peter brings me a cup of tea in bed along with the news that my brother in law had to call an ambulance for my sister at 1am. She had been out for a long walk in the heat during the day, but had drunk 2 litres of water whilst doing it. She drinks gallons of water but as she is on HRT she doesn't seem to sweat anymore. When she got home she had a banging headache followed by a bout of vomiting, which got worse, much worse.
The way my nephew described it, I know it wasn't funny but we bother roared with laughter over his description of the scene, it was as if all of the liquid in her body needed to come out through any orifice possible at exactly the same time. He said he was covered in it, it was all over the floor and up his legs. Fortunately he is an excellent First Aider and carried out some observations whilst waiting for the ambulance to come. They wanted to put her on a drip but that meant a trip to the hospital which she refused. Hospital might not be the best place for anyone with underlying medical conditions at the moment. So in the end she was left running on empty and went to bed for a few days.
In reality she should have gone on the drip, it would have made her feel much better, much quicker but I totally understand why she refused the trip to A&E.

It's another boring day in the office, I get inundated with messages from Peter about Luton Towns new Manager. They are bringing back Nathan Jones who left to go to bigger and better money at Stoke City. I don't know what sort of reception he will get, a lot of the fans felt utterly betrayed when he left. If you are not a football fan you will not understand any of this, true fans live and breathe their team. It gets right on my tits. Sure enough Peter is instantly on the computer making a video of the dog giving her opinion on this latest piece of news to put on his Facebook page.

It's the last and final clap for the NHS tonight and I miss it yet again.

One of our favourite holiday destinations, Cyprus, is opening up to tourists. They have had very few infections there and are stating that they will pay all expenses for any tourists arriving who test positive for the virus and have to go into quarantine. It's a novel way of trying to kickstart the holiday industry. It's just a shame that it doesn't apply to anyone from France, Italy, Spain or the UK, not that you can get there anyway.

One piece of news is that from Monday 1st June you can now meet up outside in groups of 6 with people not from your household.
 I thought that was what everyone was already doing on the crowded beaches?

Friday 29th May

It's that time again to go to the supermarket. I have to wait 25 minutes in a queue before I am allowed in. I whizz round like I am on race track pushing little old ladies aside to get out quickly.
I am almost finished and am approaching the final hurdle when an announcement comes across the tannoy: 'would all First Aiders go to aisle 12 immediately'. I really do not want to get involved and am on my way to the checkout when I come across the store managers in a huddle loudly discussing where their in-store First Aider was. Overhearing their agitated conversation it seems like they haven't got one in today. I relent and ask them if they would like me to go and assist and they delightedly lead me off to the casualty.
Laying flat on her face by the lemonade is an old girl, there is a customer with her who says she saw it all happen. The lady didn't hurt herself, she just sort of slithered down the front of her trolley to the ground almost in slow motion. Poor old girl, she is a bit stunned and confused. On closer questioning it turns out that she is diabetic and

hasn't taken her drugs or eaten this morning. The store manager is completely panicking which isn't helping the situation and is already on the phone dialling 999 before I have even given him any details. He starts asking me questions relating to Covid 19, I stop him in his tracks, this is nothing to do with the virus. He then starts telling me not to move her, don't touch her, don't do this, don't do that. Why do people ask you to help and then tell you what to do? Why didn't he deal with her himself as he is so knowledgeable? What she wants to do is sit up, so I ignore him and with my assistance she pushes herself up into a sitting position which immediately makes her feel a bit better.

What does concern me is that this old girl has bandages around both her lower legs. The bandages are coming off and the lint has come out of the dressings, her legs are badly ulcerated and are leaking through the bandages. It's a disgusting sight and doesn't smell great either.

Fortunately for all of us the ambulance arrives within two minutes, the station is just down the road. I hand the lady over to the crew and back off, when I get around the corner of the aisle I literally dowse myself with hand gel.

That is the fifth time I have been in that particular shop and had to do First Aid on another customer because they had no First Aiders around. They should keep me on a retainer.

After I thoroughly wash my hands at home and change my clothes, I unpack the shopping and then lay out in the garden, it's scorching again. They have visitors next door and have taken the boys over the field for a kick about leaving the women and a smaller child in the garden. You think I would be rejoicing that I have some peace but oh no, this smaller child is then allowed to kick a ball at the fence and he doesn't even live there. I retire to the serenity of my bathroom for a long soak in the tub.

As retaliation for having my afternoon in the garden spoilt, I watch the free 'Take That' concert on YouTube and sing along at the top of my voice, even Peter joins in. I haven't even had a drink but sound like I have just rolled out of the pub having consumed a bottle of gin and I hear the neighbours hastily close their patio doors.

Saturday 30th May

I spend 2.5 hours this morning doing an online Covid19 Course. It's a bit bizarre as the course is aimed at people helping out in hospitals and care homes. Not sure how knowing someones care plan and nutritional needs is going to help a drunken football fan who has fallen down the steps and cracked his head open.

It is another beautiful day in the Naam, it's also another hot and sunny day in Bedfordshire. I manage to sunbathe all afternoon, I am browner now than I was when I came home from holiday.

Peter decides that we are going to have a barbecue. He normally has real trouble with his first Summer barbecue but this year it goes off without hitch. I take my dinner down to sit on the decking. The minute I put a fork to my mouth, the boy next door and his father decide that it's that time of day to kick the ball at the fence. Within seconds they have whacked it several times, I actually shout at them but it goes unheard (or ignored), so I stomp inside to eat my dinner. It was very obvious that we were having a barbecue, the smell of cooking meat is the clue. Why do they pick that moment to make that annoying racket?

An hour later the balls are still banging so I suggest we take the dog for a walk. We are gone about an hour, when we get back the patio is on fire. Literally ON FIRE.

Peter had left the paper bag of charcoal leaning against the metal leg which had got very hot, it must have caught fire and the plastic wheels have melted into the patio, small flames are licking up around the metal legs. Peter grabs the new hose which arrived this morning and puts the fire out. The neighbours are sitting on the other side of the fence quietly eating their dinner, did they not smell it?

It has made a real mess, and no matter how hard he tries Peter cannot get the plastic up off the stone work. Surprisingly I take all this rather well, I don't get upset or scream and rant which I might have done in a previous life. What does concern me is that if he can't get the metre square size of melted plastic up, we will have to have another patio laid which will cost a fortune. Not exactly what we need at the moment.

We retire indoors, there is not much we can do today without the correct tools which Peter immediately orders from Amazon. So we lay on the sofa watching a film with a large drink each, it makes me forget about the hideous mess on the patio.

Around 11am Peter drags me out into the garden. The temperature has plummeted, it is a clear night and feels freezing, I grab a cover and wrap it around me. We are gazing into the sky, apparently looking for a spaceship that has been launched this evening, we should be able to see the vapour trails. As we are out there I spot my neighbour looking at us out of his bedroom window, probably wondering what we are doing at this time of night staring into the sky wearing a dog blanket.

We never do see the rocket.

Sunday 31st May

I have a bit of a hissy fit this morning. I put the washing in the new machine and end up putting it on the wrong programme. I then cannot get out of the new front door and Peter takes the Mickey out of me that I am hopeless with technology. (It's true but I don't want to keep being reminded of how useless I am). Looking out of the broken patio window at my black and charred York Stone patio, I totally lose it with him. What else is going to go wrong in the house?
We have words and I burst into tears. He then gets a bit upset as well. We both calm down and manage to talk about it, which is a novel thing. He admits that he is totally fed up. I am stunned, this is not something that he ever, ever, ever suffers from and it is a complete new emotion to him. He is not bored, just sick to death with the whole situation, he just wants to go back to work and see some sport at the weekends. Whereas I have a whole different sort of wants - to visit Debenhams, have a haircut, get my nails gelled and have a drink out with friends.
I know this whole Lockdown thing has been difficult for everyone and we all have individual ways of dealing with it. Talking to three of my good friends this afternoon whilst sunbathing (again), one says nothing really has changed as she works from home a lot anyway, and the other two say they are loving it and want to take early retirement. This is from three very active people who before this saga begun I couldn't imagine them wanting to stay at home permanently, they were always out and about. They are not even bothered about not being able to go out shopping or socialising.

As a special treat to myself this afternoon I decide to tackle a huge pile of ironing that has built up. It is so hot that I am still wearing my bikini whilst doing it and manage to iron myself right across the stomach. It stings like mad and I have a lovely red welt to show for it. It brings a complete new meaning to having a flat stomach.

It is the last day of May, we have all been locked indoors for 9 weeks and from tomorrow we will begin the start of the New Normal, whatever that may be.
As of today the Coronavirus has 6,104,980 confirmed cases across the globe with 370,078 deaths.
Spain, Sweden & Poland have reported their lowest number of new cases in two months. In Afghanistan, they are warning of an impending catastrophe as the number of infections keeps on rising. There is a currently a ban on travel between the different United Arab Emirates and all residents now need a permit to travel between Dubai and Abu

Dhabi. Bangladesh is lifting its lockdown despite a rise in the number of infections.

A big surprise is that Iran has had 151,000 cases and 7797 deaths, who would have thought it? Peter worked out there a few years ago and reckons it will be a lot more than that but they aren't telling.

The UK's death toll stands at 38,489 and the figures are definitely on the decline with only 113 deaths overnight. This is a really good sign but everyone is twitchy about easing the Lockdown. It could be a dangerous moment if the infection rate shoots upwards and we have a spike.

As from June, horse racing and the Premier League can resume behind locked doors which means no spectators present. The new football season which normally starts at the beginning of August will be delayed until mid September.

6 people from different households can now meet outside as long as they stay 2 metres apart and 2 people can meet indoors as long as they follow the 2m rule.

You cannot stay overnight in anyones house unless you have a really good reason.

Yes, like that's going to happen.There are a lot of people out there dying to have some nookie with their girl/boyfriend.

Getting old is not for sissies - Bette Davis

7. The New Normal

Monday 1st June

When I get into the office for some reason I am a bit emotional this morning and shed a few tears. No-one bats an eyelid, we are all having tiny meltdowns and it's my turn today. Just being able to get how you are feeling off your chest and have a sympathetic ear to listen to your whinges, quickly lift my spirits and I am back to normal in no time. Well as normal as any menopausal woman can be during an unprecedented time in history where we have all been locked indoors for months!

There is another piece of interesting news from within the company. As we are the only team still working, everyone else has been furloughed or is working from home, we will be taking on the admin for the whole of the country on a temporary basis until things get back to a sort of normal. This I think holds us all in good stead for keeping our jobs long term. Phew, we feel slightly relieved, but there has been no official announcement so far that this is going to happen and it could be a lot of work.

Danny sends me a picture of downtown Hoi An, it is another Bank Holiday there and the centre is absolutely heaving with people, all locals and other Vietnamese tourists who have descended on the town for a night out. It is mayhem. The roads are blocked and the police have been called in to disperse the traffic, Danny and his mates are stuck in a bar and cannot get out. Their idea of pure heaven.
I don't care about the traffic and pollution, I wish I was there.

Peter has gone in to London to help out a friend with his computer problems, I am still concerned about his frame of mind, I hope business will start to pick up with the opening of small shops which is now being allowed. Outdoor markets and car showrooms are now allowed to re-open, we are on our way. That also means car boot sales will soon be allowed, maybe I can get rid of all the crap in the little room? Unfortunately all the leisure side of life, swimming pools, pubs, restaurants, sports centres, gyms, cinemas, zoo's etc are still waiting to get the green light.

Tuesday 2nd June

There have been riots in the USA over the killing of George Floyd with calls for all of the officers involved to be charged with his death. Trump is threatening to call in the National Guard to keep the protestors off of the streets. It is all kicking off over there. It's certainly taken the Coronavirus off the front page of the American news, their figures are truly shocking.
And this is all happening in Trumps lead in to re-election. Surely Mickey Mouse stands a better chance of getting elected?

Wednesday 3rd June

When we get up this morning the temperature has dropped by 10C. It's hardly cold but feels really chilly after the hot weather we had in April & May. It tries to rain for most of the day but only achieves a few spits and spots. We dearly need some rain, everywhere is looking a bit dead and brown, my lawn looks positively barren.
Each time the dog rolls over on it she brings bits of straw back through the house.

I was supposed to have some system training this afternoon but none of our desk top computers have the correct software to run it, despite being told it was already loaded in the system. You'd think someone would have checked first.

It is also evident that the children in this area might not be going back to school until September. SHIT, SHIT, SHIT, that is my Summer definitely ruined.

When I get home, Peter has toiled all day with his heat lamp and scourers to clear the melted plastic off the patio. It has left a dark mark but as all the slates have a black shadow on them, unless you knew what happened you wouldn't notice the difference. He has done an excellent job but he is really tired and aches all over. He has completely softened up in the last three months and will find it hard to adjust to shifting heavy machinery around when work kicks in again.

When I come off the computer after my weekly TEAMs meeting, we watch the evening news. There have been more protests in USA and the participants are still breaking the curfew. The four officers involved in the George Floyd killing have now all been sacked and arrested on the grounds of second degree murder.

Thursday 4th June

I get a phone call this morning which leaves me feeling breathless with excitement. My hairdresser has rung saying that they might be opening on Sunday 5th July, would I like to make an appointment?
Yes Please.
When?
5th July please
So I am booked provisionally for my first professional haircut since February, she won't be able to believe how long my hair is.

I also get a strange call from my doctors surgery. I haven't had a thyroid function test for my Graves Disease since November and I really should have one to check my levels every three months. I know this but thought there were more important things going on. As I have been feeling fine, I haven't made an appointment this year. The receptionist books me in and then gives me some odd instructions:
I have to drive my car into the staff car park.
I then need to ring reception to inform them that I have arrived.
They will then send a nurse to do my blood test whilst I am sitting in my car.
I have never heard of anything quite so bizarre, I hope they don't spill blood on my new upholstery.

Peter has gone out this morning to help another friend and I am a bit bored. As I am doing my exercises laying on the lounge floor, I notice that my cream leather sofa is covered in dirty marks around the bottom. I end up sponging down my leather sofa with upholstery cleaner. Honestly what is the world coming to that I am getting so desperate for something to do?

At work I receive a phone call from the IT department. It is about the new software for my computer. The analyst starts talking to me but he might as well of been speaking Japanese for all I understood. There is no point speaking to me about thin clients and VM ware, I have no clue as to what it is. I arrive at work, sit at my desk, turn the computer on and use it, I have no idea how it all functions. I thought that was the reason why companies have an IT department full of computer geeks to do all of this for you. In the end the youngest girl in the office takes pity on me and gets it sorted out for me with the very irritated and bewildered IT guy. God bless her. And him, poor bloke.

I am totally mystified by a new ruling from the Government and rant about it to anyone who will listen (which if I am to be honest is just Peter). From next week any passenger travelling on public transport must wear a face covering. First of all why next week and not today? This has now been decided despite scientists saying that masks were no protection against the virus two months ago so the public did not bother with them. My view is that if you sneeze and are wearing a mask, the only person who will inhale your sputum is yourself. Secondly, look at Vietnam, everyone was wearing them there, you only have to look at their figures to know there is something in it.

Friday 5th June

We have all been sent a survey regarding our jobs to fill in online. It is not anonymous so you have to be careful what you say - yes I know they say they want you to be honest, but they don't really want to you to be. The first question is about what option you would prefer: to go part time, go casual, take a sabbatical etc, etc. They ask you to rate them in the order you would like. I really do not feel that at this stage I can possible comment as we have absolutely no clue as to what is happening with our jobs. Until we have more clarification, how can I possibly choose? I write all of this in the box along with a few ideas to save money and try to submit it. It will not go through until you have selected your favoured choice. So I select that I would like to work 4 days per week, which is what I already do, just to be able to send the flippin' thing. Honestly technology, sometimes it is rubbish.
I note that they are now offering unpaid sabbaticals which is what I asked for back in November and was turned down flat with mutterings about it not being something that the company offered. Well it is now! I would take some unpaid leave at the drop of a hat and head off travelling again but there is one small problem - I can't go anywhere outside of Europe and even that has it's own difficulties. There are no flights and visa restrictions are in place everywhere I would want to go. Also as we head into Summer all the places I would want to visit enter the hot, humid, rainy season, it is not the best time to for a hot hormonal woman to visit.
I would self combust.

As peace currently reigns in the garden I cut the grass and generally tidy up. It's grey and overcast but still fairly warm. Everything needs watering, the ground is bone dry. Out comes the new hose which subsequently explodes and splits as soon as I turn the water on and drenches me again. Another hose down.

I am so bored I decide it is time to clean out the filters in the tumble dryer. Oh the romance and joy of being stuck indoors! What has happened to my life? How did things come to this to amuse myself? It turns out that there is more fluff in the machine than is contained in my brain. How do these contraptions get so dirty? The machine definitely works much better afterwards, so it was worth doing.

Late afternoon the heavens open and there is a torrential downpour. The rain comes down like it does in the tropics for about 20 minutes. It doesn't take long for it to dry up and we go out for a walk with the dog. The ground isn't even damp, the rain has just evaporated on the surface.

I have a small dilemma, we have a rota in the office for buyings staffs birthday presents and it is my turn next week to purchase a gift from us all. Where the hell am I going to buy a present? And even more difficult it is for a young man. I ring the office to ask for suggestions, idea's abound but there are no shops open and I can only buy something in the supermarket. I can't risk ordering anything online at this stage as it might not turn up. I'll think about it over the weekend.

Saturday 6th June

Peter snores like a train all night, he has definitely got hay fever. I am restless and cannot relax, I toss and turn and there is a strange buzzing sensation in my ears. I am wide awake at 4am. At 5am I have had enough and get up (unheard of, me getting up that early). I sit writing on the computer until about 8am when I take Peter a cup of tea and get back into bed for an hour and realise I am frozen solid. My feet are like blocks of ice and I warm them up on Peters legs whilst he screams like a girlie and upsets the dog.

I load the washing machine which then leaks through the seal and water ends up all over the kitchen floor. Peter is really cross with me and messes up all the programmes on the machine trying to get it to spin and empty. I shove the instructions in his face as I cannot read them without my glasses but he can't be bothered to read them and carries on pressing all the buttons until something happens. What is is with men that they cannot read instructions? Panic over, a pair of my knickers has got caught in the door and that is why it has leaked. Thank god for that, I was terrified it might already be broken.

I am going to visit my family; I haven't seen my mother or sister since the beginning of February. We had planned to sit in the garden, unfortunately it's horrible outside but I am going anyway.

On the way through Hitchin there are groups of people heading towards town and there is a woman hanging a placard up outside the church. There are going to be protests about 'Black Lives Matter' across the UK, including Hitchin town centre. That will really upset some of the posh people who live there, I can instantly think of two snobby women I know who will be mortified that such a thing is going on in their town (which they think they own).

It's great to get out and give my car a burn up on the M1. When I arrive at my family home, my mother appears pleased to see me and I stay for about an hour, sitting at opposite ends of the dining table. As I drive to my sisters, the heavens open and it pours with rain. I get soaked just getting out of the car. I spend three hours catching up with my sister and nephew. He has a magnificent head of hair which he is dying to get cut. For some odd reason they all like my hair much longer, they say it makes me look softer but I am adamant it is all coming off in July. It takes so long to dry, I get arm ache holding the hair dryer. We have a bit of a laugh and a right old chin wag. My sister has still not fully recovered from her liquid episode 10 days ago and lays on the sofa underneath a blanket, but she is in good spirits.

Whilst I am there a massive storm rages outside with biblical thunder and lightening, the roads are instantly flooded as the water runs off the bone dry ground. As I drive home there are enormous puddles everywhere, but it is nice to smell the rain on the grass.

On the way home I pop into work to see Peter who is in the Call centre, he is caught up in some emergency and there is a big flap on so he doesn't have time to talk to me.

I go straight home, throw myself onto the sofa, put on an 007 film and spend all evening ogling Pierce Brosnan and drinking gin.

The perfect night in for a woman of a certain age!

Sunday 7th June

Because I was awake early yesterday, I sleep for 11 hours. This is amazing. I do have the odd hot sweat but just lay with the covers thrown back for a few minutes and manage to go straight back to sleep each time.

It's another horrible November day in June, overcast and really windy. I am determined to clear out the study, it is the last room in the house that hasn't been touched during this Lockdown. Peter puts a 'Toyah' album on to listen to whilst we wade through tonnes of paper that we seem to have accumulated. I don't mind some of her music but this is her '*Human*' stuff and I think it is dire. It is certainly an acquired taste, funnily Peter knows all of the words.

I seem to have kept every payslip going back to 2000, along with copies of all of my expenses and receipts for the last 20 years. There are manuals full of out of date material and even a folder from when Peter used to work on the ambulances 25 years ago. There are leaflets, receipts, instructions and guarantees for appliances that we don't own anymore, handouts and piles of blank forms. I appear to have all my banks statements going back ten years. All of this paper and shredded material goes into the recycling, the bin is so heavy I can hardly move it. All sorts of other crap ends up in the other bin: cables, floppy discs, plugs, stationery, how do we amass all this stuff? There must be houses across the country full of rubbish. I do love a good clear out, it clears my mind somehow. Normally my brain is whizzing from subject to subject and never stops whirring, for a few hours it calms down as we shed all this garbage. Peter even manages to put his air fix models into his display cabinet, I am so glad to get them off the sideboard in the kitchen where they were gathering a fine layer of dust.

Amongst all of this crap we find a classy Mclaren/Mercedes stationery set that Peter originally brought as a present for someone. He never did give it to them, just stuffed it in a drawer and forgot all about it. It is the perfect birthday present for the chap at work and I am vindicated.

After the effort of clearing out the study, Peter retreats to the sofa to talk to his virtual friends on his laptop. I am on a roll; I descale the kettle, steam clean the whole of the ground floor and clear the weeds again at the front of the house that no-one else in the road ever bothers to do. This is the second time during Lockdown that I have cleaned the street for the benefit of everyone else.

After lunch we need to go and pick up some dog food, so I go along for the ride, it is a change of scenery after all. Blimey what is happening with my exciting life, I have been out two days in a row! There is a big surprise waiting for me though, M&S and Matalan are open and there are no queues to get in. Forget Pets at Home, I am going in. Peter leaves me to go off to get in the queues to collect the dog food and a new windscreen wiper from Halfords.

Of course practically everything in Matalan is on sale. I would imagine most clothing stores warehouses are groaning under the weight of unsold Summer apparel. It is not a shop I normally frequent but the pure delight of wandering around looking at clothes is almost therapeutic. I don't need anything but end up buying four tops which are all half price. You cannot try anything on, so it is a bit of a gamble whether they will fit or not but it is such a novelty to be out buying for pleasure and not necessity. And anyway they are so cheap I will give them to my sister if they are too small for me rather than return them.
When I get home, fortunately they all fit perfectly.

We have had 77 more deaths in the UK, it's definitely slowing down but there is still a long way to go. The latest news is that we are the only country in the world to have had more than 40,000 deaths apart from the USA. That is not something to be proud of, our Government definitely left it too late to enforce any restrictions.
India has admitted they have over 300,000 cases which is increasing by 10,000 per day. With the huge size of their population I bet we will never find out the true figure coming out of there and I bet the authorities will never know.

Peter cooks dinner this evening, a proper meal with fish and veg. I detect that he is a bit more in the zone, he certainly seems happier. Now that the smaller shops have reopened, jobs are starting to come in and he has decided that he is coming off the furlough scheme part time. This is music to my ears: happy husband, happy life.

Monday 8th June

When I turn on my computer at work this morning, nothing works properly except the new piece of software that has been added over the weekend. All my emails have been moved around or disappeared, my favourites have all been deleted as well as my signature, and I now have a new set of logins to go through every day. I spend a frustrating half hour re-setting everything before I can do any work. I am utterly useless with technology and this gives me the right hump on a Monday morning. I try to ring IT but they are only dealing with Covid related problems over the phone and I have to leave a message which they will endeavour to get back to me asap.

When I get home, Peter has had a productive day and started building an Air-fix Mustang. But he has been to the bottle bank and cooked dinner which totally saves his life.

Tuesday 9th June

If I had still been married to my first husband it would have been our 36th wedding anniversary today. Mind you I would probably be dead by now, keeled over with boredom or died of asphyxiation smelling the booze on his breath every day. Thank God I didn't stay with him.

Peter has quite a few jobs coming in and needs to go to work. There isn't anything for the rest of his staff to do, but he is hoping in July they might be able to start up again. I am so relieved, he is one of the few people I know who genuinely loves his job and I know how much it has affected him not working. If you don't know him like I do, you would never know from his laid back demeanour that he has struggled at all with the Lockdown; you would think he has had a ball lounging around every day.

The crap news is that it doesn't look like the schools around here will be going back until September. Apart from my personal problem with footballs for the rest of the Summer, some of these kids will find it really hard to catch up. One of my friends says a lot of parents she knows have got bored with home schooling and aren't doing it anymore and the kids are running amok at home all day.
Big trouble ahead in the classrooms I think.

This afternoon there is yet another online meeting regarding the redundancies. We are a bit nervous and just want to know if we have a job or not going forward. But oh no that's not what we find out. There is a load of waffle about looking at ways to save money and we have to attend more meetings to go through any idea's we may have that could contribute to this. This is just delaying the announcement of who is going and who is staying. I know it is a legal process that any company has to go through, they already know what they are going to do, but they must be seen to be consulting with the staff first. After the meeting we discuss ways between ourselves that we think could save money and come up with some ideas to submit to the senior management. Will anyone really listen to our opinions? I honestly think they have already made up their minds and are just delaying the inevitable. We shuffle out of the meeting room, all a bit despondent.
Why don't they just put everyone out of their misery and tell us?

When I get home the gin bottle beckons.

Wednesday 10th June

Peter has gone into London to help a friend with his PC Problems. Due to the heavy G&T's last night, I don't wake up until 10 o'clock. It's a miserable wet morning and I would really love to stay in bed hidden underneath the duvet all day long.

It is the Duke of Edinburgh's 99th birthday today and a lovely photo of him with the queen has been released to mark the occasion. So he is still alive, no-one has seen him for months. He doesn't look very healthy I must say, just looking at him makes me think there is something medically wrong with him. If he makes his 100th will he get an extra special card from his wife?

In the office we have been told that H&S are coming in to do an inspection next week and someone has gone mad with the duck tape and a tape measure. All the desks have been moved around so we are 2 metres apart and not facing each other. Only one person is allowed in the kitchen at any one time. One of the mens urinals and a sink in the ladies that we have all been using for the past three months has now been taped off.
I find this is really irritating, we have been thrown together in this environment for 3 months and now someone higher up the food chain has decided to take it seriously. I enter the Call Centre, there are three people in there who shouldn't be, sitting chatting and using the computers. So apart from a bit of tape nothing has really changed.

The other bit of news from Boris today is that two households can meet up and stay overnight.
In other words illicit sex is back on the menu.

Thursday 11th June

I go for my blood test this morning. The rules have changed and I am actually allowed into the surgery. But first I have to go through the welcome screening and have my temperature taken. The nurse reads it as 34.9, this is very odd as that is technically hyperthermic and I am normally running at boiling point. She does the blood test which goes as normal and I am on my way in record time. They obviously don't want anyone hanging around so all the appointments are on time for a change.

It is another boring day in the office, I think the phone only rang four times. The air con has broken in the Control room and it is very warm in there with all of the machinery whirring away. It gets reported up the chain but to who, I don't know.

When I get in, I am really pissed off, it's been a rubbish day. Peter is laying on the sofa having not bothered to make any dinner. If he thinks I am cooking anything, he has another think coming. He opens another bottle of beer and a bag of crisps and I hit the gin.

Friday 12th June

Peters phone goes off at 9.30 and we both wake up with a bit of a start. I could easily lounge in bed for another two hours but know I must get up. When I do arise from my comfy bed I have missed a phone call from Anna. She still doesn't understand the time difference and I am always getting messages from her in the early hours. I promise to ring her tomorrow afternoon when I have a bit more time to talk.

It's that time of the week to go to the supermarket again. This time I have persuaded Peter to come and help me, why should I have to go through this fortnightly ordeal alone? Fortunately there is only a short queue, which saves me listening to him moaning about the wait.
I notice that a lot of customers are wearing masks and gloves, this seems to be increasing week on week. It is like the process is in reverse, we should all have been wearing face coverings months ago and now we should be able to remove them safely. I don't understand the wearing of gloves in a shop, each time you touch something, you then put any bacteria onto the next thing you touch and so on. It would be better to thoroughly wash your hands when you have finished.
The shopping trip is a complete disaster, I think Peter does it on purpose so that I never ask him to come again. He keeps disappearing with the trolley and then whizzing past any food that I actually want to put purchase. He spent half an hour down the crisp aisle and then what seemed like forever down the alcohol aisle comparing beer prices on the Internet on his phone. All this time I am running up and down the aisles grabbing things we actually need. When we get to the checkout he tosses everything into the bags, two bottles of wine are in with the veg, the eggs are thrown in with the toiletries and all the heavy stuff squashed down on top of the bread. He then proceeds to chuck all of the bags in the trolley. How we got home with no breakages I will never know.

Once I have unpacked the shopping chaos I set about doing the housework. It's no small feat lugging all the cleaning stuff and vacuum cleaner up and down two flights of stairs. Peter sits at the breakfast bar lovingly painting his Mustang whilst I then tackle the ironing. Around 4pm I realise I have not sat down since I got out of bed apart from the drive to the supermarket. I am just finishing the ironing when Peter asks me what I have done to my arm. Looking down I see an enormous dark brown bruise about 4 inches in diameter where I had the blood test done, that's strange it's never happened to me before. It looks like someone has grabbed me viciously and my arm is swollen and decidedly larger than the other. It has also started to ache, weird how it just appeared, it wasn't even there when I had a shower this morning.

Peter is absolved from all of his sins in the supermarket by ordering a Chinese takeaway for tea, it is so nice to have someone else to cook for me.
He spends part of the evening on yet another conference call, I listen to some of it, when someone starts banging on about political correctness, I zone out and pour myself a very large glass of wine.

Saturday 13th June

When I wake up, I have my camisole and knickers on inside out. I wonder how that happened? I also wonder in my preoccupied state how this doesn't happen more often.

There are more protests going on around Britain today. They have had to board up all the statues to protect them from the protestors (or rioters whichever way you want to look at it). We have to look forwards not backwards, you cannot change or wipe out history just because it was bad. It happened, lets work to make sure it never happens again in the future.

I manage to speak to both of my girls on FaceTime. Anna looks really well and seems very upbeat. La Vie is shouting and hollering making a complete racket in the background and is in full voice. Anna says it is very hot out there at the moment and she is struggling with the heat; welcome to my world girlie.
Greenie on the other hand sounds very low and I struggle to hear her properly as she whispers down the phone to me, I think the husband is around somewhere listening. When we finish talking she sends me a separate message saying she loves and misses me. I wish I could give

her a big hug. I wish I could give them both a hug. Breaks my heart to think I will not see them again for ages.

We are off in the car to see Peter's mum and her husband. It's another beautiful day and we sit out on the patio with Maureen 2m away. Her husband is not well at all and stays indoors the whole time, sleeping and intermittently throwing up in a bucket. It takes him a full 15 seconds before he recognises us. Poor old fella, he really should be in hospital, but Maureen is desperately trying to avoid the inevitable. One whiff of Covid and it will finish him off.
Peter helps her with a few jobs around the house and I plant her pots up for her, put some plants in the garden beds and do a bit of weeding.
She has arranged for a catering company to bring in lunch to save her time. What a lunch! Smoked salmon, fish pate, prawns in mayonnaise, cooked salmon and crusty bread all washed down with a bottle of Prosecco with chocolate brownies for afters. It was lovely sitting there overlooking the river, very calm and tranquil, shame about her husband not being well enough to join us.

When we got home Peter and I lay on the sofa together watching the very odd Covid 19 version of Trooping of the Colour from Windsor Castle. It was a very surreal experience and even the Queen looked a bit baffled by it all.

Sunday 14th June

I spend all morning sitting in the garden catching up with my friends. The conversations all follow the same pattern, what we haven't been doing. One thing that is apparent is that some of them have definitely taken to not going to work and would only be too happy to stay at home on a permanent basis.

I made an enormous pasta bake for dinner which would feed about 8 people. Feeling completely stuffed after consuming half of it, we take the dog for a walk over the fields to walk it off. Another layer to add to my increasing waistline.

Monday 15th June

I did not want to go to work today. I am fed up with the whole work/ redundancy situation, I just want to know if I have a job or not.
Everyone is on a downer in the office and morale is at a really low ebb.
I send everyone a copy of a video of our dog singing' *Sensational*' as a

little booster. The big boss snarls back that he didn't detect a lack of morale in the office when he was in. For heavens sake, what is the matter with him? He's been stomping and skulking around in the office, not speaking to anyone properly for a couple of weeks now.

Peter forwards me an email from Beds Borough Council that there is now a very high rate of the Coronavirus infection in Central Bedfordshire and would we all please try to stay at home.
Just what we need as everything is starting to come back to life.
Most shops have re-opened this morning. The queue in Bedford Town Centre to get into Primark was a mile long - really? Why?
Mind you I can't wait to go to Debenhams later this week.
Peter is planning to go back to work this week. A lot of shoe repairers have gone into their shops after two months, turned the machines on and they have gone 'Bang' and need repairs.

This evening we finish the pasta bake from Sunday. I really should have frozen some but can't be bothered and serve the whole lot up. Even Peter can't manage to finish his enormous portion. I do manage to get through the evening without the aid of an alcoholic drink or any sweets due to my stomach being overloaded.
I really can't eat much more, I am bloated and my clothes are too tight and look awful. I never carry any weight on my front but currently I have a big spare tyre that would fit my car and the most enormous love handles. I know I need to call a halt to this excess but I still cannot summon up the will power or incentive at this current time.

Tuesday 16th June

Peter got up at 5am to go to work, which awoke me and I had trouble going back to sleep. I eventually managed to sink into a deep sleep half an hour before the alarm went off. I ache all over this morning and can hardly move, I have no idea why. It is like all my joints have frozen solid and nothing is flexible. I hobbled painfully across the car park at work as my knees were locked.
It might help if I stopped wearing 4 inch high heels, but I am not quite ready at 56 years old to give them up.

I drag myself into the office where there is a huge bombshell waiting for us. The big boss (the one I called a very rude name at the Christmas party) has decided to take voluntary redundancy after a differing of opinion with his Superior. That is why he has been so grumpy and miserable lately, he's normally a good laugh. Everyone is shocked and upset and we feel there is now no protection from the vultures circling. We are certain that there will now be yet another restructuring of the company, they only did one last year. Where that now leaves us I do not know.

The heavens opened during the night and the rain was torrential. I like laying in bed in the dark listening to the rain, but it was abnormally heavy and the noise kept me awake rather that lulled me into my slumber. When I eventually slept I had some very strange dreams about some dirty old men I know. Totally random and bizarre. Don't even ask!

Wednesday 17th June

Peter somehow managed to drag himself out of bed at 4.30am to go into Central London. He snored and snorted all night long and I feel knackered this morning. I need to get up early as I have to attend a consultation meeting on ways to save money within the company. We have been split into groups and given two questions to discuss with others who were calling in online. I suggested two things that were immediately disregarded by everyone on the call, so in the end I stopped contributing to the conversation entirely. Half an hour later the Director came online and repeated almost word for word one of my suggestions. Suddenly everyone was listening and amazed at what a good idea it was. My colleague who I was with rolled his eyes and made faces at me, we both kept our mouths firmly closed for the rest of the meeting.

There is more bad news today, one of our colleagues who normally works at the other end of the building who is on furlough has been rushed into hospital with a brain tumour. I would guess she is around the same age as me, and it doesn't look good.
Maybe now is the time to re-assess our lives. I know friends are selling their houses, and giving up work. Perhaps it is our time to go off and do what we want?

After the meeting I went to Debenhams. There was no queue and once inside there was only around 20 shoppers in the whole shop. All the staff are wearing full face visors and it is all a bit odd. You have to move around the store in one direction and cannot try anything on. I end up buying a dress, a skirt and a pair of very strange camouflage jeans, which I know Peter will love. Yes they are far too young for me but I really don't care what anyone else thinks, I like them. I hope they fit as I hate taking stuff back.

I fully understand why some women dress the way they do. It has nothing to do with what anyone else thinks, if they like it they are going to wear it and stuff anyone else's opinion. These days women in their seventies are still very trendy not like my grandmother who looked old at 30 and dressed like a prim old fashioned teacher for her whole life. I am quite careful to try and not look like mutton dressed up as lamb, I follow the rules - do not show legs and cleavage at the same time, it's one or the other. But if older women want to dress up in short skirts and tight trousers with their boobs hanging out, covered in tattoo's, as long as they are confident and happy that's perfectly OK with me.

On leaving the store there is the most massive rain storm and the roads run like a river, I get absolutely drenched getting to the car. This in turn ruins my hair which I am struggling with on a daily basis to keep looking tidy. I look like I have been pulled through a hedge backwards and it has gone flat, floppy and dripping.

I then have to go back into work to do my late shift in the Call Centre. The phone rings once all afternoon. I spend a lot of my time searching for old friends on Instagram. Jackpot, I find an old friend who I was bridesmaid for about 25 years ago. He is divorced from that wife and we lost touch around the time my dad died. We reconnect and I can see he looks happy and healthy with his new wife. I hope he gets in touch, I would love to see him and meet her.

Reading through the news today, the UK has now hit over 40,000 deaths and there has indeed been an increase in infections in Bedfordshire. Worldwide there have been over 8 million cases reported and 437,722 deaths.

Beijing has had a spike with 137 new infections in a week and all travel has been banned within the city. The Chinese cancelled 1255 flights today alone. The news report says that the virus has been contracted from imported salmon on chopping boards at the biggest food market in the city. What is it with the Chinese and their food hygiene?

Back at home the Premier league has resumed behind closed doors and fans have been requested not to gather outside the grounds, to stay indoors and watch the game at home on the TV.

Poor old Wicksteed Park has gone into administration.

West End Musicals will probably not go back onto the London Stage until 2021.

Oh it is so depressing, when will it ever end?

Peter goes to bed at 10pm, he is worn out and not used to getting up in the middle of the night to go to work and the wine hasn't helped. He snores like a steam engine and makes the window rattle. I manage to stay in our bed until 1.15am when I give up and play musical beds by retiring to the downstairs bedroom where I sleep terribly again. My hot flushes are completely out of control.

I know exactly what has caused this - the increasing work uncertainty has brought back the menopausal symptoms with a vicious force.

Thursday 18th June

Peter wakes me up at 5am wanting to use the en suite shower, so I have to climb out of bed and decamp upstairs. Once in a deep sleep, the alarm goes off at 8am which is a pain in the arse as Peter has forgotten to turn it off and I don't have to be in work until 1.30pm. I lay there tossing and turning, throwing the covers off to cool down and then pulling them back again but sleep doesn't return. This ongoing tiredness results in me feeling a bit emotional and weepy for the rest of the day. It's a well known fact that if you do not get enough sleep it will eventually affect you in some way, and I am not a happy bunny today. At work our boss is in the office and is very upset that he is leaving, he refuses to tell us what has happened but something very fishy has definitely gone on behind the scenes and it leaves a bad taste in the air.

There is a certain female wafting around in the building today who is not popular with us girls in the office. I don't know what it is that she actually does, but she seems to put in an appearance every couple of weeks. She launches into a big speech about how younger people are so much quicker than the over 50's. Bearing in mind that 5 of the 8 staff in our office are over 50 she is on very dangerous ground. She doesn't heed the flashing warning signs coming off of me and rambles on about her last job where she reckons it took her 30 minutes to complete a task that took the really old people (in their 50's) at least 4 hours to complete.

I tell her that everyone in our office brings something to the table and at 56 years old I still have an overwhelming talent over some youth. She looks at me surprised and asks what that might possibly be. I state that unlike a lot of young people nowadays, I have the advantage that I can add up in my head and can spell without the aid of a computer spell checker.

She cannot think of any reply to that, leaving her with mouth agape I sweep out of the office to prepare my afternoon tea.

Boris Johnson is entertaining Emanuel Macron in London today. Top of the agenda is a discussion regarding the quarantine procedures surrounding both countries. Hold on a minute, don't we have a rule that anyone coming in from abroad must self isolate for 14 days, why does that not include Monsieur Macron???

Poor old Quanta's airlines have suspended all flights to and from Australia until October, the authorities don't want anyone bringing the virus in. More redundancies I expect.

One of the queens favourites, Vera Lynne died today.
I am sure they'll meet again some sunny day.

Friday 19th June

When I eventually arise from my slumber I take a long, hard, uncomfortable view of myself in the full length mirror. I have put on at least a stone in weight and look like a right lardy arse. With the long unkempt flat hair and the extra girth, I look terrible. I am not a pretty sight naked. Nor with my clothes on for that matter.
With my close up glasses on I do a bit of maintenance to the eyebrows and face and repaint my toenails even though I have real difficulty reaching them. That's about all I can manage on the beauty side without a full face lift, liposuction and body reconstruction.

It's my day off and I have nothing to do, nowhere to go, no-one to see. I must get out of the house and decide go to the retail park for a mooch around. People are queuing to get into Next and TK Maxx, I never buy anything in either of those shops so head directly for M&S. I am dearly in need of some new underwear so I indulge myself in their massive selection. I hope it all fits. I also buy a size 18 dress that is reduced to £9.50 which I could wear to the office and will cover my increasing bulk.
When I get home it all fits apart from the dress which is actually a bit big, but it will do for work.

Saturday 20th June

This morning I don my (very tight) volunteer uniform and go on a two day course with Peter and meet up with some friends who I haven't seen for four months. It's great to be with other people even if we have to at least try and observe the social distancing rules. Some photos find there way onto Facebook and a mighty row ensues about a picture of me feeding Peter a yoghurt. (Don't even ask!). Honestly people, mind your own business, get a life: we live & sleep together, social distancing doesn't mean a thing between me and him.

My friend Lisa states that I look so much younger with my hair a bit longer. Maybe I need to have a chat with my hairdresser about a bit of a restyle once she takes some of the weight out of it.

We get through the first day of the course and my friend Carlos has to rush off home as there has been a shooting in his village. It turns out that some idiots had driven along his road shooting out the windows of all the parked cars, one of them belonging to his mother. Have people really not got anything better to do than damage others property?

Sad bastards.

Peter is not happy either. Luton FC played their first match of the Covid season today and drew 1-1. They are in real danger of getting relegated and he has the right hump all evening. I pour us both a large glass of wine and recline my fat arse on the well used sofa.

Sunday 21st June

I am up early again for the second day of the course. Peter has snored and snorted all night and I haven't had much sleep. It looks like I am not the only one, after lunch at least three of us in the classroom are trying not to doze off.

When we get home, football noise reigns supreme out the back along with some very loud music coming from another neighbour. Maybe he is trying to drown the football noise out. The music is an interesting mix and mainly consists of Mud, Showaddywaddy and Gary Glitter. Blimey I thought no-one listened to Gary anymore, the neighbours are loudly singing along and thoroughly enjoying themselves and it makes me chuckle.

Just to add to the Covid misery and economic meltdown, someone has gone berserk in a park in Reading and stabbed a number of people, one who has now died. The police were playing the incident down as unknown but have now admitted it was a terror related attack by a Libyan national already known to them.

Spain has opened its door to tourists from the UK and I watch the aircraft landing at Alicante for the first time in months on the news. The passengers are delighted to be back, some of them had got stuck and haven't seen their families for ages.

So I am home alone this evening whilst Peter is out again. I make a decision that I am going to stop drinking, the exercise plan has gone right out of the window, and somethings got to give.
With things the way they are, let's see how long it lasts.
 I give it a week.

Monday 22nd June

 Peter struggles to get out of bed this morning for a long drive to do a machine repair. He worked all last week, was on the course over the weekend and then did a shift in the Call Centre last night. He is already tired and aches all over and it is only Monday. We also think he has hay fever which is not helping with the noise he is making whilst asleep. It is due to turn very warm today with a heatwave on the way which will make driving long distances a bit uncomfortable.

I get my blood test results which are absolutely normal. I have convinced myself that I will only ever suffer the one bad attack I had in 2017 and hopefully will never have another problem with it. Considering the strain of the last year or so, if there was going to be a flare up of my Graves disease, surely it would have happened by now?

In the office today we are preparing a party for our departing boss on Tuesday lunchtime. We spend all afternoon hanging bunting, blowing up balloons and rudely arranging them - you know what I mean, two small ones and a long one. We put photos of him all around the room and draw love hearts over them in red pen. We also have to set up the TV so other staff can ring in to the party - not my job, someone else needs to deal with the technological side. Who would have thought it, having a leaving party by social distancing and over the internet, would you believe it?

I go for a walk at lunchtime with my boss and we ponder what will happen now. It is the end of an era at work, and there is going to be a whole new world out there after Covid. She is officially care taking the big job whilst also doing her own, this will not be an easy task, there are a lot of ego's out there to deal with.

Tuesday 23rd June

Blimey there was a lot emotion on display at work today.

We have a meeting at 11am in the conference room. It is forecast to hit 30C this week and at least the air con is working in there unlike in the Call Centre where it already feels like an oven as it still has not been fixed.
It has finally been agreed that our office will do the admin for the whole country for the time being, (not permanently, yeah watch this space). No other admin staff will be brought back off of furlough until we are at full capacity and can't cope. Mind you it could be months at this rate before anyone is brought back, I have cancelled events for August, September and November only this morning.
It's a good meeting between ourselves, short and to the point with no waffle and no staff who love the sound of their own voices. Our new temporary boss is on good form and I am pretty sure we will be OK under her leadership. We know what work level we are currently at and where we need to be, we need to sit down together again to run through the new procedures and pricing structure that has been brought in.
On the plus side it certainly looks like we are going nowhere at the moment and will stay together as a team.

We are all in a buoyant mood as we arrange the banquet (we thought it was just going to be a few sandwiches) for the party. This feast has all been paid for and prepared by the Office Manager out of her own pocket, it has not been laid on by the company. She has even gone to the trouble of making a special cake and decorated it with golfing paraphernalia.
We have '*Cher*' playing loudly in the background and a few of us are boogieing around the office, (without our handbags and 2M apart obviously), having a bit of a laugh for a change.
The crowds start to gather, well there are at least 14 of us spread out across a large office. Just as we are about to start the party, Health and Safety arrive to carry out an on site inspection. They do pick their moments and the new temporary boss has to go off to appease them, whilst we spread ourselves out even more thinly around the building. Once satisfied that we are adhering to the safety regulations they leave and we call our nearly ex boss into the meeting room for his party and all pile back in to the room.
There are lots of staff calling in online, our colleague Tracey has not been able to come in as she is still shielding, but she can sort of join in and see us all. It's very odd looking at a split screen with lots of blank

faces looking back at you, but who you know can still hear every word being spoken.

We present the boss with his generous gifts and one of the senior volunteers says a few words, which mainly consists of telling us about every time they got drunk together. Afterwards we call for a speech and it is the bosses turn to speak. He starts off well but then breaks down halfway and is completely overwhelmed. It's not like him at all, he's a proper geezer and everyone doesn't know where to look. It's sad to feel that somewhere along the way he has been sidelined. I rush him over another glass of wine and call loudly for '*Cher*' on the stereo.

With the emotional bit over we tuck in to the sumptuous buffet and then pile out in to the car park to have some photos taken. I am wearing my new M&S dress and catch a glimpse of myself in the glass door. I look old and frumpy, the elastic waist is too high and keeps riding up, it really doesn't suit or fit me properly. When I get home I wash it and then give it away to one the girls in the office. Unfortunately it doesn't fit her either so I end up giving it to Maureen who it suits and fits perfectly.

We all eat far too much for a lunchtime and it is hard to get back to work and concentrate without having an afternoon nap. Our Office Manager is now in floods of tears and can't stop crying all afternoon. Our ex-boss escapes early and we are left to ponder what will happen now.

We have to admit it is the end of an era.

There is some exciting news from Boris during this afternoons final press conference of the Covid period. From 5th July all hairdressers, B&B's, pubs, hotels, restaurants, caravan and holiday parks can reopen as long as they follow the regulations. Not beauticians though, the toenails and eyelashes will have to wait a bit longer.

There is a collective sigh across the country, we can go out somewhere at last.

The advice though is to still stay alert and maintain social distancing, which is now reduced to 1M. The poor businesses and shops who have just put up 2M distancing tape will now have to redo it all.

It is made VERY CLEAR : we are not out of this yet and could have a resurgence of infections.

Talking of infections, we get a call from Maureen that her husband has collapsed and been rushed to hospital having had a suspected stroke. He fell down the gap between the toilet and shower and the Paramedic had to call for back up to help get him out of there. He collapsed, went deathly white and fell to the ground. This is the 6th time this has happened, he goes to hospital every time and they send him home again none the wiser. Fortunately the carer was there at the time so Maureen wasn't on her own to cope with the very frightening ordeal. Due to hospital restrictions, she was not allowed to accompany him to hospital, where he then waited 4 hours to get a bed on a ward and she is still waiting for a phone call to find out what the hell is going on.

Wednesday 24th June

Flipping heck it's hot today. I hate the weather in this country. You never get a chance to acclimatise to the heat as it never lasts for long enough, so when it suddenly turns warm we all suffer. I cut the grass at 9.30 and then had to lay on the cool kitchen floor in front of the fan to cool down. The sweat is dripping off of me and my hair is stuck to my head. I look really glamorous!
Whilst I am so sticky I move our air con unit from the study and wheel it into the bedroom to use tonight. It was something that Peter brought for me during that really hot Summer a few years ago and it is a Godsend whenever we have a heatwave.
So it get's used once a year!

There is some good news at least today, the lady at work who has the brain tumour has rallied round and they are looking at sending her home. A few days ago they were talking about palliative care.

I ring Maureen on the way home from work, who is in a bit of a state. The hospital has decided that it is her husbands medication that is causing the blackouts and have withdrawn his prostate and Alzheimer's drugs. Just like that. They say that is what is causing the collapses and he can go home tomorrow.
NO WAY is that going to happen. Maureen refuses to have him home until they properly investigate, it's happened too many times and needs looking into. What will happen to his PSA reading now and how will this affect his dementia?
I know the hospitals are under immense pressure but if they had investigated throughly the first time this happened, it might have possibly saved 5 further Paramedic call outs, 5 ambulance runs and 5 stays in hospital.
Fortunately Maureen is sticking to her guns and waiting for hospital welfare to ring her back with a solution. She finally acknowledges that she cannot look after him any longer at home by herself. She has slept on the sofa for the last year and has been his sole carer up until the last hospital episode when we were in Vietnam.

Enough is enough.

After the saga my family had with my old dad and mother, I am only too aware that if there is a robust spouse around, hospitals will send patients home to be cared for by them. My poor dad who had Parkinson's for 15 years, cared for solely by my mother, eventually went psychotic caused by the very strong medication he was on and had to be sectioned. It was at that point we refused to have him home as my mother had reached tipping point and I genuinely believed she would die of exhaustion if she had to cope another day with him. Sometimes you have to make some very unpleasant decisions (and I still feel really guilty even after all this time) or you could end up losing two parents instead of risking one of them.

When I get home I have my weekly online meeting. I know it sounds stupid but a lot of us are having trouble with the internet, it is so hot, does the atmospheric pressure interfere with it? Online, the conversation is much of a muchness. Some are still busy, some are bored witless and some are down in the dumps.

Thursday 25th June

I have another terrible nights sleep caused by Peters nocturnal noises which can still be heard over the roar of the air con. When he gets up I fall into a deep sleep only to be awoken half an hour later by him to say the dog had been ill - everywhere.

When I get up and go downstairs there is a faint odour of dog poo in the air. A lovely accompaniment to go with my breakfast.

Unfortunately her bad tummy isn't over with and she shits everywhere in the garden and then is sick on the backdoor mat and all over her bed. As I clean it all up, she is laying on her blanket looking really poorly and sorry for herself. I put a chair across the top of the stairs on the landing so she can't go up there and be ill on the carpet, at least downstairs it is easier to clean up on a wooden floor. Hopefully she will sleep all afternoon whilst we are at work and feel better later on.

A major incident has been called at Bournemouth beach. There are literally thousands of people clustered together enjoying the sunshine and the local NHS are struggling to cope with the amount of casualties. Several vehicles have been damaged and 22 Police have been injured at an illegal street party in Brixton.

WHAT IS THE MATTER WITH THESE STUPID PEOPLE?

There have been 49 deaths overnight and another 1118 people have tested positive just today. THIS IS NOT OVER.

In the USA the virus seems to be getting out of control despite the President now casting doubt over the number of deaths as a political move by the opposing parties to steal the election from him by over inflating the figures. That man is off his head.

In the office today the temperature is hitting 40C and is unbearable. I am in meltdown and about to self combust, I cannot find any respite from the heat, there is a river of sweat running between my shoulder blades. The air con allegedly can't be fixed, but Health and Safety have been in and put stickers all over the floors telling us all to stay 2M apart which will really help when I keel over in the heat. There are fans whirring everywhere but all they seem to do is whip up the hot air and blow it around increasing the misery. Eventually someone finds a battered old air con unit in one of the outbuildings which makes a noise equivalent to a jet engine, but at least it cools the room down a bit to a balmy 37C.
Peter is working with me this afternoon and I leave earlier than him as we are worried about the dog in this temperature. I borrow a can of air freshener from the ladies loo, just in case. Peter has detected a lot of motion on the house security camera's.

Yes a lot of motion or should I say motions. The dog had been ill all over the kitchen floor, on the front and back doormats, along the side of the sofa and by the patio windows. Somehow there was poo up the blinds as well, it obviously came out of her bum with some force. It must have been 35C in the house and the smell was suffocating. I had to scrub the floor to get it all up as it had baked on in places. Then I had to steam clean the whole bottom floor as she had walked her mess from the back doors to the front door and throughout.
Just what you want to do on the hottest day of the year.
Sweating buckets and trying not to gag on the smell, I struggled with cleaning the coir matting by the front door, I had to scrub the mats with carpet shampoo and then scrub the blinds as well. All her bedding and blankets had to go in the washing machine and she had to go in the bath as she was covered in it. Two hours later I could at last take my shoes off and get changed out of my sweaty and slightly soiled clothes.
I really didn't fancy anything to eat, even the air freshener couldn't quite mask the revolting smell and food was the last thing I fancied after all that.
Poor little dog, she was still shitting in the garden when Peter got home. He thinks she must be starving, so against my advice he cooks her some scrambled eggs, which she wolfs down.
I bet we see that again.

The slightly better news is that the hospital is keeping Maureen's husband in for investigations for a week and then hopefully moving him to Respite before a proper decision is made for the future. The down side is that Maureen cannot visit him and the hospital have advised her not to speak to him on the telephone as he is very confused.

The gut wrenching thing was that he had not mentioned her once and she is very upset.

The truth of the matter is that she might not be able to see him for weeks due to the visiting restrictions and depending on his weakening mental state he may not recognise her anyway.

What an awful situation to be in after 25 years of marriage.

Friday 26th June

Peter wakes me up early this morning with a bulletin about the dogs stomach. She has been ill yet again during the night all over the ground floor. I let him clear it up and doze off again, I did tell him not to feed her anything.

Despite the heat I have to go to the supermarket. I need to buy some more carpet shampoo and air freshener. I desperately need to kill the smell in the kitchen and hall somehow. It's officially the hottest day of the year and it registers 32C in my car. Fortunately I don't have to wait long today and I am in and out of the shop in record time.

When I get home the dog has puked up on her clean bed which has to be washed again, fortunately her back end hasn't produced any further mess in the house. When I let her in the garden she lets go of her bowels completely and I end up having to hose the lawn down to clear the diarrhoea off the grass. I keep her inside all day with the patio doors shut to keep the hot air out and have the fan going constantly in the kitchen to keep her cool.

I unpack the shopping, struggling to get anything in the freezer as I note Peter has sneakily filled it with *Magnums* and *Cornetto's*.

Around 8pm, mercifully the temperature drastically drops and the wind picks up. A storm is forecast but doesn't materialise, just a short sharp shower. Hopefully it will wash the remaining dog poo off the lawn.

When Peter gets in he feeds the dog scrambled egg again. She is absolutely starving and wolfs it down, not touching the sides.

We will pay for that later on.

Saturday 27th June

Sure enough there are some lovely parcels downstairs for us when we get up.
Out comes the *Shake and Vac* and more carpet shampoo.
A lovely aroma to eat breakfast with.

We are off to see Maureen. As could be expected she is distressed and worried about the uncertainty of the whole situation and breaks down in tears, not like her at all.
I think she may be resigning herself to the fact that her marriage is now finished. It's almost like a death except you can't really grieve. When my dad was taken into hospital he survived as a shell for 66 days. The only part of him that could move were his eyes. We could not begin to grieve though because he was still alive. It is a very strange and upsetting state of limbo to be in.
Maureen has arranged another lovely lunch along with loads of nibbles and chocolate. I managed to eat my lunch and nothing else, no alcohol was imbibed.
I am getting ready to go on a diet tomorrow.

At work they have been moving the Call Centre equipment to another office where the air con actually works. The Duty Manager has gone seriously sick with heat exhaustion and I think it was the last straw.
It is sods law that the weather has changed and is wet and windy (see what I mean by never having long enough to get used to the heat). At least it will be OK in the office now if we have another hot spell.

Sunday 28th June

Oh dear the dog has been ill yet again. Our downstairs hall and kitchen smell like a public toilet.
If she doesn't improve today, Peter will ring the vets in the morning.

I receive some pictures from Anna. She is having a few nights in a hotel in Danang with her husband and the baby. La Vie is wearing a colourful bottle green dress covered in black palm trees.
These sorts of outfits are very popular amongst the Koreans and Viets, it is very common to see whole families wearing clothes made from the same fabric. The favourite ones are covered in banana's, water melons, pineapples, red flowers or palm trees.
I make a comment to Anna that I like La Vie in the dress. She asks me if I really like it. Well I like it on La Vie but wouldn't wear it myself, but

I don't tell her this. She excitedly says that she will buy herself and me a dress like this one, so the three of us can all match when we meet up again.

Firstly, I am horror struck, she will never get one big enough.

Secondly, I will look a prize prat in it.

Oh well no-one will know me there. Peter laughs like a drain when I tell him and show him the picture.

He heads off for a ride on his motorcycle and I spend the rest of the day moping around. I have started a sugar free diet (which always works for me) and am in the hardest bit which is the three day detox. I also have not had a drink for 8 days so am suffering badly with sugar withdrawal and have a banging headache.

I feel really lonely and sad this evening and burst into tears when we go to bed. Peter pats me on the arm and tries to cheer me up by asking if it is the thought of wearing the horrible dress that has upset me which actually makes me laugh.

In a roundabout way it is the thought of the dress that has made me feel sad. I just have no idea when I will get the chance to go out with Anna and La Vie looking like a complete prat.

Monday 29th June

I feel bloody awful this morning. This is not a good start for a Monday morning as I am weepy and emotional again. My knees still hurt for some reason and I have real trouble getting down the stairs, I actually trip up at one point and have to grab the bannister to stop myself from going head over tit down the steps. Poor old girl! I am also lightheaded and hungry and can already feel another headache coming on.

This is all to do with the sugar detox.

I fill my sister in with what is going on with Maureen and chat about my nephews state of mind. She ask if I can speak to someone, anyone, about trying to keep him as an employee somewhere, even if it is part time. She is terrified if he loses his job it will push him over the edge. I don't know anyone on his side of the business to talk to and I feel a bit helpless.

Poor Peter, he was just starting to get back into the swing of going back to work but unfortunately has now run out of jobs to do and is back on part time furlough. All of this is not helped by the fact that the city of Leicester has been put into another Lockdown due to the high infection rate and he cannot even go into his factory. It's back to square one for the residents and businesses of that city.

He does make himself useful this morning by going to the bottle bank. When he takes the dog for a walk he sends me some lovely pictures of her poo which has fortunately now gone back to solid after her illness. Delightful.

Tuesday 30th June

I feel a bit more upbeat this morning, I slept well for most of the night until the dog leapt up on the bed, I let her stay, I didn't have the energy to start an argument with her at 5am. She is obviously fully recovered from her illness. I definitely don't feel half as cranky either, perhaps my body is getting used to the sugar departure, but my knees both hurt and my joints still ache.

In the office, I have two meetings to attend. One very useful, the other a load of hot air. The Management are in meeting after meeting, all day every day. I do wonder what exactly is being achieved. We have virtually no work left for July and August is not looking promising. I have even cancelled some more events for October today. The big problem is that any event in this country that wants to go ahead has to jump through so many hoops to obey the restrictions it is putting organisers off. It is far too much hassle for a little fete or gala and far too risky for a larger event and is currently against the law anyway. We already have a lot of events booked on our system for 2021, organisations have decided to give it a miss this year. Where that will leave the company financially, I do not know. D Day is on Monday 6th July when we will find out who is being made redundant.
Please God do not let it be my nephew. Or me.

Peter has a bit of good news for me, the patio window is being replaced next week, after 16 weeks of looking at a piece of black boarding, we will have proper glass again. It's been that long, I can't get too excited - it can wait.

It is the last day of June, the country has been Locked down for 15 weeks. It is slowly returning to 'normal' and most things will re-open this weekend which has been christened Super Saturday by the press. It could possibly be nothing super for the police and NHS if everyones goes mad, rushes out to the pub, gets paralytically drunk and ends up in a fight. It looks like the official day for it to all be over is 1st August.

Looking at the World Health Organisation website there has been over 10 million cases and 504,000 deaths worldwide, with nearly half of that number occurring in the USA and the Americas, where it is totally out of control.

The UK has fallen to fifth in the list of highest number of infections but is still third on the WHO chart of the highest amount of deaths with 43,575 fatalities. According to the news the UK registered death rate has now fallen back to what they would expect for 'normal' at this time of year.

Back in Vietnam they have had 355 cases to date and still no deaths. The airline pilot is still hanging on and they are fighting with everything they have to keep him alive.

The economy is in an almighty meltdown, there are so many companies struggling to stay afloat. I hope they don't all follow suit and put their prices up, it is not a good time, no-one has any money, they are all in the same boat.

Easy jet has announced that it is planning to withdraw its services from Stansted, Southend and Newcastle, which will leave another 700 unemployed.

Luckily at the moment there are still millions of staff on furlough, so technically still employed, they can stay on that scheme until October when it finishes. But then what? If business hasn't picked up, millions will be out of work, on the dole and there will be a huge recession. Not a very comforting thought.

I have got through another month without slipping back into my dark depressive state. There have been a few dark days but I am firmly holding on to my patience and sanity. Peter seems happier in himself even though business is not great.

Even though it is quiet in my office, work is very stressful and with the Groundhog sensation every week, I am bored stiff with life at the moment. Along with millions of others I want to make plans for the future, but how? And when?

As we start to move out of the Covid Lockdown, you would think things would get better for most people but no, there are some surprising scenario's that come to the fore as we move on into July.

If you want something said, ask a man. If you want something done, ask a woman - Margaret Thatcher

8. Reaching the end?

Weds 1st July - Sunday 5th July

So the first week of July passes. How can we possibly be in July already, where has the year gone? It is certainly starting to look as if we might have six months wiped off of our lifetimes. It won't make any difference to young children, they won't remember it. Teenagers might remember but will soon forget, they still have their whole lives ahead of them, what's a few months to them? Us older people, who are closer to the end of our lives than the beginning, it's valuable time we are missing out on.

I write a letter to our CEO begging for my nephews job. I know he can't really do anything about it, there are lots of other staff to consider, but at least he answers my email and it makes me feel better that I have at least tried.
This whole Covid episode and the new staff structural upheaval has made us all miserable in the office. As a team we are now a bit disjointed and barely see each other as we are all working different days and times.

I heard from both my girls this week and Eric. Anna has gone back to work for two days a week. She says it is very boring as they only have two guests in the whole hotel. When I spoke to her La Vie was shouting and screaming with glee in the background, she's OK. Greenie is still trying to hold her household together but I get the feeling it is all starting to unravel.

I at last got my airline refund from my cancelled ticket home from Vietnam. It's taken all that time but at least I have it. Now I have a huge credit on my Visa card with nothing to spend it on.

Maureen is living a nightmare. Her husband has been in hospital since 23rd of June and she has not been allowed to visit, for obvious reasons. Today she has managed to speak to him on the phone but it took a while before he recognised her voice. The hospital say he is extremely confused and unsteady on his feet. He is allegedly being moved to a care home this week but poor Maureen is pulling her hair out at the lack of information. I know Covid is the priority for every hospital but there are still people out there with normal lives and problems not connected to Covid that still need dealing with.

I am still tackling the diet, but it is very hard. I haven't cheated yet and most surprisingly I haven't had a drink for nearly a fortnight. My stomach has definitely reduced in size, so something is working. The problem with this diet is that one mouthful of doughnut and the sugar cravings will come rushing straight back. But as I am now comfortably in the sugar free zone and starting to see some weight loss, I will be able to stick it out, for a few more weeks at least.

I did actually go out on Saturday. I went to Luton Town Football as a volunteer. It felt really good to get out and see my friends; Carlos and Rachel. The downside was that we had to take the temperature of all the visitors to the ground, around 200 people in all, whilst dressed in PPE. Boy was I sweating and it wasn't even particularly warm. I also managed to have a good long chat with my favourite Paramedic which put a big smile on my face. He does make me laugh.

There was also a nasty surprise waiting up in the stands for me. Peter had paid for two huge cardboard cut outs of us to be put on two of the seats. It is a small way for the club to make a bit of cash and it makes it look like there were some people in the crowd, despite there being no noise. All at £25 a pop! Unfortunately the photo he had chosen of me was awful and very unflattering. All my friends who were watching the game on the Internet said the camera's kept repeatedly showing our cut outs. In full glorious detail. It is sods law when you have a ghastly photo of yourself and it gets repeatedly shown across the nation.

It was an odd experience being at a football match in an empty stadium which normally has 10,000 cheering and chanting fans in attendance. To try and make a bit of an atmosphere they played canned crowd noise during the game, which was very strange as it was out of sync with what was going on on the pitch. As there was no cheering, and I was so busy chatting with my friends, I failed to notice that we got beaten 5-0. Peter did though, and sulked all evening.

Most of the pubs re-opened on Saturday night to great fanfare. I understand all the extra police and ambulance resources that were laid on were a waste of time as in most towns it was all a bit of a damp squib. In Luton and Bedford there were balls of imaginary tumble weed blowing around the streets it was so quiet. I did wonder if that is because Bedfordshire still has a fairly high rate of infection and people are just being cautious. Everywhere across the country was quiet, except Londons Soho where everyone went mad out on the lash.

The most exciting event of the week was my haircut, which I hate.

Mon 6th July to Sunday 12th July

So this weeks most exciting event was that the back door was finally fixed. Because I am so dappy I now keep telling Peter to shut the door - it is already shut but I am so used to seeing the dark plastic sheeting when it is closed, I now can't tell the difference.

The weather has been miserable and overcast most of the weekdays, but quite humid. On Thursday it rained really hard on my way home at 8pm. It was coming down so hard on the A1, despite having my windscreen wipers on double fast, I could not see where I was going. My new car is so low to the ground it doesn't cope well with lots of surface water and it was sliding all over the place. It was very scary and I lost control twice as I hit a huge river of water. Fortunately there was very little traffic and I wasn't in danger of hitting anyone as I swerved about.

Work has been awful. I have never felt so demoralised in my whole working life.
We have managed to hang on to our jobs for now. Moving forward it transpires that they may also require us to work on busy weekends from 8am until midnight on a shift system. As we are now covering London this could potentially be every weekend from Easter until Christmas including New Years Eve. We cannot get any clarification as to how many days this might involve and it is all a bit hazy, but they are rushing this through and want us to sign up to a change of contracts. We have asked for a description of exactly what it is that they want us to do on these 'weekend' shifts but we still have not had a proper answer. A vague 'Admin support' was all we could get.
They should be warned: they are dealing with four hormonal women here, we won't do anything we are not happy with.

 Four offices are to be closed, we will struggle with the amount of work if we ever get up to speed again as we are not getting any extra staff. We should all be thrilled to bits but we are not happy bunnies. Things should start to improve for us but it just keeps getting worse.
We keep getting emails stating that our thoughts are so important. We are being invited to consultation meetings to 'honestly ' discuss our roles. They know exactly what they want and these meetings are the legal consultations that they have two go through, they don't really want to hear our opinions.

One of the meetings was about our job titles. We were asked what we would like to be called. Various suggestions were made and a list was compiled which we had to vote on. All four of us voted for the same one which unanimously won. But oh no, we get another email with a few more suggestions and could we all please vote again. We all voted for the same one - again. Mysteriously that name could not be considered even though it was on the list. Another list was then sent round which we deleted without voting. CALL ME WHAT YOU WANT - I DON'T CARE ANYMORE.

The Directors came to visit us last week. This is the first time since the Covid crisis hit back in March that they have been able to visit. Half an hour before they are due to arrive, we get a call from someone who was working in the Call Centre last weekend who had just tested positive for Covid. All hell breaks loose and everyone is running around with sprays and wipes cleaning every conceivable surface before the senior bods arrived.

There are a lot of frightened and nervous people out there. Some people still do not want to leave their houses they are so scared of catching the virus. Agoraphobia seems to have taken seed. One of my friends has only been out three times in 4 months and won't leave the house, she is terrified. One of my colleagues says both her sisters will not go out and won't even open the front door to her, all post has to be left on the doorstep for three days before it is retrieved. The Lockdown has really seen some changes in people habits. Social people who used to be out all the time, now prefer to stay isolated indoors. It is going to be a hard and difficult slog to get these frightened people back to work and out of their safe havens.

Poor Maureen. What a hideous week for her.
Her husband was eventually moved to a care home 40 miles from her house. She had specified that she needs him within a ten mile radius of her house. At 82 she cannot be driving an 80 mile round trip every time she wants to see him.
When he was taken by ambulance to the home, she was at last able to see him outside in the car park before they admitted him, she was not allowed to accompany him inside or help get him settled. He didn't have a clue who she was and she was deeply upset.
The following morning she received a call from the home that her husbands needs are too great and they do not have the skills or staff to look after someone with such high dependency. An ambulance was called for and he was carted off back to hospital.

Next morning she receives a call from the same home stating that an ambulance had arrived again this morning with her husband on board. The staff are refusing to take him in and are in a heated debate with the ambulance crew in the car park to take him back to hospital. As if Maureen had any control over this!

Maureen is straight on the phone to the hospital to find out what the hell they are playing at. How can they do this? Where is the dignity and care that all hospitals harp on about? A very poorly, frail and senile old man is being treated like delivery of a bag of shopping. She is informed by the member of staff that he will be moved to another care home tomorrow morning. Slightly placated she calms down only to find out that the next day they have only tried to send him back to the same home that he has already been refused entry to twice! By my estimation that is 6 wasted ambulance journeys and a bed clogged up in the hospital.

Maureen is passed being upset now, she has cried buckets this week, now she is boiling mad and absolutely furious. She rings the hospital with a list of care homes nearer to her home that would be suitable. She is told that none of them have any vacancies. This she finds exceedingly odd as she has rung all of them herself this morning and every one of them has beds available. The hospital promise to get back to her.

In the mean time she is at last allowed to go and visit him as some of the restrictions are easing. After 20 minutes he eventually realises who she is and they even manage a little doddery dance around the ward. Maureen came over to us for lunch on Saturday, we let her talk and talk, she needed to let off some steam.

I desperately need to get out of the house. I decided to go and see my friend Elaine who lives in Bedford. It's been a while since I have actually been to her house and I couldn't remember where it was! I had somehow left my glasses at home so couldn't type it into my phone and drove around in circles until I gave in and had to ring Peter for instructions. Of course he assumed I was having a menopausal moment. And of course he was right as usual.

I myself haven't had a good week. I should feel great, I have kept my job at least, but I feel terrible. On top of every thing else, the problems with Maureen's husband have brought back all the angst I went through with hospitals and care homes before my dad died and my eyes fill up every time someone talks to me. I couldn't stop crying on Sunday afternoon when Peter went out and I was left on my own. I sobbed for England and had very dark thoughts running through my head. I can honestly say I have no enjoyment or interest in my life at the moment. Maybe that is how the rest of the population are feeling.

I also have had a stomach upset for 5 days now, it is probably just stress but I don't feel well at all. On the upside, at least I am losing weight! I manage to somehow get through each Groundhog day and just want to go to bed and sleep, which is easier than it sounds. Peters snoring has ramped up yet again and my night sweats are off the temperature scale. Combined with the electricity buzzing around in my brain over my job, I feel emotionally exhausted. After the initial few months of actually sleeping very well, being tired is becoming the norm for me again.The black cloud has definitely landed and I can't shake it off any longer. That small black dog of depression is wagging his tail at me.

None of this is helped by the fact that I cannot sit and relax in my garden for longer than fifteen minutes without a leather football being whacked about next door or headed over the fence breaking my plants and ornaments. This weekend my patience finally snapped and I shouted at HIM. Two minutes later his father comes around to complain about it. He was quite aggressive and it was wrong of him to come round when Peter was out. On the other hand we had it out. I am not advocating that the boy does not play in his garden, just that on some days he doesn't and gives it a rest now and then. I am pretty certain that they are not even aware of the noise he makes and did not believe me when I said he can do this up to 14 times per day (I had recorded this in my notebook). What difference it will make, who knows?

Two days later he apologises to Peter for badly handling the conversation with me. Hmm what was the use of that, it is me who he should say sorry to.

Stress and worrying are two things that do not afflict my husband and he doesn't really understand why I am so fragile at the moment. He says we have no control over this situation and to stop worrying about it as I cannot change anything. Mind you I can't really pinpoint it myself. I suppose that is the thing with mental health, there is no clear cut explanation why you feel great one day and rubbish the next. There is certainly no clarification as far as the menopause is concerned with regard to the depression and mood swings. Some women get it, some don't.

Once of my friends sailed through it, her family said that apart from being a bit ratty occasionally they never really noticed any change in her at all. Another woman I know suffered so badly that her husband left her and her children stopped talking to her altogether because her behaviour was so appalling. Some women suffer so badly and become so difficult to live with it ends up ruining all of their relationships. Fortunately for me, as far as I am aware, all of my friends and family are still talking to me even if I do behave like I am from another planet somedays.

What I really need to give me a bit of a lift is a change of scenery. I have a diary full of TEAMS meetings but no actual outings arranged with real people, it is a virtual world out there. Mary rings me, she has finally made it to her place in the South of France from Dublin and invites me to come over. I look up flights from Luton airport for the last week of July - £468.00. That's just not doable, I could get to Vietnam for that sort of money.

Peter in the end books us up for a weekend in the New Forest at the end of July. It may not be as glamorous as the South of France but will make a nice change from the boring routine we are now in. I will wait and see what happens in the next few months and then hopefully go and visit Mary later on in the year.

On a more positive note, the airline pilot who was fighting for his life in a Vietnamese hospital has recovered enough to be able to go home, leaving Vietnam with a zero death rate out of their 382 cases.

As a matter of interest there has now been 14 million cases and 600,000 deaths worldwide. The UK lays ninth in the list of countries with the highest number of infections but still third with the most amount of deaths.

I am aware that my reports are beginning to sound like the 'Hunger Games'.

The Government are now making a lot of noise about the public needing to wear masks when in shops and offices. Perhaps if they had done this four months ago instead of waving the idea aside as useless, they might not have these sort of horrendous statistics.

Horse, Gate and Bolted are three words that spring to mind.

Monday 14th July to Sunday 19th July

After the beautiful few months we had, the weather in July has been a bit ropey. It poured with rain again for two days solid, at least the grass is green again. But it is dull and overcast like the mood of the nation.

Peter got up at 1.45am on Tuesday to drive to Glasgow. He has cricked his neck and can't turn his head around, that will be handy on the long drive there and back. He says it will be OK as he is going in a straight line on the motorway and doesn't need to turn around!

On Wednesday a very strange thing happened. I could hear someone had their TV on very loud, I went into the garden but the neighbours had all their doors shut and the sound was not coming from outside in any case. I went upstairs and our TV had turned itself on in the lounge. We have not used that room for ages and it was a bit of a mystery which spooked me a bit. It also pissed me off a tad, I can't even turn it on with the proper remote yet it can turn itself on at a whim when I don't want it to.

On Wednesday evening I thought I was cracking up until I spoke to my nephew - who was. I guessed he was drunk from his slightly odd behaviour on our TEAMS meeting. I finished the call quickly so that I could ring him.
He was sobbing his heart out and drunk as a skunk. He still doesn't know about his job and it was getting to him. He was also distressed that a few of us on the call were a bit upset about things and he was ranting about the unfairness of life in general. Peter brought me over a large glass of wine and I broke my alcohol curfew whilst I listened with my head in my hands.
My sister and her husband are away for a few days so I am keeping an eye on him. Next morning he puts a photo of his head on our WhatsApp group. He had gone out for a walk at 3am, fallen over, cracked his head open and had to go to hospital for stitches and a CT scan. Please don't tell my sister.
I went to see him on Friday, he was absolutely fine, physically and mentally.
Mental health : the highs and lows: up one minute, down in the doldrums the next.
We had a pleasant afternoon sitting in the garden and he even cooked me some lunch.

On the way home I got caught in a traffic jam. This was a novel experience which was one thing I had not missed in the last 5 months. It took me 1 hour to go 3 miles.
As I was running a bit late, I decided to pop into a supermarket in Luton to pick up some shopping rather than going to my local.
Well, there was no social distancing going on in there from the people of Luton. No one seemed to give a stuff about anyone else, I was pushed out of the way several times, leant over to get to the shelves and

all the customers were going down any aisle they liked in the wrong direction.

That will explain why Luton has currently got one of the largest infection rates in the whole country.

I spoke to Anna this week on Face time. Her family are in mourning as her grandfather has died (the one married to the walking skeleton) and she is very sad. La Vie has no such cares and is banging around and yelling her head off, it looks like she will be walking very soon. She will be such a handful once she gets mobile.

I can't get hold of Greenie, she is not answering my calls and has not read my messages either. I drop Eric a line to see if he has seen her recently, he thinks her Internet is not working. This happened once before, her phone had broken, so I am not unduly worried at the moment.

We spent the whole day with Maureen on Saturday. She was very emotional and bawled her eyes out several times. Her husbands dementia has now regressed back to his childhood and he keeps asking for his mum and dad. He is still in hospital and the Doctors have decided that at the moment he is too ill to move. None of this has been helped by the constant upheaval backwards and forwards to care homes that don't want him. Maureen is going to take it up with the hospital Ombudsman. Too right, it has been a catalogue of disgraceful care.

We have a lovely lunch out on the patio and then Peter and I set about the garden. We cut down trees and bushes that have got overgrown, Maureen joins in and it takes her away from her worries for a while. She is much brighter when we leave.

Due to the lovely lunch, dessert and a bottle of Prosecco, the diet has taken a battering today. I am awake all night, I end up sleeping downstairs but it doesn't make any difference - I think it is the sugar surging around my organs.

I spent all day Sunday sitting in the garden with not a sound from next door. It is all I need, if only one day a week, to be able to sit out there not tensing up every half hour for the next round of football noise. It definitely puts me in a better frame of mind and with yet another glass of wine inside me, I feel more relaxed than I have done for a few weeks.

Monday 20th July - Sunday 26th July

Scientists have announced that the Coronavirus will not be gone by Christmas and is here to stay. Whether we have another huge influx of infections remains to be seen. Hopefully they will come up with a vaccine soon, that is if the Russians don't steal the idea as allegedly stated on the news. The UK Government has already ordered hundreds of millions of doses of any vaccine created.

It made the BBC news tonight about the big surge of new infections in Luton. They are all in once place which will remain nameless but has been mentioned once or twice already as ignoring any of the restrictions. My friends in the ambulance service say it has gone mad again down there.

Where did Peter go then on Wednesday evening? Right into the centre of it all to Luton Towns football stadium. It's down to the wire as to whether the team stays in the Championship, Peter has spent the last few days working out the permutations of all the different clubs in the relegation zone. He is obsessed and I keep telling him he cannot control the un-controllables. Which is more or less what he tells me when I get stressed and worried about something.

When he gets home he has lost his voice as he was shouting and cheering so much. Fortunately Luton won their game and will not get relegated. Bloody good job, I hate seeing grown men cry. Football is the only sport where you see men crying when they win and crying when they lose. Peter and our Paramedic friends have shed many a tear on the terraces.

I read an article today that the sales of tea and coffee have gone up by £43 million in the last three months. Apparently all that most people have wanted through Lockdown is a nice cuppa, a biscuit and a good book. I better get a move on and get my first book published. Someone might buy a copy.

Maureen's husband has at last been moved to a more suitable care home in Cambridge. She is still not allowed to see him but feels happier that he is at least settled somewhere nearer to her and much nicer than the other place.

Watch this space.

My friends, Julie and Martin, have managed to sell their house and can now start to plan their big adventure of buying a yacht and sailing around the world for their retirement.

I am thrilled for them but this good news has a quite negative affect on me.

I also want to move house and start making plans for the next phase of my life as I head for retirement but Peter won't hear of it at the moment, he is not ready and he does not think we are old enough.

At the weekend we go for a car ride to the back of beyond in Lincolnshire to look at a new van for Peters business. It is a miserable day and pours with rain all the way there and back, not sure where the Summer has gone.

He gets a cracking deal on a new electric/petrol van. The Government is giving a £7000 incentive to anyone who buys one and Peter snaps the deal up. He ends up paying less for the new 4x 4 van than we paid for my Mini.

We decide to go to the Springfield's outlet centre for something to eat. It is very busy, everyone is wearing masks and there is a queue outside every shop. I end up breaking my diet (which I am still trying to stick to) and have scampi and chips. It is delicious.

(When we get home I break it again by having half a pizza, a huge bowl of ice cream and three glasses of fizz. Well, if you are going to break it do it in a spectacular way).

We do manage to have a look around the shops whilst we at Springfields as it had emptied out a bit when we left the restaurant. I don't buy anything even though there are some lovely clothes around and the Summer sales are on. I have nowhere to go which needs anything new and this stupid rule of not being able to try anything on is definitely not helping. I always try clothes on before I purchase anything and rarely shop online. I can't be bothered to buy clothes if I need to send them back when they do not fit and with my increasing girth at the moment it is a real gamble.

On Sunday afternoon Peter is besides himself with glee as Watford FC get knocked out of the Premier league. Watford are Lutons biggest footballing rivals and it means we will be playing them twice next season. My dad would have been delighted, he was a huge Watford fan, and he and Peter used to have some very friendly banter over the games, he would have loved watching them play together.

That will be two big punch ups to look forward to when the new season starts: whenever that will be.

There is big trouble brewing in Spanish holiday destinations as there has been a surge in Covid infections in Europe and the British Government have said all people coming in from there will need to quarantine for 14 days when they arrive back in the UK. The foreign office is advising that people do not go there unless absolutely necessary. I watched the beetroot red holidaymakers whingeing on the news about how hard done by they all are.

Honestly people, you knew the risks in going there, the Covid figures are not a secret, stop moaning about the consequences.

Monday 27th July to Sunday 2nd August

As I was getting into to bed on Sunday evening, Peter left to drive to Stranraer to catch the early ferry to Northern Ireland to deliver some machinery and was away for two nights. The best two nights sleep I have had in weeks.

Apart that is from Anna ringing me at 3.30am worried sick because they had reported 24 new Coronavirus cases in the area and the city of Danang and Hoi An had gone into total Lockdown. I look up the figures, they still have had only 459 cases in the whole country. I tell her not to worry, no-one has died so far and the figures are so small compared to the UK, but that doesn't help with her panic and concerns. I am still worried as I cannot get hold of Greenie, she has not read any of my messages and there is no answer when I ring. I hope she is OK.

We had the final consultation meeting regarding the redundancies this week. Huddled around someones laptop, as no other system works any longer in the building, we listened to the directors plans. It was the strangest meeting. At the end not one person asked a single question or uttered a word. A day later an announcement was made on the Companies Intranet site about the re-structure. Apparently us ladies in the office will be working shifts of 7am-11pm, 7 days a week.

That is news to us. That was definitely not what we agreed to.

And it is not going to happen.

I had at last managed to book some appointments with my beautician to get various much needed maintenance done to my nails and face which I was looking forward to. Unfortunately Boris changed the rules on Saturday with very little notice and they rang me to cancel everything except my toenails, which apparently are safe to do!

We have all managed to cope with being locked up for three months but even now we still do not have the freedom to live our lives and it is getting to us all.

My friend Lisa is about to celebrate her 50th birthday and nowhere will let them book a meal for 30 people. Yet Peter and I went into a restaurant on Saturday in Spalding where there must have been 40 people eating. Lisa has been told that all diners in a restaurant are not socialising or talking to other tables which is what would happen at a birthday dinner so it is not allowed.

My volunteer group were going to meet in a park for a picnic this week, all sitting on separate blankets with our own food. We were really looking forward to seeing each other after the long hiatus. Due to the virus spiking in Luton, there was some confusion over whether our members from there could actually attend, the last thing we wanted was to be reported to the police as having a mass gathering. After a bit of investigation the rule still is that only 6 people can meet up outside from 2 different households, so we would have been breaking the restrictions anyway.

Peter has booked us into a hotel in the New Forest for a change of scenery, the weather is set to change and it is going to be scorching. So we set off on our weekend trip, sitting on the M25 on the hottest day of the year with the dog puffing and panting in the back. The room in the hotel was the smallest room I have ever stayed in. I have bigger wardrobes at home. It consisted of an enormous bed which took up all the floor space and a tiny bathroom which was covered in limescale. Every time you tried to navigate around the room you banged into the wooden bed frame. It is not the most romantic of bedrooms. I took a sleeping tablet both nights and knocked myself out, otherwise I would never have slept in that pokey place with a temperature of 80C. We did manage to sit on the beach on Saturday which was lovely with a good breeze blowing and I topped up my tan. Even the dog behaved herself and didn't get into any fights with other animals. Unfortunately on both evenings I had far too much to drink and started an argument. So it wasn't the greatest weekend ever but I appreciated the effort.

One good thing did happen, Greenie got back in touch. Her phone had broken and she had been waiting to get it back. I secretly think she had not paid the bill and they cut her off but she was saving face by saying it was broken.

She told me that things in Hoi An are very bad. This second Lockdown is much more severe than the last one and they have now had several deaths. They had tried so hard to keep the infection at bay and it looked like they were succeeding and now this.

The authorities have traced the cause of the new infections to a group of Chinese who had been smuggled into Danang City illegally by some Vietnamese criminals. What complete idiots, they have now ruined it for everyone, I hope they go to prison for what they have done to the people there. The children are off school again, the airports are closed, all bars & restaurants shut, no-one who works in the tourist industry has a job and my girls have no money. Vietnam only properly opened up to tourists in 1993 and I am seriously worried that they might keep the doors closed permanently for the near future. Currently you can't leave the country or get in.

Danny is still out there, completely fed up and miserable as he can't go out boozing, schmoozing or partying. Perhaps he now understands how we feel in the UK after 4 months of it.

Monday 3rd August to Sunday 9th August

After the dodgy weekend I went into work on Monday like a bear with a sore head.

Part way through the day we had the final consultation regarding the redundancies and restructure. Honestly some of the titles given to some of these new roles, they might as well have been written in Swahili, I have no idea what the jobs were or what they would be doing.

It's also come to light that from next week we **will** be doing all bookings for smaller events for the whole country. When it comes to the handover it is apparent that some of the staff in other offices have misunderstood our new roles and seem to be tossing everything at us to sort out. That's fine we will just toss it back. There are a lot of tossers around at the moment!

This week restaurants across the country are offering 50% of meals mid week, subsidised by the Government. It is a plan to get the hospitality trade restarted. Peter books us into the local pub for dinner on Tuesday. Unlike the weekend where we ended up winding each other up, we manage to have a very civilised conversation. Miracle of miracles he can now see where I am coming from about a few things. I had felt like I was banging my head against a wall to get him to see certain things from my side instead of his own rosy view. Positivity all round.

On Wednesday a huge tanker exploded in Beirut causing massive destruction and wreaking havoc throughout the city. Unfortunately the tanker was full of 2750 tonnes of ammonium nitrate which was why it went off with such force. 137 people have died and at least 5000 are injured. Someone had videoed the explosion on their cell phone. The blast literally vaporised anything in its path. Some people are still un-accounted for. There is now a big investigation as to why this chemical was stored in such a huge quantity.

After a relatively quiet and settled week, Maureen's husband is back in hospital with problems eating and a chest infection. The poor man has been moved from pillar to post and doesn't have a clue where he is or who anyone is. The hospital also seem to think he has been overdosed on his drugs in the care home. They have rung Maureen twice to ask her what the actual dose should be, surely his GP should be able to tell them? Maureen has now reached the difficult decision to put him on to palliative care and let him go naturally. As long as he is not in any pain she wants him to go to sleep holding her hand. I really hope it happens fast, my dad lasted 66 days on palliative care and it was harrowing to watch.

It has been boiling hot this week, some days reaching 36C. It's really weird but everyone is complaining about the heat at work, beetroot red and sweating buckets. To me it is just how I feel normally so I am not suffering quite so much!
We have had the air con unit on at night in our bedroom. It must be the envy of the street. Everyone else is not sleeping but we are snuggled up every night under the duvet in Arctic conditions.
Poor Peter got stuck on the A1M on Friday for three hours after a lorry went over and blocked all three lanes. The temperature reached 90C. The police were handing out bottled water to all the stranded drivers.

After many a re-write, my first book was actually published on Amazon. *'I'm not dead yet - the adventures of a menopausal woman'*. So 2020 has been a complete wash out but at least I have achieved something and it gives me an amazing lift. I feel better in myself than I have for months. It might not be every readers cup of tea but I am immensely proud of it. It is all my own work and I have edited it and published it myself (with some help from Peter). My friend Kirsty designed the cover which looks amazing and is very eye catching. My husband has put it on his Facebook page and we have lots of messages from friends saying they have brought it and recommended it to other friends.
I know I will never be J.K.Rowling but it is very satisfying seeing your own work in proper print.
It was a bit difficult trying to explain it to Greenie and Anna, I am pretty sure they didn't understand what I was on about. Anyway they are too busy worrying about the virus in Vietnam. They have now had 759 cases, the figure has doubled in 2 weeks, and they now have lost 10 people. They are in serious Lockdown, no-one will break the rules there. It's still a drop in the ocean compared to the UK and the rest of Europe though.

On Saturday, I decided enough was enough, we needed to see our friends, so I invited my friend Lisa and her husband Jez over for a barbecue. She can't have any sort of proper celebration for her 50th so I made a bit of an effort and even put on a nice dress and a trowel full of make up. It was lovely to have company and to be able to sit out in the garden until it got dark. It was a lovely evening, another thing to improve my mood.

I paid for it later as I laid awake half the night after consuming 1.5 bottles of fizz!

Monday 10th August to Sunday 16th August

So this week the office hours go back to normal. Hurrah! 9-5 again. Unfortunately this means I have to get up at 7.15 fours days in a row and by Friday I am dead beat! It also means I have to cook dinner four evenings in a row. I am so out of practice, I can't think of what to make and we have some very strange concoctions.

It is very quiet at work, this is normal for August, but now eerily so. The phone did ring several times during the week and we all jumped out of our skin.

I sneaked off to the pub on Monday lunchtime with our boss and we sat there putting the world to rights. Also made a nice change.

Good news though, my nephew has gone back to work. Hooray! He has kept his job and is pleased as punch.

All of his family and friends breathe a huge sigh of relief.

Visiting France is now off the menu again and holiday makers were returning in their droves to avoid being quarantined for another 14 days when they get back to the UK. Except that is my brother and his family, they are having such a lovely time they are staying put out there. He runs his own business so can please himself when he goes back to work.

Peter has been spending all his spare time in the garage putting in a special electric plug to charge up his new electric car when it arrives. Of course it has a gadget involved and even a remote control, wouldn't you know it, but it has kept him out of mischief for a few days.

My friend Rachel came round on Monday evening and we laid on the floor in the lounge, allegedly doing a pilates class that we follow on Youtube, but mainly having a massive gossip and catch up. It was good to see her and I did ache a bit the morning so we must have done some exercise.

The good weather broke up this week. Definitely looks like Summer may be over. There were huge storms across the country, strangely it never happened in our village. We had some rain but no lightening or thunder. On the way to work on Thursday the heavens opened and the roads were completely flooded within minutes. You needed a boat to get into the car park. I got soaked going between my car and the door. One of the girls had walked from the station and got caught in it. She was standing in reception dripping water everywhere. She was wearing those fluffy mules that seem to be very fashionable at the moment (I would not be seen dead in them), and they looked like two wet dead rats. She had to get her mum to bring her a change of clothes, she was soaked to the skin.

I am still getting good feedback about my book. I had edited it myself and a few people have pointed out a few errors and some dodgy grammar, so Peter corrected them and we republished it.

At the weekend I went to stay with my friend Jane. She has just brought a caravan at a site in Northampton as a weekend bolthole. The weather was miserable on the way there but as I approached the site the skies cleared and the sun came out. We spent the afternoon and evening sitting out on the decking drinking wine and gossiping. We had a very nice evening though I really struggled to get up in the morning. Jane is a morning person and I am definitely not.
We went into Northampton town centre which is on the hot list of increasing infections. I can see why, it was very busy and lots of people were not wearing masks or really observing any sort of social distancing. The restaurant we had lunch in was full with no spare tables. We had a good mooch about in my favourite shop - Debenhams. Unfortunately we still cannot try clothes on which completely puts me off buying anything.
For some strange reason we ended up in the Ann Summers shop, it was a good job I had a mask on as my mouth was constantly agape. Who buys this stuff? And blimey, it is not cheap. Well someone must be purchasing it as the shop was doing a brisk trade. Not youngsters mind you, all women of a certain age. I ended up at the back of the shop where the more serious sexual enhancement tools were for sale. Do you know you can buy a set of electronic eggs that you put up your whatsit and are operated by remote control?
So whilst you are doing the ironing in the kitchen your partner can give you an orgasm whilst they are washing the car. Amazing!

The students are all up in arms over their exam results being calculated by an algorithm. Well, that was always going to be an unfair way of assessing their work. All the schools were empty by the end of March, the exams could have been arranged during the Summer, spreading the students out over several rooms and then there would not be this huge fuss which is going to rage on and on.

Monday 17th August to Sunday 22nd August

I don't know what's come over me this week, I must have had a personality transplant; I actually feel better than I have for about 16 months. Has the menopause finally chewed me up, spat me out and decided it has had enough of me and moved on to ruin another woman's life?
The weekend away lifted my spirits, actually publishing my first book has given me a renewed purpose (I did my first autograph!!!) and Peter and I are getting on fabulously again. He has not read the book and says he won't as he has a good idea of what is in it about him and admits that it is all true, I have not made anything up about him. (I haven't).
I also seem to have got back my sense of humour as I proved in the office on Monday when I described in great detail the visit to the Ann Summers shop to my work colleagues. We were all howling and crying with laughter, God it felt great to really belly laugh again. On Tuesday we moved on to talking about shellfish, another hilarious conversation which turned a bit naughty. It was a good way to start the week.

I had family visitors at home this week. My sister and brother in law came over on Friday and then on Saturday my mother and her husband came for lunch. My mother is really interested in my book and positively encouraging me to write another.
This is it - enjoy.

I had a mad moment on Thursday whilst cooking dinner. I put a gammon joint in the oven and noted the time it would take whilst I prepared the veg. I cooked all the veg beautifully and then realised the gammon had another hour in the oven. So we ate the veg and an hour later ate the meat. Who says the menopausal fruit loop episodes are over?

Most of the weekend was taken up with me not feeling too great. I had gone down with a water/kidney infection. Fortunately I had the antibiotics that I got in Vietnam and took them which saved me having to go to the Doctors. I knew my illegal drugs would come in useful.

Monday 23rd August to Monday 31st August

So it's the end of August - 6 months into the Covid world meltdown.

Work was interesting at the start of the week, no-one knows what they are doing, so no change there then. I actually sat at my desk with my head in my hands as I did not understand what I was supposed to be doing, everything is still changing on a daily basis. There have been some interesting staff movements as well, which raised a few eyebrows. All in all we are all in a slightly better frame of mind even if it is still organised chaos in the office. We still have very few events that are going ahead, so all that business as usual stuff from 1st July was a load of rubbish (and a waste of man hours).

I was on holiday for the latter part of the week and managed to catch up with a lot of my good friends. I had lunch with Carlos and his mother on Saturday lunchtime. He is still on furlough from his job at Luton airport and it's not looking too hopeful that he will actually be going back. So he is busy trying to find something else, unfortunately when furlough ends in October, there are going to be a lot of people out of work, all in the same boat.

I went to Nottingham on Wednesday to see my best friend Julie, who I have not seen since February. Peter had a job in the city so he dropped me off for a few hours. We spent all day putting the world to rights as well as discussing their house sale and plans to buy a yacht to sail around the Mediterranean for their retirement. It's all very exciting and also a bit daunting. They have to get rid of most of their possessions, so their house is one big sale. I did come away with a few bits as Julie has excellent taste.
We ended up having lunch in the pub and Julies husband came home and Peter turned up to pick me up to find us both half cut sprawled across the sofa's. We have offered them a temporary home for as long as it takes to get them sorted out before they depart the country. I really hope they come to us for a while as I will get some proper time with Julie before they disappear for their great adventure. I know I will still see them probably once or twice a year, but she's my best friend and I will miss her being at the end of the phone. But technology is so advanced I am sure we will be able to talk to them on the boat.

Peter took me to Freeport village in Braintree on Thursday. It was very busy but we did not have to queue to get in any of the shops. Most of the shops are practically giving away their Summer clothes and I did get a few bargains which I gambled on fitting me. Peter also brought me the most divine red Osprey leather handbag as a belated Birthday/Anniversary present which I love.

Our old friends Elaine and Clive came for dinner on Friday, it's only the second time I have seen them this year as well. It was great to catch up with them. We have been going on holiday with them every year for about 10 years but in 2020 it is not going to happen. We also went to Lisa and Jez' house on Saturday for dinner and to see their lovely extension that has now at long last been finished. I got completely dressed up for a change and felt a bit more like a proper woman than a drudge.

Maureen's lovely husband died on Saturday. Poor man he was just worn out with it all. He was still in hospital and his family had requested that they stop filling him up with drugs and let him go. It was peaceful enough at the end but very quick, Maureen unfortunately didn't get there in time. She is obviously very sad but says it is an enormous relief not to have to watch him in that state anymore. There will be no funeral. He had left his body for scientific experiments but no-one is taking bodies at the moment so Maureen has to pay for a private cremation. He was adamant that no money be spent on a big funeral. Good thing really as at the moment only 10 people could attend anyway.
It's an odd thing though when there is no funeral. We never got to say goodbye as we could not visit him in hospital, so it is almost surreal that he has gone.

I spoke to Mary in the South of France, she is having a lovely time and says it is quieter than usual but the infection rate is rising due to visiting holiday makers from all over Europe. She says the rate is up in Dublin as well and most of the people contracting the virus are under 45 but with very few symptoms. More people are catching it but the death rate is down, that also seems to be the story here. Has the virus mutated or are our immune systems dealing with it better?

Trump is on the presidential campaign trail this week. He's already claiming that if he loses the re-election it is because it has been illegally fixed.
That man is not right in the head.

It takes a great deal of courage to stand up to your enemies, but even more to stand up to your friends - J.K. Rowling

9. Onwards and upwards

So it's September already.
We've had 6 months of abnormality and it's gone a bit back to normal.
If you can call wearing a mask everywhere normal, or being restricted to who comes into your home, or being turfed out of the pub at 10pm, or not being allowed to go abroad, the list is endless….
We know we are still not out of the woods and the NHS are predicting bad things for the coming months.
Please, we can't take much more.

Tuesday 1st September - Sunday 6th September

On Wednesday Peter went to Jersey to do a job on a machine in St Helier. What a performance. He had to pay £95 to have a COVID test which he said was not a pleasant experience and made him gag. He was in Jersey for just 3 hours and only got the all clear message when he had been home indoors for 6 hours.

At work we have all been asked to fill out a survey as to why the Company got such a slating over some questions that went out a few weeks ago. One of the key things to come out of it was that no-one feels safe to speak out within the organisation. So someone has come up with yet another survey to find out why.
It is really simple, you do not need to be a highly paid executive to work this one out: in this current climate people are concerned for their livelihoods and do not feel free to speak up about any subject as it might put their job in jeopardy.
We ladies in the office are adamantly refusing to do it.
This is going to cause trouble, I can feel it in my water.

I have news from best friend Julie that their house is coming up to exchange and they will be technically homeless until they sort out their new life in Greece. As I have offered up our home to them it sends Peter and myself into a frenzy of new bathroom fittings, decorating and moving stuff around the house, loft, shed & garage to make some space.

My mother and I met up on Friday and went for a mooch around the shops and lunch. She has at last had her tooth fixed and it looks really good. I am pretty sure we were the only customers in Debenhams where there were racks and racks of clothes all massively reduced. But as you still cannot try anything on it is all a bit of guesswork so we don't buy anything.

There have been huge protests in Hong Kong relating to the postponed elections, allegedly due to Covid, and everyone is out on the street in uproar. Thousands of police have been drafted in to contain the crowds. That won't help with their infection rate.

Monday 7th - Sunday 13th September

I had a day out of the office this week, I went to swanky Ipswich!
We are assisting the office there in what was supposed to be a seamless handover which has in fact turned into a complete car crash. Our office has been told to stop doing certain support work which is now going to be handled by another team. Only no-one has informed or trained the new team who are taking to over, so we are off to give them a hand. It is apparent from the minute we arrive that the two staff are already completely overloaded and do not have time for any this.
The only benefit of the day is that we do pop in to see a colleague who lives in Stowmarket and he provides a lovely lunch on the way home.

On our return to the office we have all had an email demanding that we fill out the survey. We are then asked three times during the following week to fill it out by three separate senior managers and still we adamantly refuse.
I told you it was going to cause trouble.

I went to get my hair cut again. I have had enough of this long style and get the whole lot cut off, it is a huge weight off of my head and takes three minutes to blow dry.

Monday 14th - Sunday 20th September

Everyone is demotivated this week. We are called before the bench in a TEAMS meeting to answer for not filling out the survey. They really, genuinely, honestly, want to know our feelings, pretty please.

So we let them have it right between the eyes:
Lack of support of any kind from Senior Management or HR since the big boss was made redundant. Working shifts, working in the Call Centre weekends & lates with no consultation. All sorts of people wandering around the supposedly 'Covid ' secure building. Constantly being asked to carry out tasks that are not part of our job with no training. Having bits of our jobs suddenly being done by other higher paid staff. All having to attend the office daily and (some of us) not

being allowed to work from home like everyone else. The constant changing of the goalposts and swapping around of jobs and titles. Having daily meetings that are a complete waste of everyones time. Being asked for our opinion in meetings and then being run rough shod over. The difficulties of taking on all the countries event admin at the drop of a hat. Trying to work several different systems depending in which area you are dealing with. The constant worry about keeping our jobs in this current climate. The Staff Wellbeing completely ignored. The list went on and on.

And went down like a shit sandwich.

As I said they don't really want to hear it. There will be repercussions from this.

We did at least manage to sneak off to 'Chicago's for lunch one day this week. It was surprising how many people were in there. Nice to have a change of surroundings though.

Worryingly the infection rate is on the rise again. Last Friday there were 3539 cases reported which was 600 up from the previous day. Some people think it is due to the much better testing system that is now in place. The scientists and boffins are saying yes it's good news but a huge bulk of the population are testing positive, especially in the 20-29 year group. It seems to be affecting younger people and particularly hitting the North of the country. This is probably due to the University students returning and the socialising that **I KNOW** goes on even though the students have all been told to curb their nocturnal activities. The rule of 6 has been brought in again to try and restrict the number of people that can gather together.

Oh and it looks like Christmas might be cancelled.

I manage to speak to Anna on Tuesday. What she tells me breaks my heart.

Most of the hotels in Hoi An are closed, they are now coming into the rainy season so even the Vietnamese will not be travelling anywhere. She cannot find any work in a town that relies 100% on tourist trade so she is now reduced to selling soup and coffee by the side of the road to earn money for things for La Vie. I am completely horrified. This is a University graduate who can speak 4 languages. I instantly offer her money which she immediately refuses on the grounds that we are friends.

I am so upset that my friend Kirsty, who sits next to me in the office has to give me a little talking to. I know Anna and Greenie are not my responsibility. I just feel helpless that I cannot help them.

Somehow my husband, who likes a gadget or two, manages to mess up all the electronic locks in the house with his new phone. He can only reset them using my phone, his doesn't work. So all afternoon he is messing about with the front door whilst I completely empty our spare bedroom so that our friends can move in. I am such a tidy person and hate clutter, I have a feeling that on top of everything else this might do my head in.

Monday 21st - Saturday 26th September

So this week we have another influx of cancellations due to the new rule of 6.
Firework displays and Remembrance parades are all cancelled and it is very depressing for everyone concerned; our business, the volunteers, the employees and of course the event organisers.

Peter made an executive decision a few weeks ago and has booked a man to cut the trees down at the bottom of our garden. Fortunately I am not at home to see the almighty mess they create in my pristine garden. We get away lightly, they only break the roof of the shed, smash one of my ornaments and obliterate a huge shrub!
He's also been financially industrious and changed our Internet provider and we now have a new home phone number. After having the same one for 15 years what are the chances of me ever remembering it?

There are bewildering figures being circulated in the press today. They are saying we could be having as many as 80,000 new cases a day in the coming Winter months and the Excel centre is being un-mothballed as a precaution. This is so frightening. The Government are asking all people who can to work from home to please do so again. We decide that this is something we can manage in our office now that the workload is a bit slimmer, but oh no, the senior Management are having none of it and say we have to stay working in the office. So against what Boris has said they know what is best for us 4 women despite all the Senior Directorate and most other staff working from home.
This I fear is the payback for not filling out the bloody online survey.

On a separate note, Peter and I went to help out at a behind closed doors football match between Luton and Manchester United. There is huge excitement to be playing such a prestigious club who have one player alone who is worth more than Lutons whole team and ground combined. When the coach arrived at the ground there were at least 300 local youths crowded into the road and crushed up together against the Man United team bus. Not a face mask in sight, no social distancing whatsoever. The infection rate is still extremely high in Luton.

I rest my case m'lord.

On a less serious note, they had set up a temporary changing room for the away team, as due to Covid they cannot share. It was basically a shed made of plywood and held together haphazardly with duck tape. As we left the stadium I saw members of the Man United team naked in the showers through a 6 inch gap. It must have been a big culture shock for them to be showering in a wooden shack compared to their luxurious bathrooms at Old Trafford.

It was also a bit of a shock for me to see a £65 million penis.

But in a nice way.

I spent all of my day off decorating the spare room we have cleared for our friends. It is the room we have been using as a study and is the only room in the whole house that has never been decorated in the 15 years we have been there and is still a bland 'magnolia'. As Julie says she might be here for a while I give it a fresh coat of paint to brighten it up and cover all the holes where we have taken the pictures down. I will decorate it properly when they leave.

We had lunch with Maureen on Saturday, she seems OK if a little sad. But she is a trooper, keeping busy and starting to go out again, enjoying life after the trauma of the last few years. She misses her husband but no-one wanted him to live like that. At least she is surrounded by friends and good neighbours where she lives which is a relief to us that she has people around during the week.

Sunday 27th September to Sunday 4rd October

We both need a holiday, we normally go to Peter's friends luxury apartment in Cyprus at this time of year and have a glorious time. This time of year the weather is usually perfect, and we relish our time spent there.

Due to recent circumstances all we can manage is six days in a wooden cabin in Scotland by the side of Lock Linhe with the dog.

Scotland was closed.

The scenery was magnificent, the weather was kind, most places were shut and the dog hated every single second of it and sulked all week. I have never spent so much money in six days, ever. Did I feel relaxed and rejuvenated when I got home after a round trip of 1200 miles in the car?
What do you think?

When we got home our house had been taken over by Julie and her husband and there were boxes piled up everywhere and they had gone off to Greece to buy a yacht.
Like you do!

The rest of the weekend culminated in Peter and I being sick. Peter puked up everywhere on Sunday afternoon and I was ill on Monday just as I arrived back at work, so I had to turn round and go home again. Goodness knows what caused that, it must have been something we had eaten, boy I felt rough. Maybe it was the huge amount of shellfish we ate whilst in Scotland, maybe we had eaten a dodgy scallop or two. It finished off the holiday week in true style!

I went to the supermarket on Sunday afternoon and golly, tempers were frayed in there. There was road rage in the car park and people were shouting at each other inside. It didn't help that the queues went half way down the aisles, due to half the checkouts being closed, it took longer to pay than it did to do the actual shopping. I also noticed that there was no toilet roll on the shelves.
Surely not that old pony again?

Funny how things come back to bite you on the bum. Donald Trump has tested positive for Coronavirus and has to spend three days in hospital as a precaution.
As he returns to the Whitehouse, looking fit as a fiddle, acting like Zorro he dramatically whips his mask off on the balcony.
Publicity stunt or what?

Monday 5th October to Sunday 11th October

Julie has returned to our house, but her husband is staying in Greece sorting out the boat purchase. I love having her here, I have only seen her twice this year and it cheers me up no end. Unfortunately we hit the gin every night which I am not sure is such a good thing and we have been in an alcoholic haze all week.

I have started to help her sort out some of her clothes, shoes & makeup. She knows she has to get rid of most of these along with all their other possessions as they just will not have the space on the boat, but it is a very difficult thing for any woman to do, and I can see she is struggling with it.

I come out of it alright though - 3 pairs of shoes, 1 handbag, 3 dresses, a jacket, 2 shirts, 2 T shirts and a box of toiletries.

Thank heavens we went to Scotland last week. Nicola Sturgeon has announced much tighter restrictions across the country due to a high rise in new infections. The new rules there are completely baffling but I get the general gist of it - you can't have a drink in Scotland outside of your home. Anywhere.

In the UK Boris has announced a new three tier system of restrictions dependant on how bad the infection rate is in your area. They are totally confusing but whatever tier your town ends up in, it will stay there for 28 days. There are the usual exceptions and currently it looks like Bedfordshire is only on tier one, so we are relatively safe to still go out and about.

Will this all end in tiers?

Julie has only been back two days and somehow has managed to break one of the toilet seats, it has a huge crack across it. Peter sits on it two days later and the whole thing breaks in half which gives him a jolt mid stream. He mischievously leaves half of it outside her bedroom door (it resembles an half smile) which makes us all roar with laughter.

Peter spends all weekend in the garden building some new decking where the Leylandii trees used to be; banging, hammering and having a generally lovely time making a mess.

Us girls help out by getting completely rat arsed on gin and heckle him from the comfort of the sofa.

Monday 12th October to Sunday 18th October

Julie has flown off to Greece today to get their Greek residency card sorted out. So I am without my playmate but at least I give my liver a rest and dry out this week.

On Tuesday we are all invited to a mysterious meeting at work. No-one in the office has received any forewarning and hasn't a clue what it is about. When I look at the names of the people invited, there is an HR person involved. This does not bode well. We can get no information off of anyone, everyone is pleading ignorance.

So it is obviously bad news.

Sure enough we are all put on redundancy consultation again. The decision has been taken due to the downturn in the events side of the business and lack of income, they only want one office to cover the whole country. As we are already in place and covering the whole country already, surely it is a no brainer.

But apparently it isn't. And it does not make economic sense.

Despite there currently being only one member of staff still working in the other office, we are all advised to put a business case forward to save our jobs. Incidentally the 'other' office is the one the Management work out of, (they would need to recruit 4 new staff if they get rid of us and have the office there permanently).

Well sodding hell, it's just what we don't need.

We are all allowed to go home for the afternoon to 'reflect' on this news. I go straight into the garden and furiously set about oiling the new decking to let off steam. 10 minutes after I finish the heavens open and it pours with rain.

It then takes a full three days to dry out.

A bit like myself.

It's Greenies birthday this week and I make a little video of me wishing her Happy Birthday. I'd love to give her a big hug, she sounds so fed up, hopefully it cheers her up a bit that I have remembered.

It's also Maureen's Birthday and she comes to stay for the weekend. We had a huge Indian takeaway, it wasn't quite a special treat but I think Maureen appreciated it. She also tells me that if I have written anything in my book that criticises her precious son I am in deep trouble.

Oh shit, I better start running!

Monday 19th to Sunday 25th October

So this week the Coronavirus is officially on the rampage again and some of the larger cities are having much tighter restrictions imposed. Dublin is in complete Lockdown. Manchester is in revolt with the Government.

Wales is under much tighter restrictions along with Scotland.

My friend Mary is still in France, she doesn't want to go back to Ireland and sit in her house on her own for the Winter so she is staying put. She also has a cute new French boyfriend, go girl!

We are thoroughly cheesed off and depressed at work about the whole job situation. We are such a good team and the thought of looking for another position in the current economic climate is gloomy and a little bit daunting. I could not bear to end up working with another spiteful woman or control freak like I did in my last two jobs.

Weirdly I get several messages from people who I used to work with about how they are loving my book and that my descriptions of the staff I used to work with are spot on. Strangely enough there is a really nasty and spiteful review on Amazon today. It is not a review of my book, it is a personal comment about me.

It can only be one of two people and I know who they both are.

My friends are both back from Greece and spend their days sorting out their stuff and selling most of it on Ebay. I rescued several boxes of housewares that was going to the tip. It must be really painful for them to get rid of all these possessions and this is quality stuff not rubbish. They cannot take it with them and currently the charity shops are only accepting clothes so they have to dispose of it somehow. I whisk it all away to my sister and she redistributes it to a lot of needy people that she knows.

I have had quite a few messages from Greenie and Anna this week. The weather is the worst they have had in 20 years and the water is knee high across town. There are boats paddling up and down the streets. It always rains a lot in October but this year it is non stop, just what they don't need. When it eventually stops raining there will have to be a big clean up, all the muck will come out of the rivers, and the raging sea always dumps a load of sand along the coast road. Mind you it doesn't seem to have stopped Danny going out and getting drunk, some places must still be open for business. He also seems to have picked up a Vietnamese lady friend along the way, something he always maintained that he would never do. I suppose with the lack of Western tourists around he has had to go native for female company!

There has been a horrendous terrorist attack in Nice, near to where Mary lives. A man armed with a gun and knife has run amok at the Notre Dame Basilica and three people are dead, one of them almost decapitated.

For heavens sake don't we have enough to worry about in the world at the moment without religious fanatics causing mayhem?

Two good things happen this week. One is that a book critic has read my book and written a five star review on Amazon and also on her social media pages.

I am thrilled to bits about it. It's one thing for your friends and family to read it and comment, but when a complete strangers loves your work it is amazing.

The second is that the best programme on British TV is back. '*Strictly Come Dancing*' has restarted, at least that's something to warm the cockles of my heart through these long dark evenings. It will be an unusual format due to everyone living separately to adhere to the social distancing rules.

They have gone with the flow and introduced a female couple, which whilst I have no problems with anyones sexuality, is a bit odd to think of two women doing the rumba or a romantic waltz.

Let's see how it pans out!

Monday 26th October to 1st November

Monday morning the depression sets in. I was in tears all day, there are rumours circulating in the media that another Lockdown is on the way. I do not want to live like this anymore, I can't stand having my freedom taken away.

My pathetic woe is soon put into perspective when an enormous and powerful typhoon hits central Vietnam where my friends live. 14 people are dead - some are still missing, trees are uprooted, buildings and businesses are completely destroyed, it knocks the power out for days, causes huge flooding everywhere, the beach is decimated yet again and it is pure misery for everyone. So not only do they have no work or any money, some of them now have no roof and are wading around in their homes in three feet of dirty water. At least I have a roof, money, electricity, and all my family and friends here are accounted for.

Peter has a job in Glasgow so he gets up at 2am, drives there and back and completes the job in one day. How does he do that at 54 years of age? Julie hasn't left the house since Sunday and I am hardly busy, yet we are both exhausted by bedtime each evening and we haven't been anywhere.

Another week in Paradise at work.

New financial policies are brought in. They send them out three times containing errors before the correct one is circulated - by then I have lost the will to live and can't be bothered to read them.

I met up with my friend Elaine for lunch. The shops are full of Christmas trees and decorations. At least they weren't playing Christmas music throughout the store yet, I honestly don't think anyone is in the mood. I thought I had a miserable time last Christmas, this one is looking even worse. We sit in the cafe for three hours nattering, I have jaw ache when I get home and cannot sleep due to having drunk three coffees.

So on Halloween (which is another damp squib for the kids), holding up the start of 'Strictly Come Dancing', Boris calls a press conference and announces a four week emergency Lockdown starting from next week. The latest figures make grim reading. The UK has had 1.3 million infections, 51,300 deaths and the daily infection rate is rising heavily with 25,000 new cases in just one day. The scientists predict that we could have up to 4,000 deaths a day if we do not put in a four week circuit breaker. He also says that if we adhere to the rules we should be able to have a normal as Christmas as is possible. There are the usual bewildering instructions about going out but not going out, going to work but not going to work, yeah we've heard it all before, we know the spiel by now.
The rumours were right; I knew something was up when there was a long queue to get into Aldi this morning.

This causes huge problems for my house guests. Martin is off to Greece on Sunday, they now have to decide if Julie goes with him. Unfortunately there are still a lot of loose ends to tie up here and Julie is still working from our home. After a lot of conversation they make the decision for him to go and she will join him at the beginning of December. None of this is then helped a few days later when Greece goes into a three week National Lockdown so Martin ends up house bound in another country. I have everything crossed for them that the Lockdowns will be eased in a few weeks time or they are buggered.

Mysterious parcels have been arriving all week, which then get secreted somewhere in the garage never to be seen again. I guess Peter has started his Christmas shopping and they are weird and wonderful gifts for me - if he can remember where he put them. Quite often I get a festive present at Easter that he has found after having a clear up which he had forgotten about.

Maureen was on the phone on Sunday in bits. The 007 actor, Sean Connery, has passed away. Women of a certain age will understand why she was so upset!

Later that morning there is a loud bang and the kettle blows up, probably from over use in the last few months. Peter and I go off to purchase a new one. Somehow we also end up buying 36 bottles of wine, a litre of gin, a litre of Baileys and three cases of beer.
Well there will be nothing else to do for the next four weeks!

People are going to judge you anyway, so you might as well do what you want - Taylor Swift

10. Lockdown Mark 2

Monday 2nd November to Sunday 8th November

Work on Monday morning consists of cancelling any remaining Remembrance Parades and firework events that are still on the books. Remembrance day is important to a lot of people and now it won't happen and it is very poignant.

We are ushered into a top secret meeting on Tuesday and it is announced that our organisation is going to be involved with the National Covid vaccinations, but it is all hush hush. That won't stay under wraps for long within this organisation. NOTHING stays secret, we have some of the most indiscreet people you could ever wish to meet. We have been asked to recruit and train 30,000 volunteers to help with the massive project of vaccinating the British population. We are all urged to volunteer to assist, whilst our paid jobs dangle up in the air.

On that note we still have not had any answers to our questions or proposals regarding the employment consultations. It has all gone very quiet on the Western front. Later in the week it becomes obvious why. The Government extends the furlough scheme until the Spring to keep people from losing their jobs, the organisation could now furlough all of us until March with little cost to themselves. Also it now transpires that they will need administration staff to assist with the vaccination programme, they could redeploy us for a few months. So there are now two options on the table for them to go down before even considering redundancy at this time.
But we hear nothing, there is unconditional radio silence with huge balls of tumble weed floating around the airwaves.

There is another awful terrorist incident, this time in Vienna. 4 people are dead and the murderer has been shot by the police. Isis are claiming full responsibility.
I hate it when they do that as if it is something to be proud of.

During the last Lockdown you could hear a pin drop and not see another car or person for miles. I drove to the supermarket on Friday and there were people and traffic everywhere. Peter says his journey home on Friday evening was the worst traffic he had seen for months. When we went out for a long walk on Saturday with the dog, I have never seen so many people out, I didn't know that many people lived in our village. Hmm Lockdown, what Lockdown?

On an amusing but slightly terrifying note the American elections are taking place and Trump is on a high, insisting that has has won and getting a legal team involved to prove it. It is a really close call and on Friday Trump is still celebrating and refusing to acknowledge that he might have lost. On Saturday it is certainly starting to look as if Biden has won after one of the most contentious elections in living memory. Temper tantrums all round in the Whitehouse I bet.

It's really mild at the moment and my flushes have ramped up with the central heating being switched on. I haven't slept well for a few nights and feel lousy.
The high alcohol content of my blood is probably responsible.
I have also done some strange things recently. There was a pint of milk in the cupboard with the mugs. I turned the house upside down looking for my watch only to find it in my cardigan pocket. And I spent all day wearing my knickers the wrong way round and wondered why they were cutting me in half!
Answers on a postcard please.

Monday 9th November to Sunday 15th November

Last weekend Julie and I embarked on a Pilates fest and have been trying to do some exercise each day, by Tuesday we can hardly move, every muscle aches and we have to lay on the sofa all evening eating chocolate and drinking gin.
Come on it's good for the soul! (probably not the arse though).

For some strange reason Peter has replaced all the lights under our kitchen cabinets. Don't know why, the old ones were fine. Now with (yet another) remote control you can have a blaze of disco lights whilst you are cooking or doing the washing up. He's even got it to respond to music by Toyah.
So between trying not to have a seizure caused by the flashing colours and preparing dinner by disco light, I have to contend with '*It's a Mystery*' blaring out every five minutes.

I have to go into work for two days as I cannot seem to do specific things from my computer at home, which is certainly a complete mystery to me. I spend the other two days 'working' from home which basically consists of keeping an eye on the emails as there is nothing else going on.

It does give me a bit of time to get on with this second book, which I suppose is a bonus, though unlikely it will be out before Christmas or next the way the Covid is hanging around.

As of this week there have been 52 million cases across the world and 1.3 million deaths. I take a look at Vietnams latest figures - 1253 cases with 35 deaths. I know it's gone up but how is that low figure even possible in such a populated 3rd world country? The USA leads the way with 10 million cases and 245,000 deaths, how can that be possible in the richest country in the world?

Talking about Vietnam, I spoke to Greenie on Friday, she was so upset. Her gambler of a husband has borrowed some money without telling her and now she doesn't know how they will be able to pay it back as they have no work. Please don't let it be from an unscrupulous money lender. I'm going to have to do something about this and think very carefully about how to handle it.

Trump is still refusing to concede that he has lost the election to Joe Biden. They may have to get the bailiffs in to remove him from the Whitehouse, he is acting as if nothing has changed! I must say his much younger and beautiful wife must be mightily relieved it is all over, if the rumours are right she never wanted him to be President in the first place.

On a political note Dominic Cummings, the MP who broke all the last Lockdown rules with a day trip to Barnard Castle, has at last been sacked by Boris. If you believe the press reports it's not because of any political reason but over a disagreement about Mr Johnson's girlfriends influence over the PM.
Who knows what shenanigans go on behind the door of No.10.

The attacker who went mad in June in a park in Reading stabbing several people has been found guilty of the attacks. You don't say, they had him bang to rights.
Peter Sutcliffe, the Yorkshire Ripper, has died in prison. He had a suspected heart attack and then tested positive for Covid. This evil man murdered at least 13 women and has been at her Majesty's leisure since 1981. I am not going to get all political here but we have all been paying for this for nearly 40 years. A lot of good things could have been purchased with the amount of cash it has taken to keep him alive behind bars.
End of rant.

It's been really mild all week. There have been some sunny days with lots of fog and mist in the early mornings because the ground is so warm. With the central heating on in the evenings, the house is very warm at bedtime and I need the ceiling fan on every night. I would switch the heating off completely but Julie feels the cold and sits all day huddled up. So whilst she is wrapped up in a blanket on the sofa, I wander around in my underwear. Even Peter has stopped dressing for bed as if he is on a Polar expedition.

I receive a lot of messages this week from my friends in Vietnam worrying about me again because they know the virus is on the rise again here. I send them all messages that I have barricaded myself in the house, I am not going out at all and have no chance of catching the virus.
I know it's not true but it gives them one less thing to worry about.

Peter, Julie & I spend part of the weekend discussing the merits of decomposing toilets versus marine toilets for the boat and researching them on the Internet. This is a very serious matter, but there was much hilarity during the discussions. They will need to get this sorted out before Peter and I go out there for a holiday, Peter will spend a lot of time sitting on the loo.
What is it with us British that we find it so amusing talking about poo and wee?

My favourite TV programme, 'Strictly', is now in Covid disarray. The female couple have pulled out due to Katya Jones testing positive. The 'It Takes Two' presenter, Rylan Clark-Neal, is under quarantine at home as he has had contact with an infected person. And now one of the judges, Motsi Mabusi, has gone home to Germany to deal with an emergency and will miss two weeks of the show as she will have to quarantine for 14 days when she returns.
The good news is that the fabulous Anton Du Bec will temporarily be on the judging panel, and on the brilliant Saturday show he goes down a storm.
Please can we keep him?

Des O'Connor died this week. Peter spent part of his weekend replaying clips of the Morecambe and Wise show featuring Des. Peter idolised Eric Morecambe as he was a huge Luton Town supporter and he spends all Sunday afternoon chuckling away to himself in front of his laptop.

Those of you who have no idea who I am talking about, look them up - they were a British Institution and at one time had the most popular TV programme in the whole country. Mind you there was only 4 channels on the TV at that time to choose from.

Peter has lost his patience with the consultancy process for my job, he can see that despite putting on a brave face it is starting to get me down and I am feeling quite ill with the stress of it all. I am certainly ill several times a day in the toilet, (Too Much Information as they say). Peter says the consultations should have been halted two weeks ago when the furlough scheme was extended, they have no reason to make us redundant now.
Watch this space.

Monday 16th November to Sunday 22nd November

So it's D-Day and we will learn our fate in the office.
Hurrah, the redundancy consultation has been paused until the end of February.
Boo & hiss we will then have to go through the consultation process all over again.
In the meantime we are being re-deployed to the top secret Vaccination Programme. It is so secret that it was on the news and in all the papers on Tuesday. The press were very well informed, they even had a copy of the job descriptions, someone has been very indiscreet.

Unfortunately no-one can give us any details of how/what/when/where these 'temporary' jobs will occur and we have to wait until later in the week for any details.
They are still adamant that one of the offices will have to close down in the Spring to save money and reading between the lines they definitely want it to be us. But we will not go without a fight and I think that is the problem. Some of us have forgotten more about this business than some of the other staff know and I don't think they like it. They would rather have a completely new workforce that they can mould and shape to their way of working rather than an experienced but extremely vocal and opinionated team.
Four menopausal women in one office is more than they can bear and they hate our guts.

The short straw goes to our Office Manager who will be the sole person dealing with small events for the whole country whilst we are seconded, she will have to do everything. Despite there already being 300 events booked for 2021 the management are adamant that we won't have any work for the next six months. Not sure who is feeding them that incorrect information but I have a feeling that our Office Manager has been stitched up like a kipper.

But it gives us the rest of us a bit of breathing space and another five months salary in the bank before we have to go through this wretched process again.

At this current Covid time who knows what will happen next week let alone in February?

We all receive a copy of a strange and messy document listing all our private and confidential proposals and questions with answers attached regarding the redundancy consultation. The way it has been written you can work out who has said what, not sure if that is appropriate with each persons individual consultation supposedly being private to them.

Whoever wrote it obviously got bored towards the end of the document and has given the same answer to about 20 of the suggestions! Somehow even with all this spiel they have still not answered a lot of the questions and have missed a huge chunk out of one of my proposals. We are not too worried at the moment, we file it all away and then we will just ask all the same questions again in February.

Did you know that on Tuesday 17th November it is a whole year since the first case of Covid was revealed in China. Blimey where has that 365 days gone?

There is talk circulating in the media that we will be able to see family at Christmas but might have to pay in January with another Lockdown. What is the point of getting it under control in early December to then let it go rife again over Christmas week? I don't see any sense it that.

Peter has been to Belfast overnight (he is still on part time furlough) and got stopped by the border police on the way back. Fortunately he is still working some of the time and the business has not had to completely shut down like last time. Apparently if you are a shop that sells any item of ironmongery you can stay open. So as all the shoe repair shops sell padlocks they can keep going. Good thing really as so many of these shops are 'Independents' and will not survive another closure.

So on Thursday we have our first meeting with the Vaccination Project Leads. It is actually the first work meeting that I have attended during this Covid 2020 nightmare that I came out feeling positive about. We are asked to choose what we would like to do and also what hours we would prefer as this is going to be a 7 day week operation. Our present management don't get a look in or get to offer any opinion - we are allowed to choose.

Friday and I am off to the supermarket again. It's coming to something when the highlight of the week is a trip to Asda. My mother gets excited at going to Wilko's, my sister prefers Morrisons. Oh the thrill of it all! God we are all such saddo's.

Anna rang me and I was put onto video to see La Vie who is walking now and was chattering away, completely oblivious to the financial difficulties faced by her parents. I tentatively offer to send Anna some money. I've tried this before and knew I was on a sticky wicket, she refuses point blank - again. Funnily enough I get the same response when I offer Greenie money as well. Despite what a lot of people secretly believe, these particular Vietnamese don't actually want anything from me except our friendship.
It leaves a lovely feeling but also a bit worrying that they won't let me help them in any way.

On Saturday we went to help with LTFC behind closed doors (at least we went out). I had a long chat with my Paramedic friend about the vaccinations. He says all the sceptics who say it hasn't been tested properly, it's too fast, it won't work, they are not going to have it etc etc, should sit and watch someone seriously ill with Covid and listen to them trying to breathe, it would change their mind instantly.
I would be first in the queue for the jab if it was offered to me.

It's Sunday and Julie and I go out to M&S to buy some Christmas cards.
Is it classed as an essential item?
Yes, it is something to relieve the mind numbing boredom of being locked indoors and at least all the relatives will get their cards early rather than on the 24th December.

Monday 23rd November to Sunday 29th November

I feel like I am losing my marbles today.We have still not been officially seconded over to the Vaccination Programme and are stuck in limbo work land. I know there are people out there who would only be glad to be at home doing nothing on full pay, but I don't function like that, it's really not my bag. It's not good for me to sit and twiddle my thumbs especially when I know there is a humongous task waiting for us, I am climbing the walls with boredom.

I decide that I will try to volunteer to assist with the Vaccination Programme (a completely separate issue from my paid job) and end up being sent 12 emails asking me for a reference, DBS, occupational health details and asking for a phone interview. I am already a member of staff and have been a volunteer for 30 years, yet I am being asked to give information already recorded on the HR system. At the end of a long and frustrating day trying to sign up I am told that I have been unsuccessful only to then be told I have been sent the wrong email (twice) and they do actually want me.
God help us, who knows what will happen when we try to take on 30,000 people from outside the organisation, the process will be endless.

Peter is working at home today, so along with Julie, there are three of us trying to run all our devices off of our already slow Internet.
It is computer hell.

There were rumours circulating at the weekend that Boris is going to extend the Lockdown, but luckily it looks like fake news. Boris calls another press conference and confirms that the Lockdown will definitely finish on 2nd December. Depending on where you live and how high the infections are in your area will depend on how much freedom you will get. Even football matches can have small crowds back. As the rate in Luton is so high I cannot imagine that LTFC will be allowed any spectators but somehow they are. There will be a stricter three tier system in place and everyone will still have to adhere to the rule of no more than three bubbles gathering together. So it's looking like no large family get togethers for Christmas.
I bet some people are actually relieved they haven't got to have a house full of people they can't stand and only see once a year. They can sit in front of the telly in their pyjamas, stuff their face full of Quality Street and get pissed like other people do.

Excellent news is that the Oxford (Astra Zeneca) Covid vaccine has proved 70% successful against keeping the dreaded virus at bay and hopefully will be rolled out in the new year, pending license.
A few interesting facts were brought to the fore by this announcement:
  1. Apparently the current flu vaccine that everyone is clamouring for is only 50% successful at keeping flu away, so this new jab has better

coverage over the Coronavirus than the flu jab has over flu. Does that make sense?

2. The reason that this drug is being produced and tested so fast is purely down to the enormous amount of money that has been thrown at it. Normally new drugs can take years to get tried and tested because each laboratory will be on a budget or rely on funding. This isn't happening with this virus, it is so important to get this vaccine out to the public that funding is not an issue.

3. The Government ordered 400 million doses of the vaccine last March before it was even invented. (This is one thing you cannot criticise them for).

4.The other plus is that it does not need to be kept at Arctic temperatures, which would need specialist equipment to store it, and is much cheaper than some other vaccines that have been created across the world.

Trust the British to come up with something cheap.

A brand new Samsung Galaxy phone has arrived from work which I will need for my new role, followed three days late by a brand new laptop computer. Peter and Julie chuckle quietly to each other, they are very aware that I have only just mastered my iPhone.

Fortunately they help me set both devices up and I am ready and raring to go.

Restaurants are going to be allowed to open next week with rigid rules regarding alcohol and 'substantial' meals. This starts a British debate as to what constitutes a substantial meal. Funnily a Scotch egg does?

I have managed to book a night out with Julie next week before she leaves me and flies off to start her new life in Greece.

The poor publican in our village has lost the will to live and has put out a message that they are not going to reopen in the near future, the rules are so restrictive they are not going to bother, not even for Christmas. What a crying shame.

I receive a really sad message from Greenie, her exact words were that she and her husband were having 'rifts'. She has no close family, lives with her husbands parents, has no job, no money and doesn't know what to do about her marital situation. I try to explain the term' sit it out'. It is a long and complicated conversation due to the language barrier and I advise her not to do anything rash. No-one is in any position to do anything at the moment.

I think she understands.

So as at the end of November there have been recorded 74 million cases and 1.6 million deaths across the planet. Back in my Vietnamese spiritual home there have been 1400 cases and still only 35 deaths. The death rate for only today in the UK was 610, which is the highest day since March. I just can't get my head around this enormous figure and it is very alarming, yet the Government is allowing everything to open up next week and families will be able to get together at Christmas over a five day period.

I hope and pray we won't all have to pay for this with another Lockdown in the new year when the Winter flu hits the population along with another rise in Covid.

And bloody hell, everyone has gone mad with the Christmas lights on their houses and in the gardens, it's like a magical fairy land in our village.

Shame, I'm just not in the mood.

What makes you different or weird, that's your strength - Meryl Streep

11. Christmas

Monday 30th November to Sunday 6th December

So the great day has dawned and I am now part of the Vaccination Programme to save humanity. Vaccination Support Team to be correct. We are there to answer any queries or complaints regarding the enrolment process. Except we have no idea of what we are doing and are flailing around in the dark at the moment until we get bedded in properly. The aim is to get 30,000 volunteers enrolled, interviewed, vetted and trained to assist with the Covid vaccinations scheduled across the country throughout next year. The figures are huge and it is a mammoth task.

The Pfizer Vaccine has arrived in the UK and looks like it will be rolled out to the elderly as early as next week. 800,000 vaccines are on their way here with another 40 million due in the new year, that's enough for 20 million people as everyone needs two jabs. Even her Majesty will be having hers before Christmas. The main problem with this Pfizer vaccine is that is has to be kept a sub zero temperatures so the storage is really important. Having done my online training, I realise that the fridge is a critical and vitally important key to keeping this particular vaccination fresh.
Who will be the first numpty to pull the plug out to put the kettle on or charge up their mobile?

The Lockdown was finally over on Wednesday and it seemed like everyone celebrated by going out shopping. Julie had to go to Milton Keynes for a Covid test, before her flight to Greece on Friday, she said it was heaving with shoppers and the car parks were full to bursting. On a more serious note we then spent a very tense 36 hours waiting for her test results. She didn't get them until past midnight and she was leaving our house at 8am. If she had tested positive, she would not have been able to fly and all their plans would have fallen apart like a pack of cards.

Poor old Debenhams, who are in financial trouble yet again, have started massively discounting their goods and there were queues around the block to get in. Everyone is panicking about their Christmas shopping. The biggest queue's were reserved for Primark - I still don't get that - WHY?

So Julie and I went for our big night out. I can't really say say it was our final night out when in fact it was the only night out since she came here. It was nice to get dressed up and put on a bit of slap. It was partially spoilt by having to wear a mask to get in and out of the restaurant and to go the toilet. I thought it would be heaving, this place is always fully booked and it's normally difficult to get a table, but it was half empty. It's a really funky place set up in an old Victorian ballroom but as you couldn't stand at the bar and the tables were so far apart, there was no interaction with anyone else so the atmosphere was a little flat. We made the most of it by getting total wasted, I can't even remember Peter picking us up, the journey home in the car or getting into bed.

I'm trying to cover up how upset I am that she is going, it has been great having someone else in the house and we have got on really well. It's a fabulous adventure for them but I will miss her like crazy. Sure enough when it is time for her to leave the next day, I am inconsolable and bawl my eyes out after she leaves.

There is a small black dog prowling around the house all day long.

I spend the weekend clearing out the spare room, doing 6 loads of washing and giving the house a really good clean. It takes me all day, I am absolutely knackered and have to spend all evening horizontal on the sofa with a glass of fizz. At least it stops me reflecting on how empty the house is and the black dog has gone back in its basket.

Monday 7th December to Sunday 13th December

Back on the menu this week is Brexit. They still can't agree, no change there then.
The hitch this time is something to do with fishing rights, I have lost the will to live with it all.
Also back on the menu is the R rate which is on the alarming rise again one week after the end of the previous Lockdown. Wales are already saying they will be going into another full Lockdown. Somehow Nottingham City Council approved a Christmas market in the city centre which was then so busy it had to be shut down after just one day. There was also allegedly a report that the council shut all the public toilets in the area and some people were urinating and defecating in the streets!
And wouldn't you know it, the gleeful press is full of two people who suffered a reaction to their first vaccination. Both of these patients had pre-existing allergies and had their own auto injectors to treat

themselves and were fine. Strangely enough there were no reports of the figures for how many people have been given the vaccine successfully who haven't reacted. Funny that.

Looking at the current list of criteria for receiving the jab I am in 8th position as I am over 56 years old. So sometime next Summer then?

Boris makes a big announcement that all families can meet up with three bubbles over a five day period during the Christmas holiday as long as everyone is careful. It causes a bit of confusion with some families. One of my friends has to sit and draw a diagram to explain how it works to her husband, he thinks they can meet up with two different bubbles each day. NO, the rules are that only three bubbles can mix over the five days. It causes a lot of family arguments as to who is seeing who (not in our house though). Do you invite grandparents or siblings, do you have your children's partners or do you invite your in-laws? I cannot comprehend any of this, the R rate is on the rise, let's not make it worse by allowing everyone to mix for what is only a few days. Peter and I have no such problem, no-one in my family celebrates Christmas so there will be just be the two of us and Peters mum.

The Office Manager at work (the one who got stitched up like a kipper) is giddy with excitement, this is what she has been hoping and praying for. She can now go to Scotland to spend Christmas with her daughter and grandson, and she goes off on a massive spending spree to Debenhams.

Blimey it's been a busy old week at work on this new role, I even had to work on Sunday morning. The amount of emails I have answered which could have been avoided are too numerous to count, mainly system or user error. I feel like we are fighting fire with fire. Whenever I get asked about a technical error it is like speaking a foreign language to me; I have only just figured out how to use the Amazon button on the TV remote control. Oh but what joy I experience when I answer someones system error email and they get it to work, I feel like an IT wizard. Peter chuckles softly to himself in the corner.

I actually put up our Christmas tree on Friday and sprinkled some decorations around the house, last year I was not in the mood and could not be bothered. A lot of the villagers have really gone to town with the lights on their houses, - I manage a light up polar bear on the porch. I have some new multi coloured tree lights and all the baubles I have collected over the years and my tree looks really lovely in the corner of our extension. I send a picture of it to all my Vietnamese friends and they are all duly impressed. They are all OK but still out of work, at least I know they will not go hungry even if they have no money, the Vietnamese Government would not let that happen.

I go out Christmas shopping, I don't have much to get and am usually finished by the end of November but this year I am way behind. I head off to the Galleria at Hatfield which turns into a disappointing morning. I haven't been there for a year and at least half of the shops are boarded up and empty, all a result of the Covid situation. I come home pretty much empty handed.
When I get home, my sister and her husband turn up with fish and chips for lunch.
It is really lovely to see them and they stay for the afternoon. My sister and are are so unalike in many ways but we do have the same sense of humour and we both cry with laughter over a joke I try to tell her.
It's only when they have left that I realise we have actually broken the Covid rules. I thought you could have another bubble of people in your house but no, not in this area (Tier 2). Oops, sorry!

Sad news this week, the glorious Dame Barbara Windsor died in a nursing home where she had been since July suffering from dementia. A tiny feisty woman who was a massive star of the Carry on films and a brilliant actress in Eastenders, it made me feel really sad.

We went to Luton Town football on Saturday, they had allowed 1000 fans in to watch. It does make a huge difference to the atmosphere to have a real crowd and we win 3-0. No sulking from Peters side of the sofa tonight, he is elated.

It's also the semi final of 'Strictly' and I sit and watch agog with excitement.
The phone rings three times during the show which I refuse to answer. Peter sits in front of his laptop with his head phones on watching Lutons three goals on a repeat loop. And he cooks the tea. And washes up. Result.

I get a very odd and strange message from someone I have absolutely no wish to see or speak to ever again, who suddenly wants to meet up with me. I seek advice from my close friends and husband who all tell me to ignore it, so I delete it from my phone. I suppose some people have had nearly a whole year to reflect on their previous actions and now want some absolution.
I'm sorry but not this person, not now, or in a million years.

Monday 14th to Sunday 20th December

Bloody hell, on Monday morning the email box is full again with people trying to assist with this Vaccine Programme. The computer systems are not working properly due to the huge volume of inquiries. We understandably are starting to get some very cross and angry emails from some very frustrated people. Unfortunately we do not have any answers to their queries as the Project team are struggling to sort these errors out and we end up having to apologise to everyone and file the emails to await a reply.

There is also a grand selection of weird emails from the public quoting the bible, talking about Armageddon, querying the safety and ingredients of the vaccines, wanting to know how many animals the vaccine has been tested on, asking to see all the Pfizer testing papers and one particularly lovely message that told us to go F..k ourselves. Very cheerful and very helpful in the most difficult year anyone can remember since the war. Thanks for that, much appreciated.

Donald Trump has eventually conceded that he has lost his Presidency. It has only taken him four weeks to accept that he lost!

Julie has finally finished work and is now officially retired. They are in full Lockdown in Greece too and therefore cannot get to their boat. To top it off it has rained torrentially all week and they have been stuck indoors in a one bed flat that they are renting. At least she is there and they are together, it's got to be better than being here.

I manage to finish my Christmas shopping and get most of the food stuff done too, I just need to pick up a few bits next week. All the presents are wrapped and are under the tree. Looking at the tree I feel tinged with sadness that there is nothing for my girls and their children in Vietnam, I would gladly swap every single one of my presents so that they could have something, but it's not to be.

Not this year anyway.

I have spent the afternoon making a huge ice-cream Christmas pudding that would feed 20 people, Peter and I will be eating it for weeks. The freezer is stuffed to the brim and the garage is full of booze.

Yep I am ready, I am feeling good, bring it on.

There is huge speculation mounting this week that there will be another Lockdown after Christmas, the R rate is rising rapidly and there is talk of a new strain of the virus. The press are having another field day. Sure enough on Friday a huge part of the country is put into Tier 3, Bedfordshire amongst them.

At the weekend there is even worse news to come.

On Saturday Boris calls a press conference at tea time and basically cancels Christmas.

Just like that.

8 days after he said everyone could see their families over a five day period (which I always thought was a bit rash) he's changed his mind. Not only that, some of the country is moving up into Tier 4 with a hard set of restrictions, Bedfordshire amongst them. London is closed down for the foreseeable future.

The worst thing about the new rules is that anyone in tier 4 cannot mix with any other bubble over Christmas, they can see no-one. You shouldn't really even be driving in to a tier 4 area unless you have a very good reason. If you are in tier three you can see one other bubble on Christmas Day (no-one can stay overnight) but the Government would prefer you didn't mix with anyone at all. Lots of my friends now cannot see their children or grandchildren and people are not happy.

After being told it was possible, people have made travel plans, spent money on presents and provisions and now it is all scrapped.

It certainly looks like Covid is again on the rampage and I understand the restrictions but they could have stopped this a week ago and not got peoples hopes up. 8 days ago the public would have been disappointed but maybe more accepting of the situation, now some people are boiling mad and extremely upset.

I am not a political animal and think whoever is in power at the moment has a mammoth task on their hands. All parties would have made mistakes along the way, but this is a ridiculous cruel turnaround and could have been avoided if they had not promised anything in the first place.

I do get it, but it now needs to be enforced in certain places, bring in the Army I say. As Peter and I left LTFC on Saturday we drove through an area of Luton where all the shops were open and we could see no masks on anyone. Shame on you.

It's called Habituation. This is when we get bored of stuff and react less to a stimuli after repeated presentations. Basically everyone has Pandemic fatigue, we are all fed up with it and the repeated Lockdowns. Some people don't believe it exists as it has not affected them in any way and are wanting to carry on as normal.

On Saturday evening at 9pm I receive a phone call that my training day that was booked for Sunday morning has been cancelled and could I please rebook. I feel like complaining to the Support Team but the email will only end up with me answering myself. I rebook for 30th December.

Looking at the figures worldwide there have been 77 million cases and 1.7 million deaths. The UK had its highest day of new infections on Sunday with 36,000 new cases. We have lost over 67,000 people in this country from Covid and 2 million people have tested positive. The USA has lost 300,000 people.

I have never been very worried about catching it. Apart from the menopause, which contrary to popular belief is not an illness, I am very healthy, but this weekend I do feel a frisson of fear go up my spine.

At least one good thing happens this week - Bill Bailey aged 55, beats a group of talented youngsters to win the Strictly Glitterball. I was in total heaven.

Hurrah, there is hope for all of us.

On Sunday after the new restrictions announcement, the railways and Heathrow airport are rammed with people trying to get home for Christmas which as previously stated has been officially quashed this year by the Government.

I watch lots of cars coming in and out of our road with families unloading presents on their doorsteps, it's gonna be such a weird holiday.

Monday 21st to Sunday 27th December

Monday morning and there are three of us working out of our team of 8 (the others are on pre-booked holiday) and we are overrun with emails. Most of them are of the same theme: the systems are not working. We are all working from home now, not something I particularly relish, for the next few months. And guess what? The whole programme is now working on a skeleton staff for the next two weeks over the holidays!

By Tuesday it's so bad that I decide to put a call in to one of the Project Managers to report our concerns. When we opened up in the morning there were 500 unopened emails, the three of us work all day and at 5pm there are still 505 new messages (a drop in the ocean as we later discover). We cannot stop the flow. Most of them are technical issues that none of us are qualified to answer and need to be rectified. Fast.

All non-essential foreign travel has been banned and the ports have been closed for a few days. The French send a team over to assist with testing all lorry drivers before they are allowed to continue on their journey into Europe and as usual all the roads are blocked near Dover. Nicola Sturgeon has confirmed all of Scotland will now go into tier 4 along with most of Southern England from 26th December. That will mean 24 million people are basically in a Lockdown again.

Apparently there is a virulent new strain of Covid which seems to have arrived into the UK from South Africa. Suddenly most countries and airlines that were still allowing flights to and from the UK have shut up shop and now will not allow entry.

The hospital figures are awful and make sombre reading, there has been a 57% rise in hospital admissions in the last week, that is the highest since April.

I am furiously tapping out answers to emails all day long but it is overwhelming. I am the last person to be working on Wednesday evening and when I close down there are 682 unanswered messages in the box. At this rate there will be several thousand by next week when there is another skeleton staff on. Oh and my training for 30th has also been cancelled and I have rebooked (again) for 9th January.

Another furious email goes off to myself!

I have a pounding headache and my eyes hurt. When I stop work at 6pm I go downstairs to find my mother in law installed on the sofa and I have to make polite conversation all evening when all I really want to do is go to sleep.

I end up getting slightly tipsy with Maureen and pass out on the sofa about 9pm.

Christmas Eve dawns, it has rained all week and there is water everywhere when we go for a walk over the fields. The mud is up to your crotch and we are all filthy when we get back, especially the dog who has changed colour from white to a scummy brown. The River Ouse runs through Bedfordshire into Cambridgeshire and there are flood warnings issued as the water rises to dangerous levels.

I had been feeling OK and quite positive until I speak separately by video to Anna, Greenie & Eric in Vietnam. I really shouldn't have done it, I am my own worse enemy.

Anna is selling flowers by the road side on Christmas day to earn a few quid, Greenie and Eric are not working at all. To see their little faces was heartbreaking and it basically sent me off into a dark place and lets the black dog well and truly out of it's kennel. Good old Danny - he didn't help the situation either. After not hearing from him for ages, he sends me numerous photos of Hoi An lit up with Christmas lights whilst he parties hard with his friends.

So it's Christmas Day and probably along with the rest of the population I can't say I feel very festive. The house looks lovely, I receive some beautiful presents, Peter cooks a delicious dinner and washes up (bonus), but I can't shake the blackness and numbness that is enveloping me. It's Maureen's first Christmas without her husband and I try to make an effort by putting on a nice dress and a load of slap but by lunchtime I cannot hold back the tears.
Why now, I had been doing so well recently?
I put it down to a slow build up over the last few months. Julie going to live in Greece, the whole shitty redundancy process, the overwhelming new job, Tier 4 restrictions, not seeing my friends or family, the mammoth vitally essential task of getting everyone in the UK vaccinated twice, the ongoing menopause and absolutely no chance of being able to go to Vietnam in the near future. Or anywhere else for that matter.
We end up watching my favourite film,'*White Christmas*' and then repeats of '*Top Gear*' on the TV. Peter thinks he is helping me when he puts the '*Vietnam Special*' on. That just about finishes me off and I retreat to bed leaving Peter and his mother watching ' *The Gentleman*'. It is a hilarious film, Hugh Grant is brilliant, but the foul language is off the scale.

Boxing Day and more of the same, there is water everywhere. The town centre of Bedford and the outlying villages are flooded and the council has set up two rest centres. The Covid restrictions are lifted for all people where the flood warning is high so obviously they all set off to stay with their relatives and the rest centre only gets 4 visitors all day. What a waste of time and effort!

Overnight there is a vicious storm. More rain and 90 mile winds hit the side of the house all night long. We sleep on the top floor of a three storey townhouse and it sounds like the roof is going to come off. I can't swap beds like I usually do because Maureen is in the spare bedroom. I contemplate sleeping downstairs in the lounge but all the duvets and blankets are underneath Maureen's bed so I just have to put up with the noise and I am awake all night long. The storm abates around 5am and when we eventually get up you would never know it had happened.

Peter takes Maureen home on Sunday, she lives near the river in Cambridgeshire and the water is flowing fast and high. I hope the flood defences hold up. That would be all she needs to find her mobile home floating away. Peter spends all afternoon with her setting up her Alexa (one of our presents to her) and fitting a new light in her bedroom. I stay at home having a bit of a tidy up wrapped in my total and overwhelming misery.

Monday 28th December to Thursday 31st December

A bit of good news early this week is that the Oxford-Astra Zeneca Vaccine should arrive and will be rolled out next week. The Government have ordered 100 million doses and the good thing is that it does not need to be kept at sub zero temperatures like the Pfizer one. The not so good news is that the scientists and Doctors have decided to try to get everyone done with one jab and wait 12 weeks until they have the second booster, it is supposed to be three weeks in between. This new variant is vicious and the thinking behind it is that at least more people will have some protection with the one dose.

I actually left the house to visit Homebase to buy some paint. There is not exactly going to be much to do in the next few weeks so I might as well paint the room Julie was using now that it is empty. I buy another tin of grey paint, out house is now painted predominantly 50 shades of grey or white, is that telling me something? It is the only room in our house that has not been decorated since we moved in 16 years ago and it desperately needs new carpet too. Each time I walk on it there is a crunching noise as the underlay disintegrates beneath my feet. But carpet is not deemed a necessity and everywhere is closed so it will have to wait.

On Tuesday it is Peters 55th Birthday and normally we would be seeing friends for drinks or a meal. So what do we do instead? We head off to Luton Town Football Club (no crowd allowed now under the latest rules), at least we will get to see a couple of friends over a cup of tea and a Jammy Dodger. I am returning from the ticket office to base with my friend Lisa when a panicky message comes from Peter over the radio that there is a huge fight going on outside the ground and could we return to help out. When we get back there is a lad on the ground covered in blood with stab wounds to his head. Our colleagues had locked themselves in the ticket office until the fight was over and there are now armed police everywhere.

Apparently 4 men carrying knives chased another man up the road who was armed with a baseball bat. After beating the shit out of him they scarpered off down an alley leaving the bleeding man and the assault weapon on the ground. They were obviously not criminal masterminds as it was all done in front of the Clubs CCTV cameras and the police have the whole thing on tape and know exactly who was involved and what happened.

It is also classed as attempted murder and the whole place is sealed off.

It made for an exciting start to the evening.

It also delays the start of the game so we don't get home until late.

The press are at it again and there are reports that the Nightingale hospitals are being un-mothballed and being readied for use. The press are also saying that there are no staff to man them because the NHS is completely overwhelmed with the normal Winter pressures and Covid, so I am not sure who I believe. But looking at the latest figures it could be true.

The rumour mill is at work talking about a new tier 5 which could be brought in the New Year which would mean another total Lockdown like we had last Spring.

It is certainly looking like the schools will be delaying the start of term, and upper schools are planning to test all students for Covid when classes resume.

More areas in England are going into tier 4 and now the whole of Ireland is in complete Lockdown. You can bet that we will follow suit at some point.

Mind you it looks like the post Brexit trade deal has been agreed at last and been approved by 521 votes to 73 in Parliament.

Thank god that's over but what happens now? How is it all going to work?

I've started painting the empty bedroom and Peter has been fitting a vanity unit and new bath panel in the top bathroom. It keeps us busy for a few hours and also keeps us off of the sofa and out of the drinks cupboard.

My drinking has gone through the roof again, I can actually drink a whole bottle of wine to myself along with a few espresso martinis in an evening and not feel drunk - just a bit tired. Along with the increasing size of my arse and spare tyre around my middle from the amount of chocolate I have been eating, I know I am not in a healthy zone.

I need to break this cycle and vow to diet properly in January.

Along with the rest of the UK population.

The New Years Honours are announced.

Lewis Hamilton and Sam Mendes have been knighted. Can't wait to see what outfit Sir Lewis wears to the palace. Olivia Newton John is made a dame. She's the one that they want!

So, 2020 has been the most boring year I have ever experienced, or most of us for that matter. What a waste of a whole year of our lives. The entire planet in meltdown due to some hungry Chinese person eating a bat.

From my own personal perspective, the menopausal symptoms are definitely starting to abate apart from the hot flushes and small bouts of depression. I've obviously got to suffer a bit more and wait a bit longer for those to go away.

I have managed to avoid going to the doctors for anything.

Peter and I have survived being stuck in the house together and only had a few rows earlier on, I think we have now reached a calm understanding.

It's too cold for the kid next door to play football in the garden.

I have redecorated most of the house and Peter has changed most of the bathroom fittings.

We still have our own teeth and hair.

My boobs are the biggest they have ever been and I could give a Page three model a run for her money. (Only on the boobs side, not unfortunately the rest of the body). I am not sure how women with enormous boobs cope, I don't know what to do with mine!

I am still employed and therefore still earning, so my bank balance is enormous.

Peter is still on part time furlough so he is still paying the bills.

I've had some lovely feedback and sold quite a few copies of my first book. I now have the tidy sum of £98.42 in royalties - JK Rowling, eat your heart out!

I have learnt that clothes, make up, jewellery and shoes don't account for diddly squat if you cannot go anywhere to wear them.

My friends and family are all safe, there are at least some things to be grateful for.

As of 31st December 2020, Covid is out of control across the globe and dangerously on the rise again in the UK. There were 57,000 new cases here yesterday and 600 deaths. Across the rest of the world there have been 86.9 million cases and 1.86 million deaths. There is now talk of another new variant from Brazil along with the South African one.

The world economy is in meltdown and millions have lost their livelihoods.
Everyone on the planets future is resting on the vaccine and getting it out to everyone as soon as possible, which is going to be an overwhelming task.

Until that happens I fear for the next few months.

Be a first rate version of yourself instead of a second rate version of somebody else - Judy Garland

12. A New Year, a New start 2021?

Friday 1st to Sunday 3rd January 2021

We spend a quiet weekend, there is literally nowhere you can go and no-one you can visit. I take all the Christmas decorations down, it's funny how bare it all looks when they are gone, and spend the rest of the time painting the spare room. Peter amuses himself by pottering around in the garage and takes a few rides out on his motorbike. All very boring and mundane. The football at Luton is cancelled today, something to do with some of the players having tested positive for Covid!

There is a huge debate in the news about delaying and staggering the start of the new school term. It is finally decided on Sunday morning that the upper schools will not go back until the 18th but the lowers schools will return on Monday 4th January.

Somehow I manage to talk Peter into watching the Korean Oscar winning film '*Parasite*' with me on Prime. You may recall I watched it what seems like a lifetime ago on the flight to Vietnam last year. I thoroughly enjoy it but he is completely bemused and thinks the film is truly awful. It shows how two people watching the same thing can come away with such differing opinions. He makes me swear never to make him watch it again. Next time he annoys me I might watch it again.

It's been cold outside but I manage to take a walk every day, it really does help to clear the head. It doesn't help when we somehow manage to drink 3 bottles of rose wine on Sunday evening which gives me insomnia and I am awake all night.
That finally does it, Monday morning I am giving up alcohol.

Monday 4th to Sunday 10th January

When I log into our email box on Monday morning, sitting alone in my snug little study at home, there are over 3000 messages waiting. The team valiantly try to answer them but the tide is against us and we are overwhelmed. When I shut down, after 8 of us have worked our socks off all day, there are over 4000 unopened messages. It is like a tsunami and we cannot stop the enormous waves.

I certainly picked the wrong day to quit drinking.

Boris has called a news briefing for 8pm. Oh dear this cannot be good news.

It's not.

This new Brazilian variant is 50-70% more transmissible than the last one. There are 27,000 people in hospital with Covid which is 40% higher than back in April and deaths are up by 20%. The NHS is overwhelmed already with the Winter pressures and the figures can only get worse. If we keep going at this rate, in two weeks time the hospital admissions will be even greater, so the Government must take some serious steps right now to try to avoid this getting any worse.

So from Wednesday we are in another full National Lockdown and must not leave home except :

To shop for food

To go to work if it is not possible to work from home.

To take exercise

To obtain medical assistance

To escape domestic abuse (which after getting though Christmas with these dark cold nights I imagine will now go through the roof).

All clinically vulnerable people must start shielding again.

All shops/hairdressers/gyms/beauticians will be closed

All schools, colleges and universities will be closed, except for key workers children. This is after they said yesterday that they wanted to do everything in their power to keep the schools open. So after 1 day back and two weeks holiday, all the kids are now off until at least the end of February to be educated remotely and home schooled by their parents. All exams will be cancelled this Summer.

OH MY GOD - Please not again.

We are back to Groundhog Day, back to where we were 9 months ago, but this time it's even worse.

The only beacon of light that is shining brightly is the hopeful success of the Covid vaccinations. Boris is stating that they hope to get everyone in the top 4 groups inoculated by February. This would be all people in care homes, anyone over 70, all frontline health workers and the clinically unwell or vulnerable. Blimey that's a big ask. Then they will all need another jab three weeks later to boost the immunity.

So far 1 million people have received the vaccination.

Boris urges everyone to pull together and whatever criticisms you have of the Governments handling of this, he is right. There have been

58,784 new cases alone today, it's not showing any sign of slowing down. London is entirely in it's grip and is basically closed for business. It has dawned on me that the <u>ONLY</u> way out of this hideous situation is to get us all vaccinated and strangely it urges me on as I plough my way through our thousands of emails.

The only businesses that must be rubbing their hands together and chortling with glee are the supermarkets. Figures released this week showed that they are all making mega profits and over the Christmas period the British public spent more than ever.
Bet most of it was on booze.
Unfortunately it hits Peters business again; he is back on furlough and stuck indoors with me most days. At least I get a cup of tea at regular intervals.
Mid week the new cases in the UK hits over 60,000 with a record number of deaths in a single day.
Could things look any more dismal?

America is in the news again. Trump supporters storm Congress protesting that he has been cheated out of the Presidency. Of course he is loving the attention and is all over social media with his vitriol. The riot police are brought in and 4 people are shot dead. How did they get inside the Whitehouse in the first place? This should be the most secure building in the world, it's not like you can just leave the door on the latch. The cheerful news is that Trump has been banned from social media until his Presidency is over for his comments.
Thank God for small mercies.

There was a real comical moment when I had a TEAMS meeting on Friday morning. Peter and I had only just got up after a long lie in. I accidentally switched the camera on and everyone saw Peter and myself faffing around in our dressing gowns.
Oh how they laughed!

It has been absolutely freezing this week, on Saturday it did not get above minus 2 degrees all day and the damp fog never cleared. That was very unfortunate as I actually went for my training day (not cancelled this time) and we had to keep the windows and doors open to let the 'Covid' air blow through.
Even the hottest woman in the world felt cold and had to lay on the sofa wrapped in a blanket for the rest of the evening when she got home (Me).

In Madrid of all places they have had freak weather conditions and heavy snow. No sign of any snow here, it's just grey and dreary.

I finished all the painting on Sunday. I can't do anything else until the shops reopen and I can buy some new carpet. That's it. I now have nothing outside of work except this book to occupy my time for the next two months. Fortunately I have managed to volunteer on my day off next week at the Vaccination Centre that is opening in Stevenage on Monday.
So I am working 5 full days, volunteering for 1 day and doing my household chores for the other.
Can't say that is the life I imagined for myself.

Monday 11th to Sunday 17th January

On Monday morning, the news is full of the 7 Vaccination Centres that opened today across England. Birmingham, London, Stevenage, Bristol, Manchester, Newcastle & Epsom all opened their doors to the 80's plus to get their jabs. Bristol and Tottenham have offered their football grounds up as new venues and many other places will be opening up throughout the coming months. The Governments target is to get 14 million people inoculated by February.
Peter was at Stevenage for the opening and will be there most of the week. He said they had a few teething issues but by the second day it worked perfectly. If you listened to the press coverage you would think it had been a complete disaster. The TV coverage showed queues of people standing outside in the cold. This was mainly because people had turned up willy nilly without appointments and caused a huge backlog, not any fault of the staff at the centre (just so you know for the record).
The good thing was that Peter had his first vaccination whilst he was there. Well, there has to be some sort of bonus for giving up your free time to help!
The downside was that he did have some side effects and didn't feel very well the day after and lay on the sofa wrapped up in a blanket feeling very sorry for himself. I stayed out of his way in my office - tap, tap, tapping on the key board all day long.

The quicker we get this big job done the better, the figures this week are really grim. New infections are hitting 60,000 each day. On Wednesday the deaths were 1564, which is higher than any day in the first Lockdown last Spring. In fact it is more deaths than Australia have had as a whole since the outbreak began. There are now 30,000 people in hospital with Covid which is a rise of 80% since Christmas, and probably down to everyone who broke the rules over the Yuletide period.

Anna's been on at me again today. The Vietnamese news is full of this new Covid variant coming in from Brazil and she is terrified for me. I keep telling her that I have hardly left the house since before Christmas and have seen no-one and been nowhere, but it is falling on deaf ears. I really think she believes if I leave the house and breathe in the outside air I will drop down dead.
She also complains about how cold it is in Vietnam and sends me pictures of her and La Vie wrapped up in heavy coats and blankets. It's a balmy 17 degrees !

Donald Trump has made the news again. He is the first President in history to be impeached for a second time. He is charged with insurrection and if found guilty will not be able to hold any sort of office in Government again.
I expect it will all be someone else's fault !

So at the weekend the Government decided to close all the travel corridors.
At long last.
Sorry, but this should have happened right at the beginning, it's a bit late now to start getting this ambitious, the disease is unrestrained in our country and we have several new variants that have been brought in.
All arriving travellers into the UK will now have to prove they have had a negative Covid test 72 hours before departure and will have to self isolate for ten days. All travellers from South Africa, Portugal and South America are totally banned from travelling here.

A group of 72 professional tennis players on their way to the Australian Open are all now quarantined at the Grand Hyatt in Melbourne for the next 14 days and are not allowed to train. I bet they are all going mad, climbing the walls. Mind you not such a bad hotel to isolate in, it's hardly Beryl and Sid's B&B.

I am beginning to get cabin Fever. I have been trying to get out everyday for a walk but get so wrapped up in work that it's sometimes dark before I give myself a breather. This is unusual for me, I cannot seem to switch off from my job. Outside it is typical British weather; wet, windy but fairly mild for January. Up North they have had bad snow, not here, it is just grey gloom.

The big day out dawned, I was off to the Vaccination Centre in Stevenage. First shock of the day was getting up at 6am, I haven't got up that early all year! I was going to see what the fuss was all about. Second shock of the day was having to have a Lateral flow test; sticking a long cotton bud up your nose doesn't half make you cough. Negative, thank goodness.

Then into the Vaccination hall itself. It was separated into three parts, arrivals, vaccinations and aftercare. I have to say we spent the majority of the day cleaning the seats after people left but it was a strangely rewarding experience. Not quite sure if I really needed to do 14 hours online training and a half day practical session to be qualified to wipe chairs but it is what it is.

The joy and relief of some of these people, some who had not left their homes since last March, to at last get the vaccination and hopefully a way back to seeing their friends and relatives was a beautiful thing. Some of them wanted to stay all day and chat. One old boy was showing me pictures of his dead wife and Peter got into a long conversation with a chap who was out in Malaya during the 2nd World War. There were two brothers who came in separately unaware they would both be there, who hadn't seen each other for nearly a year. Two old girls were dressed up in their best frocks for their big day out together, their first in 9 months. The funniest couple bought their lunch and a Thermos with them, along with a huge thick blanket. They had seen the News report on Monday and thought they would be waiting outside in the cold for hours. Whilst I was there the longest wait time was 10 minutes. It was extremely efficiently well run and the patients were delighted.

I can honestly say it was the best experience I had had in months, I've signed up for every Friday now until the end of February.

And the cherry on the cake? I got my jab before I left for the day. Bonus.

And another thing, lots of people including Peter, had some side effects to the vaccine, not me - I was right as rain.

On Sunday I cleaned the house within an inch of its life, it is hard work with three floors to do and I eventually finished at 4pm. The willpower broke this evening and I had a glass of wine and a small piece of chocolate. Mind you after the week I had that's pretty admirable and I am very pleased with myself. Not drinking hasn't reduced the size of my arse though.

We spoke to Julie and Martin, they are still in indefinite Lockdown in Greece; not what they planned for their retirement.

Monday 18th to Sunday 24th January

In the last few weeks I have got into Ebay. I must be the last person in the whole country to enter this selling phenomenon. I am starting to shed things from the house, so far I have managed to sell two wool coats and a ski suit. I made a profit of £17. I know that's not a lot but it's more than I would get at a car boot sale. I have set up a savings account for Greenie and Anna, all the profit goes in there. I cannot get it to them but at least next time I see them I can give them both a big wad of cash. And they won't be able to refuse it if I put it into their hands. I have a huge mountain of things I want to get rid of and it's more money for them.

We have 7 new people join our virtual team at work and still we cannot stop the tide of emails. There is just no let up. I am worn out this week, apparently we are on target to have answered 40,000 emails by the end of the month, along with the difficult phone calls we are making. I have square eyes, a permanent headache and am answering emails in my sleep. I feel like I have answered every one 40,000 messages.
Back down on the ground, out in the centres, things are shaping up but no-one is admitting that our application process is a bit of a nightmare. We still cannot answer some of the questions, and now everyone wants to know how they book shifts. Basically the computer system doesn't work properly for everyone and some areas are having to do it manually by spreadsheet. They have had to bring in more temporary admin staff to help with this supposedly all singing and dancing App. It also does not work internally on anything except a company laptop or phone. Last year the company had a phone/computer amnesty to try and save money, now they are buying Tech willy nilly for this operation.

I get a very strange message out of the blue, through LinkedIn, from a former colleague I used to work with in my last shitty job. It is something to do with her taking our former employers to court regarding their treatment of her when they locked her in an office and refused to let her out. She wants me to write a statement of what it was like to be a woman working for them for her hearing. I can't say I really want to get involved, I have left them far behind me.
But I will say they were probably one of worst companies I have ever worked for and nothing would ever surprise me if they are found guilty.

There is huge security in Washington for Joe Bidens inauguration on Wednesday. He will be the 46th President to be sworn in. Trump has flounced out of the Whitehouse without a backward glance and flown to his luxurious Florida home and is not attending the ceremony. He will be the first ex President to miss an inauguration since 1869. Honestly he is like a large, spoilt child who doesn't want to play anymore. Mind you his wife looks delighted to be leaving, she was wearing dark glasses so the press couldn't see the glee in her eyes.

Joe Biden spends his first day in office undoing most of Trumps policies.

There are ominous skies this week, the weather is awful. Another storm rages throughout Thursday night and there are 200 flood mornings from the East Midlands right up to the Lake District, the rest of the country is under a blanket of snow.

Just what everyone doesn't need at the moment is to have their homes flooded and all the farmers livestock to be stranded.

Someone up above really hates us.

Back in October 2019, 39 dead bodies were found in the back of a lorry in Essex. They were a group of Vietnamese who had paid big sums of money (huge for a Viet) to unscrupulous people to bring them to the UK. They had been promised a pot of gold at the end of the rainbow but died of suffocation and hypothermia in transit. The people traffickers who smuggled them into the Country have been found guilty of 39 counts of manslaughter and sentenced to long imprisonments.

I remember reading about this horrible story, it sent shivers up my spine. They were simple people from the villages not the big cities, thinking they would have a better life here. Their families would have saved for years to scrape together the money to send them here.

What a terrible tragedy and waste of life.

Boris is back on the TV again. The Government are obviously getting a bit of backlash over the vaccinations and whether we should really be waiting 12 weeks to get the second one. All the Scientists and Doctors are debating the subject.

I don't know who to believe.

The arguments for :it will be more beneficial for a patient to have the second jab within the 3-6 weeks as per the original guidance and get much greater protection.

The arguments against : are that if we inject everyone once, the majority will achieve some protection against the virus with up to 50% coverage. If we were to give everyone their second jab in the three week window it would mean more people would be waiting longer for their first one, leaving them still very open to pick up the infection in the mean time.

I am not very clever but this makes sense to me. Gathering from the news today these new variants from South Africa and South America are more likely to kill 14 people /100 rather than the original infection which would kill 10/100. At least everyone would have some sort of coverage. If they catch it they will more likely get flu like symptoms, be unwell and then recover, not die.

Depending on what you believe there is also a shortage of glass phials in Europe which is causing a delay in the Pfizer vaccine getting here. Smells like a Brexit backlash to me.

I am very bored and have proper cabin fever, I actually think I am going slightly mad. Going to the supermarket on Saturday afternoon was such a luxury to get out of the house after working all day, such a treat.

I know I am stressed at the moment as my night flushes have ramped up and I spend half the night awake laying in a pool of sweat **OR** I am answering emails in my sleep **OR** I am staring up at the ceiling listening to my husband snoring his head off.

I completely crack on Thursday evening and have two glasses of red wine and a huge bar of chocolate.

It's a short lived delight: it keeps me awake all night.

On Sunday it actually snowed, so everything looked very pretty from the sofa as I looked down the garden. I spoke to Anna and Greenie and showed them the snow, they are still shivering in temperatures of 20 degrees. I spent most of the day binge watching 8 episodes of "*Pillars of the Earth*' apart from a short interlude when Peter needed to watch Chelsea versus Luton in a round of the FA cup. He got so cross over one of the goals we had to turn it off to stop him hyperventilating. He then spent the rest of the day putting in remote control lights in the kitchen and bedroom so he can control everything from his phone.

If anything ever happens to him or he loses his phone, we will not be able to do anything inside our own house!

Monday 25th to Sunday 31st January

I managed to get out on Monday and did a lap of the village. It was extremely icy underfoot and I was very careful where I walked. Can you imagine falling over and breaking something at the moment and needing to go to A&E?

It doesn't even bear thinking about.

Mind you, doesn't it show your age when you start worrying about breaking your hip on a bit of ice? When you were younger you would run at it to see how far you could skid. Now I look like a dressage pony, daintily picking up my feet with every step.

There is a tiny bit of positivity this morning, the infection rate is showing some signs of slowing down, the infection rate has dropped slightly, this Lockdown is obviously staring to have some effect. The bad news is that Domestic violence, child abuse and the number of family murders have gone up.

Apparently the USA have now passed over 26 million cases. From their first case last January it took 311 days to reach 13 million.
It then only took 64 days for that figure to double.

There has been a big row regarding the Covid vaccine being sent to Northern Ireland. The EU wants to tighten its controls on the vaccine entering NI in a bid to control the jabs being exported from the EU to prevent shipment to the UK mainland. Basically it's Brexit sour grapes and there is uproar about it. On Sunday there is a huge u-turn and the EU backs off. NI was being used as a political football and it was disgraceful.
From my own naive point of view, the UK ordered millions of vaccines last Spring and is way ahead of any other country in the world (except Israel) with its vaccine rollout, as of today 8.3 million have had their first dose. Other countries are now saying it's not fair and it should all be spread out around the world. Blame their own Governments lack of foresight, don't start trying to take it away from us.

The travel corridor has tightened and anyone coming into the UK from certain area's will have to quarantine in a hotel for ten days at their own expense. Hmm, how are they going to police that? And why wait until we are a whole year into the Pandemic before they thought this would be a good idea? It should have happened months ago.

Priti Patel, Secretary of State for the Home Department, was on the news today saying that going on holiday is not classed as essential travel - you don't say.
It would appear that didn't reach the ears of 96 people who were caught in the ski resort of St Anton enjoying themselves out on the Piste.
The British police have confirmed that so far this month they have handed out 250 fines of over £10,000 each to organisers of events and parties that have illegally gone ahead.

Don't these stupid and extremely selfish people get it? These new variants are unrestrained. Until it personally affects them they just don't seem to appreciate how bad this is.

I spoke to my friend Mary this week. She has managed to get back to France from Dublin and is now staying put until this is all over. She says the cafe's and markets are still open but there is a 6pm curfew. She's happy enough tucked up in her lovely home with her new beau and at least the weather is brighter than back in Ireland.

My friend Danny is ranting on Facebook this week about Boris. I tend to agree with most of what he is saying but can't help feeling that if he was here in the UK instead of out partying in the sunshine, he might have a little bit more tolerance and understanding of exactly what is going on here and what we are all dealing with.

I feel like I am in a bad movie that is on constant repeat. Work, eat, sleep. Nothing to look forward to, zilch on the horizon. I have no idea of the date and can only work out what day of the week it is when the bin men come, when I know it is definitely Wednesday.
I know everyone is in the same situation but bloody hell it is starting to get to me now. The black dog of depression is sniffing around my ankles yet again.

Peter is quite happy though, I think he is living in the Vaccination Centre at the moment. At least he is keeping busy whilst he has very little work. He knows all the nurses, security staff, car park attendants and most important of all - the person who knows where the jelly beans are kept. It gets him out of the house but it's a bit lonely for me stuck indoors all day.
He has further depressed me by telling me that hairdressers will not be open until at least April. That's all I need trying to cope with a huge mop of hair again!

Well that is January over, normally the worst and most depressing month of the year, this year was no exception. I didn't quite manage a dry January, more of a partially damp one. I have only drunk red wine though and not touched the gin, so I do get a gold star.

Roll on February, I imagine that won't be any better.
It's Not.

By helping others you will learn how to help yourself - Aung San Suu Kyi

Monday 1st to Sunday 7th February

So it is 2 years to the day that I left the UK on my fantastic, never to be forgotten, three month solitary trip to Asia, visiting Burma first. When I turn on the radio this morning there has been a military coup there and Aung San Suu Kyi (the countries extremely popular leader) has been detained. There is huge public anger that this happened so soon after the elections where her party won 70% of the vote. The TV is off air and all telephone and mobile networks have been shut down. Burma is a fabulous country and I feel so sad for the Burmese people, they hoped and prayed that it wouldn't happen again but most of them always suspected it would.
Britain and nations across the world are calling for Suu to be released and the state of emergency ceased. It will fall on deaf ears, I hope there is not more bloodshed.

I haven't been sleeping very well as I said earlier. Peter valiantly offers to sleep downstairs for two nights to give me a break, fortunately the dog goes with him and I get two delicious nights sleep in our bed. I roll backwards and forwards into the cold spots all night long. I sleep so well Tuesday night that I don't wake up until 9:24am next morning: I am due to start work at 9:30. Fortunately this working from home lark means you can sit in your pyjamas all day if necessary and I just stroll across the landing to the study, looking like a down and out, and switch on the computer.

There is very sad news this week with the death of Sir Captain Tom, he eventually succumbed to Covid in Bedford hospital.
A old friend of ours also died and another friend is in hospital on a ventilator. The UK variant has mutated again and is vicious.

Work is just another round of problems, we answered 37,000 emails last month. There are 28,000 people in the system altogether, so statistically speaking every one of those has had at least one problem and sent an email. They have brought in an outside call centre to assist us who are acting from written scripts. Unfortunately these don't answer some of the technical questions and part of the time they don't answer the phone anyway, so the callers then send us yet another email complaint that no-one is answering their phone calls. I have picked up messages where candidates have sent over 10 emails to various departments and still not had any answer.

Unfortunately some of these people are getting very fed up and are extremely rude. I picked up someone on Wednesday evening who I actually rang to try and help. She was so rude to me that in the end I suggested she withdraw from the programme, we really don't need people with that sort of attitude doing this important task. A drastic change of plan is called for and we end up having several TEAMS meetings to discuss the best way forward, our brilliant manager is pulling her hair out as she keeps hitting obstacle after obstacle.

Surely someone up the food chain should be sacked for taking on such a huge job without putting in the infrastructure first.

Sure enough he suddenly announces he is leaving. Yep, leaving the rest of us to sort out this bloody awful mess.

Because the computer says NO, I cannot go to the Vaccination Centre this week. My booked voluntary shifts have been deleted in error and someone else has jumped in to take my place. It is my only respite from this house and the incessant tapping on the keyboard. I am furious and spitting feathers; it is the final insult.

I feel like writing another email to myself to complain but I probably wouldn't know the answer anyway:

'Thank you for your email, I apologise that you are having difficulties but I am afraid the problem is out of my hands'!

The Government and scientists are still confusing everyone with the vaccination data. Some are saying that the Astra Zeneca jab cuts the chances of catching Covid by 60% and some are saying it isn't that effective. One in 7 people in Britain have now had Covid and over 10 million have been vaccinated. I don't think it matters which jab you've had, it **MUST** be some protection from the virus even if it is short-lived and we all end up having to be vaccinated annually.

At least Maureen and my mother have had their first dose, so it's a bit of a worry off their minds for the time being. My mother is doing OK, she at least has her husband for company. Maureen is completely alone and we cannot see her, but she is managing, she is a whizz on Zoom and it keeps her in touch with her friends.

Some towns across the UK are now having 'surge' testing where there have been outbreaks of the new variant. Testing kits are also being sent out in the post. We have a bundle in the kitchen drawer.

There is a ridiculous story at the weekend, which makes me seethe with rage, about 14 adults and 10 children who crammed into a flat to celebrate a one year old's birthday. What on earth were they thinking of? I could almost understand it if it was a 21st or 40th, but 1 year??? The baby won't ever remember any of it, but the grown ups will never forget.The police fined the adults £800 each.
Too right, when the rest of us have not seen our friends and families for months.

So it is Friday and the start of TET (Chinese New Year) in Vietnam. Everyone is on holiday and they will all be having a lovely time (if they can afford it). I really feel it today: it is almost palpable, an icy grip around my heart.
It's nearly a year since I was last there and we all know how that ended. I would honestly walk there if I thought they would let me in, but no chance of that happening. The country is still locked to the outside world. I am hoping that this 'Covid passport' thing might allow me to travel in the Summer, but Peter keeps saying it will not happen, it will be too soon for the Vietnamese authorities to allow us germ infested foreigners in.

On Sunday we take the dog for a walk. It is freezing cold and snow is forecast, although we have not seen a flake all day. The fields are still flooded and we have to wade through 8 inches of water and three inches of mud.
I am wearing a pair of faded blue wellingtons, an old parka, a tatty scarf, not a scrap of makeup and my hair is a mess. I look like Worzel Gummidge on a bad day.
Whatever happened to the smart and elegant woman I used to be?

I am also seriously worried that I won't ever remember how to walk in a pair of stiletto's.

Monday 8th to Sunday 14th February

It is Monday. Again. I drag myself out from underneath the duvet (where I could have stayed all day), cross the landing, ignoring the black dog of depression that is sitting on the stairs, flick on the computer and we are off. It is yet another week of pure agony.
At least the view from the window has changed, it snowed during the night and looks very pretty outside. The snow lays around for the rest of the week. In fact the temperature does not get above freezing during the

day and plummets at night time. Braemar in Scotland recorded the lowest temperature at - 22.5 C. I am bundled up in an old jumper and cardigan, at least with it being this cold it stops the incessant hot flushes which just do not seem to abate. I look like a bag lady with my scruffy long grey hair and hideous clothes. I catch sight of myself in the hall mirror and wonder who that old, pale faced, miserable looking women is and then I remember. It is me.
Note to self - burn all these Covid clothes when this is over.

I have managed to sell my exercise bike this week, I am so glad to get it out of the house, it was sitting in the corner covered in dust with a cobweb hanging from the handle bars. The money goes direct to Anna & Greenies account.

So the big debate rages on with everyone arguing over the effectiveness of the Astra Zeneca vaccine against the South African variant. Scientists are saying that 2 doses does not show protection against mild and moderate cases of this new strain.
Oh Joy, does that mean I am not actually covered? I am at the stage where I do not know who or what to believe, all the data is so complex. The press do not help at all with everyone's confusion.
At least the infection rate is definitely dropping. So something positive at last, if you can call 8000 new infections today and 330 deaths good news.

Something interesting came to my notice today, curtesy of my brother in law. According to the News there are still 20,000 passengers passing through the UK's airports every day. How can that still be possible? Where are they going? What are they doing? Surely it can't all be business? I am totally mystified by this.
A close friend of mine says her brother in-law, who has an American girlfriend, has managed to fly her over here every month for a long weekend since April 2020 and she has never been stopped or questioned at Heathrow. Another friend says you can still go anywhere if you have enough money to hire a private aircraft. Only last Thursday a very rich couple flew into Luton airport from a holiday in Dubai on their Lear jet, no questions asked. No wonder we can't beat this disease with that selfish attitude.

Supposedly starting next week all passengers coming in from a RED country will have to fork out £1750 to go into a hotel for 10 days quarantine. As most of these are 'airport' hotels are decorated in fifty shades of beige, only the most desperate are going to incarcerate themselves in one of these 'cells'. Aren't they?

So people will be telling porkies no doubt to avoid the cost and the Hell of 10 days cooped up in an insipid hotel room.

The Government are advising everyone not to book any holidays for the Summer, there is no guarantee they will be able to go. Strangely enough the UK holiday market is booming and getting thousands of bookings already.

The gloom and doom department is also predicting that this is the worst economic slump in 300 years. You don't need to be an educated economist to suss that out.

It is a thoroughly brutal week at work. The outside agency brought in to help is causing more problems than it solves. Strange blanket emails are going out in their thousands from our email address but it is not us who has sent them, this then creates a load more queries which we cannot answer. It is a totally farcical situation and we are all beginning to feel the strain of continuous fire fighting. Our lovely manager is fighting our corner every day. The only helpful thing that occurs is that some of us in the team are given access to the HR system. Being able to see where the applicants are in the process is very useful. Honestly if they had done this at the beginning of the project it might have saved a lot of time.

I had to chuckle: some of the Management, who put us under redundancy consultation, have been drafted in to help out HR who have a nine day wait on answering their emails, at least now we are only 6 days behind.

By Wednesday I crack completely and walk to the village shop and purchase two bags of nuts, a huge pack of liquorice and a whacking big bar of chocolate. I then proceed to stuff my face on the walk home. I end up sitting on the seat at the bus stop, swinging my legs under the bench and throwing chilli nuts down my throat by the handful. I then spend all evening feeling extremely sick.

And spend all the following morning on the toilet (TMI).

There is a partial respite from the monotony on Friday, I am in the Vaccination Centre again with two of my best mates - Lisa and Carlos. Despite having to get up at the crack of dawn, I actually put some slap on and do my hair. I have to say it is very quiet in there and we had a lot of time to stand around and chat. Carlos and I disappeared to the break room for 40 minutes putting the world to rights whilst Lisa stood with her legs crossed dying to go to the loo. Blimey we got told off when we got back!

We are all suffering in one way or another. Carlos is bored at work and only has his mother for company in the evenings, Lisa works in a school and spends all day cleaning, not teaching, and can't see her granddaughter. As for me, well, we all know how I am coping.

My friend who was in hospital last week with Covid has now had a stroke which has affected his peripheral vision. Apparently the virus causes the blood to thicken and he has a blood clot on his brain. He is my age with no underlying medical issues.

Another person, that Lisa and I know who says Covid is not real and is a Government conspiracy to control us all, was taken by ambulance to hospital last week screaming and shouting. Maybe she should go and sit in the ward with my friend, she might stop being so bloody stupid.

Sunday is Valentines Day and Peter cooks a nice dinner and buys me a lovely bunch of flowers. We venture out for a walk but with the wind chill it feels like -10C so we don't stay out for long, I have icicles growing on my nose. We spend the whole day talking about our jobs, despite me repeatedly trying to change the subject. Peter retires to bed at 8.30 as he has to get up early to go to Wales to carry out a huge job for his company at an orthopaedic factory (yes he has permission and all of the permits), at least he is working this week. I try to switch off completely by watching 'Pretty Woman' followed by'Mama Mia' and roll up to bed at midnight. It hasn't really helped, I bawl my eyes out at both films.

Partly due to the fact that I would like to snog Pierce Brosnan myself and know I will never get the opportunity.

Monday 15th to Sunday 21st February

Monday morning starts with me having an enormous, gigantic, spectacular meltdown. I was in floods of tears. Not a good start to the week.

Our lovely boss is taking a few days off for half term to spend some time with her children and has left three of us in charge of the team of 18. Somehow I pull myself together and we get through the week, (which comes with a new set of problems), without causing her any further issues and manage to hold the team together.

The temperature has switched from an icy -4 to a balmy 13 degrees. The house is like a greenhouse and I can't breathe. I go around switching off all the radiators and wander around in my underwear, it will be sods law, as soon as the house cools down it will turn cold again.

The fantastic news this week is that 15 million people so far have received the vaccination. So that's 15 million in two months. We have another 45 million to go and then times all that times 2. The other bit of positivity is that the infection rate is still dropping and there has been a fall of a third in new cases.
Boris is going to announce the Governments 'Roadmap' out of this Lockdown next Monday. I won't hold my breath, we can't possibly release Lockdown until we are absolutely sure we can do safely. I would rather stay like this than be allowed out and then locked up again in a few months. Blimey did I really say that out loud?

On another note, John Lewis is in trouble and are looking to close 8 of their stores. Along with my beloved Debenhams going, what on earth is the High Street going to look like when we get back to normality?
It will be full of second hand shops and cheap young trendy stores for teenagers. There will be nothing left for women of my age. I will have to start wearing bright pink velour tracksuits, push up padded bra's, nylon thongs and glittery trainers.

The first air travellers arrived into their 10 day quarantine hotels from the RED countries. Of course some of them tried to slip the net and got caught at Birmingham airport and been fined £10,000 each. Arseholes. What is going to become of the airline & holiday industry, how much longer can it survive? Data released this week was that the impact of Covid on tourism has dropped the airline business by 98%. I knew it was bad but that figure is astounding. All the holiday companies are itching to start taking foreign bookings, they are desperate for a Summer season, but will it happen? I don't think so.

I spoke to Anna and Greenie this week. It turns out that Chinese New Year in Vietnam this year has been a bit of a damp squib.They have been allowed to mix with their families but advised not to gather in large groups and all the normally spectacular fireworks and social gatherings were cancelled (allegedly due to finances).
I suppose it was a bit like cancelling Christmas here.

So Peter is in Wales and apart from a quick pee in the garden our miserable little dog has not moved from her bed for two whole days. She looks away every time I speak to her, won't eat her dinner, refuses to sit with me and won't even take a treat. Peter gets home late on

Tuesday evening and she goes ballistic. Running around, jumping all over him, licking his face and then wolfs her dinner down.
Little bitch.

News from Buckingham Palace is that Prince Phillip has been admitted to hospital with a pre-existing condition. The press go into overdrive, has he got Covid? Is he about to die? The Palace say no. Thank goodness for that. Then he gets a visit from Prince Charles which sets the press off again. It must be something serious for HRH to have his son visit him when no-one else can have visitors. Watch this space.
I like the Royal family, I am not keen on a few of them and think they could be streamlined a bit. There is nothing the Royals do better that a Ceremonial occasion. I always feel that the Americans are fascinated by our 1200 year Royal history. I cannot guess what will happen to the monarchy when the queen dies. Some of her children and grandchildren haven't exactly done her many favours over the years. Apparently the 'Decree Absolute' has come through for Megan and Harry. The Queen has reviewed their situation and says they cannot carry on with any of their official roles (they wanted to keep some of them) as they have made themselves voluntarily un-royal.
You are either Royal or not.
You are either in or out.
And her Majesty says you are OUT.

On Friday, after working in the Vaccination Centre, I break the rules and meet up outside with a friend to go for a 3 mile walk. I know it's not technically allowed but my mental health is not good today and I need to engage with a real person. We don't stop to draw breath on the amble around our village, we have so much to say. It is fabulous to see her, we have not seen each other since the beginning of December and I definitely feel much better afterwards.

Scanning the latest news from Burma, the military are back in full control of the country and have decreed a year long state of emergency. They have charged Aung San Suu Kyi with some ridiculous charge of illegally importing walkie talkies and she is under house arrest along with many other party officials. There have been huge public demonstrations against the coup, despite the military forbidding such gatherings, and two protestors were killed and 20 injured at a rally in Mandalay when the police opened fire.
I have a real fascination for Suu and her life story. I am also intrigued by the story of Eva Peron. The military hated both of these very different women but they were both loved and adored by the people.

Honestly the things we now get excited by. On Saturday it was announced that on 8th March one nominated person can visit relatives in a care home and can hold their hand. No hugging or kissing allowed though. The news is full of it.
Whoopedoo.

Apparently Nasa has managed to land a rover on Mars. I watched it on the news, everyone was elated and talking in fast squeaky voices about their fabulous achievement. I myself was less than impressed by the pictures showing a boring and bumpy lunar landscape. If ET or Paul the Alien had popped up on the film I might have been moved a bit more.

Peter has gone to Jersey over the weekend with his business partner to carry out an annual job that is financially necessary to their business. They have had to jump through bureaucratic hoops to be allowed to go and booked 3 Covid tests at a cost to their company of £500. He has an enormous folder full of passes/permits/tickets/Covid certificates and other company documentation which they have to show to any official that asks. They are travelling by freight ferry and have to isolate in separate cabins for the 10 hour journey, with cabin service only for food and drink. When they get to Jersey they have to go straight to the hotel and isolate again with room service for meals. They are not permitted to go to the restaurant or bar. If they leave the hotel for any other reason than to go to the job in hand the staff have to ring the police, they are not even allowed to go for a walk in the evening. Such a shame as they are in one of the loveliest hotels in St Helier, right on the seafront. When he rings me it appears that they are the only two guests in the whole hotel and the staff were waiting to lock them up when they arrived. Fortunately they have given them the best rooms in the hotel so they have plenty of space for their isolation. He spends all his leisure time either watching downloads of movies or sleeping.
The dog sulks permanently.
I at least get three nights undisturbed sleep.

That is until my work phone starts ringing early on Sunday Morning. I end up getting involved in a problem with a volunteer who has previously been seriously messed about and is now in tears after being refused entry to her training session. There is no senior manager on call that I am aware of to speak to so I make the decision to speak to the trainer myself and ask that the lady is let on the course. I have no authority to do this, I just want to help her but I know it will back fire on me.

(Sure enough I get an email on Tuesday backing up the trainers actions informing me that I am basically in the wrong. I knew it would happen - **NO-ONE** involved in this programme will take ownership of the errors and admit that their department may have made a mistake.)

The weather stays very mild and in the afternoon I manage to get out in the garden for the first time in months to have a tidy up and put in some Spring plants that I bought at the supermarket. I have only been outside for half an hour when guess who puts in an appearance and starts kicking his ball around the garden?
I leave my house and amble off around the village for a three mile walk stopping en route to buy a big bag of wine gums that I fill my face with on the way home.

Peter is now locked in his cabin for the next 16 hours on the freight ferry for his return journey. He is perving over videos of his favourite pop star, Toyah, bouncing around her kitchen on Youtube in a very skimpy outfit with no bra.
Should keep him amused for hours.

Monday 22nd to Sunday 28th February

Today is Boris' big announcement and we wait with bated breath for a sign that we are nearing the end of our year long imprisonment.
There is a four step 'roadmap' to guide us to Freedom.

March 8th - Schools and universities will return. All exams have been cancelled and it will be down to real human beings to grade the students, not a computer algorithm.
AND huge excitement: you will be able to meet outside with another person not from your household.
The stay/work at home rules apply until 29th March when, Oh the joy, 6 people or two households can meet up outside, outside sport can recommence and you will legally be able to travel out of your area.
12th April - shops, hairdressers (can't wait), gyms, outside hospitality (beer gardens & cafe's) and some holiday accommodation can reopen.
17th May - 6 people or two households can mix indoors, indoor hospitality and hotels can open and most social contact rules ceased.
International travel rules will be lifted (Covid passports are mentioned but we don't know where that leaves anyone wanting to go on holiday abroad).
21st June - all limits on social contact lifted and everything, allegedly, back to normal. Allegedly.

This all hinges on the Vaccination Programme going to plan, the vaccine showing results in the reduced deaths and hospital admissions, no further surge in infections and lastly, **no more variants**. Boris reiterates that nothing is guaranteed and the scientists and Government will be carefully checking all the data and the impact between each 5 week step.

The furlough scheme will be extended to September. That is good news. So the end is in sight, even if you can only see it through powerful binoculars.

70,000 fines have so far been handed out to people breaking the rules, 275 are for £10,000 each, mainly for organisers of illegal raves and parties.
£54 billion has been paid out on furlough and we are now officially £2 trillion in debt.

What is interesting is that the UK has a population of 65 million and 122,000 people have died, whereas India has a population of one billion people and they have only had 157,000 deaths. How can that even be possible? I suppose India is a vast country and they are spread out, even though the big cities are crammed to capacity.
As we all know now, India was a slow starter with Covid.
Worldwide there have been 114 million cases with 2.5 million deaths.
The USA still leads the way with the highest figures in all areas.

Boris' big announcement results in an enormous 1000% surge in holiday bookings for the Summer. Well 1000% is a big improvement on zero.

I also get an exciting call from my hairdresser and have a haircut booked in for 16th April. I am almost back to where I was last Summer with a huge grey mop on my head. Well, at least I haven't tried cutting it myself this time, so it still has it's shape even if it is a bit long.

The Duke of Edinburgh is still in hospital, I told you to watch this space. The Palace have now admitted he is suffering from an infection but is doing well.
So they haven't thrown him out of hospital too early and sent him home for his elderly wife and family to deal with then?

The golfer, Tiger Woods, is lucky to be alive after being in a horrendous car crash in LA and has serious injuries to his legs. He is due to have a fifth operation on his back as well so I imagine that may well be the end of his glittering sporting career.

600,000 doses of the Covid vaccine have been sent to Ghana this week as part of the richer Nations sharing with poorer countries.
Please send some to Vietnam.

It has been very Springlike this week, the sunshine has been lovely and warm. Unfortunately it is really too early to switch the heating off completely, so I have had a few sweaty nights and our ceiling fan has been turned on. Peter is still going to bed with his socks on and moans constantly that he is frozen under the paper thin duvet.

I have been working from home now for two and a half months and still hate every second of it. I have developed a problem with my knees which I put down to sitting in the same position in a cramped room at a funny angle for hours on end. Sometimes when I get up I can hardly move. My knees seem to lock up also when I turn over in bed, one night I actually cried out in pain. Is this what the so called glorious golden years are all about? Two plastic kneecaps for me in the future maybe?

Work has been another week of gloriousness, the only good sign is that the incoming emails are slowing down with only 400 unanswered messages in the box. On the downside we are receiving some extremely bad tempered emails and it is not easy to talk to some people. I know they are volunteers and extremely frustrated but it does not give anyone the right to speak to us in the manner they do. I have been reported to the CEO, threatened with escalation to other Senior Management (numerous times), huffed and puffed at down the phone, told that I am stupid, incompetent and (my personal favourite) worse than useless, all because I cannot personally change the system.

Mind you, even without all of this we are not looking forward to going back to working in our previous jobs, talking of which we have heard ZERO. We are supposed to go back under redundancy consultation this week, but there is a noisy silence. In the end we get an email from a senior Manager via a third party to say the consultation is over. On further questioning we are just told that it is finished. Surely we are entitled to know the outcome of the process. It is reiterated again that it is over with no explanations, so God know what that means.

Our new temporary boss is on the case and at least we are staying with her until 1st April. After that who knows?

I am back in the Vaccination Centre on Friday, but it's all been moved around and no-one has cared to share this new system with us. A very, very bossy Council volunteer then tries to tell us how we are going to run our area. We are then joined by another lady who causes pandemonium and two of my colleagues threaten to walk out if someone doesn't intervene. That's the problem, there is no designated manager for the volunteers and it is certainly not me, but I end up having to get involved and sort it all out. Not what I want to do on my day off, I just want to help a few old girls and boys on their way after their jabs.

In the evening my friend Tracey, who has been put on redundancy three times by our organisation, has decided to call it a day and we end up having a very strange but hilarious online leaving party. There is a quiz and much laughter and I remember why we were such a great team, it is such a shame we have all been separated. It feels once again like the end of an era and we will miss her like mad.

The sad funeral of Captain Tom takes place. Considering most people can only have 20 people at the death of a loved one, the worlds press attend his and there is an RAF flypast and Michael Buble sends a special recording.
No less than Captain Tom deserved.

It is a glorious Spring weekend and the weather is balmy. I manage to get out in the garden and prune my bushes to the sound of someones burglar alarm that rings for three solid hours before it gets turned off by an engineer.
I am dog tired and a bit emotional. I think I know exactly what is causing it. It is the culmination of the recent heavy workload, the stress over possible redundancy, the excruciating boredom of Lockdown, only having one day off a week, not sleeping properly, not having anything to look forward to and now it is all catching up with me. I am ratty and bad tempered. Poor Peter can't do anything right and buries himself in his computer all weekend which just winds me up even more.
I hit the red wine and chocolate. I know I am in a spiral of self decline. I look a complete mess, I have put on at least a stone in weight, I haven't worn anything nice for months, some mornings I can't even be bothered to shower or wash my hair, I have lost the will to do any exercise, I am so over doing any housework and have no enthusiasm for anything.

I finally acknowledge the true reason why I am so low. Exactly one year ago today I was on my way to Vietnam.

FULL CIRCLE.

A woman is like a teabag - you never know how strong she is until she gets into hot water - Eleanor Roosevelt

13. Springtime

March

Boris kicks off the month by giving the nurses a 'generous' 1% pay rise. Honestly can't he do better than that after everything they have been through?
Scottish nurses will get 4%.
It has also been shown that the Test & Trace system has been virtually useless.
Really? You don't say.

At the start of March, 20 Million people in the UK had received their first Vaccine so the Government are on target with their projected figures. Unfortunately this new Brazilian variant has arrived and there have been 6 cases so far, unfortunately the Scientists don't know enough about it and cannot say whether the vaccine will cover us for this variant. But there has been a big fall in the number of deaths and infections here which is really good news.
On a political note, it is the Budget this month, I bet we all end up paying more for everything.

The Duke of Edinburgh has been transferred to St Barts Hospital in London, it has now been revealed that he is to be operated on due to a pre-existing heart condition. The Press are on it like a rat up a drain pipe. HE DOES NOT HAVE COVID, the Palace are very keen to point out. It appears that all of his children have visited him in hospital which is unheard of, usually the Royal Family keep a stiff upper lip and stay away. I always thought it was odd they don't visit each other in hospital. At the end of the month he is then taken to Windsor Castle to recover from his operation and spend private time with the Queen. I saw the TV footage of him in the back of his limo, he looked truly awful. I wasn't sure if he was dead already and someone had just propped him up on the back seat. I hope he recovers but at 99?

There has been a massive public fallout regarding an interview that Harry and Meghan did with Oprah Winfrey. What on earth were they thinking? Who advised them that this was a good idea? They made some slightly strange allegations and comments that didn't really add up. Come on you two, I get it, you don't want to do the Royal thing anymore and want your family to live in privacy in America. That is completely your choice and fair play to you for making the decision. But you cannot go on Prime time TV which then gets transmitted across the world and slate the Royal Family.

Look at the fallout after Princess Diana did her interview, there are still repercussions over that and it happened in1995.

Go to the USA by all means, live quietly like you want to and stop moaning.

There has been more violence in Burma, where this is all going to end I don't know. Men, women & children have been killed during the ongoing protests regarding Aung San Suu Kyi's arrest. She had been summoned to appear in court but was refused access to see her legal team. She has since been seen by Video link, but it has not been revealed where she has been detained. Strangely enough her popularity has soared even more within Burma since her arrest despite her International reputation still being tarnished by the Rohingya Muslim crisis.

Peter has been driving all over the country giving vaccinations. He is still on part time furlough, there is very little paid work out there for him at the moment. I have done a few voluntary shifts recently in some centres and unfortunately some of the staff appear to be totally in the dark as to what we are supposed to be there for. I have been asked to do satisfaction surveys on an iPad, asked whether I am there for car park duty and in another place, all they wanted me to do was open and close the door - for 6 hours! Not quite what I did all that training for. Then to top it all, someone within the organisation mistakenly presses a button (again) and cancels all future shifts I put my name down for, so now I cannot volunteer anyway as it is impossible to get any sort of booking for the next few weeks.

I am still at home tapping out email after email to our vaccination volunteers. The emails are now down to a more manageable level per day. We have heard a rumour that we may be going back to our normal jobs in April, but nothing is yet confirmed. It goes down like a lead balloon, we like working for our temporary manager even if the whole redeployment has been gruelling, she is one of the best managers I have ever worked with. Her style suits me down to the ground.

She says it like it is, no bullshit, no flattery, no lies, just facts. And she values your opinion, of which I never usually hold back on.

The weather has been a proper Spring mix. We had some lovely sunny days and some freezing cold ones. So it has been possible to get out in the garden, cut the grass and do a bit of pruning but still have to scrape the ice off the car in the mornings. Not much rain though, such a shame as my lawn dries out really quickly with the dog peeing on it all the time.

I am still selling my possessions on Ebay. Everything has sold bar one item. I am now on first name terms with the bloke in the Post Office having been in there so many times recently. Once I can get some new carpet and get these rooms re-arranged I know there is a load more junk in the loft that I can get down and flog. There is a nice little nest egg building up in the account for my girls and it is growing every week. They are both anxiously looking for work, any work, to get them through the rest of this year. It should be peak season in Vietnam now and they would normally be run off their feet with visitors. It is not looking like tourism will recommence anytime soon there despite what may be planned for the rest of the world as the Lockdowns start to ease.

Elsewhere in the world France has seen a huge rise of 135% in Covid cases and it looks like there might be a third wave across the rest of Europe. My friend Mary says that the French are all sceptics and are waiting for the Moderna Vaccine and are refusing to have any of the others. There has been some evidence of the Astra Zeneca vaccine causing blood clots and some people are frightened to have it, even here in the UK. A lot of the vaccination centres had a flurry of cancellations when the news came out and some of the vaccine had to be destroyed. Honestly, it has affected such a small number of people, you have a much greater chance of getting a blood clot if you get pregnant or are on the pill.
It won't stop women having sex though will it?

In Greece my friends cannot get the vaccine despite their valiant efforts and might have to wait until they come back to the UK in the Summer, fingers crossed that they actually get here. Greece has so far only vaccinated 1 million people and COVID is still rampant in the major cities. They are still in full Lockdown with a 6pm curfew despite the Greek Government advocating a Summer season starting on 17th May. Not sure who is going to want to go there anyway with their high infection rate. Not sure if anyone will be allowed either.

On 21st March we managed to vaccinate 800,000 people in one single day in the UK, which is amazing. The bad news then hits that there are huge problems with the vaccine production in India and the programme almost comes to a shuddering halt at the end of the month. A large number of the mass Vaccination Centres are to close for the bulk of April. All second vaccines will be honoured but no new appointments can be made until more vaccine arrives into the country.

The only good thing about these cancellations is that I got a call from Peter, whilst he was helping at a Drs surgery, to say people had not turned up for their appointment and would I like to have my second jab now instead of the vaccine being wasted.

Blimey, I have never moved so fast in my life, straight in the car at supersonic speed to Dunstable, in and out in 5 minutes flat.

So I have now been double dipped.

An enormous 400 metre long container ship has somehow got itself wedged in the Suez Canal blocking any other boats from getting through. It ran aground due to poor visibility from a sandstorm caused by high winds. The only other route is around the Cape of Good Hope which adds another 3500 nautical miles and 9 days to the journey. A very costly detour. Salvage experts have removed the 18,000 containers that the ship was carrying to lighten its load to try and refloat it.

I never realised how important the Suez Canal is, apparently 12% of the total global trade goes through it every year. This current blockage is holding up an estimate $9.6 billion of goods every day.

Oops, I bet that Captain is not popular.

On the 8th March the Children finally went back to school, there was a huge audible sigh of relief from parents which was felt across the country.

On 27th March the stay at home rule finally ended and people can officially travel into other areas (that was already happening). All the parks across the country were packed with people having picnics and enjoying their freedom. Unfortunately some people went mad and two parks in Nottingham had to be closed due to high numbers of misbehaviour and drunken teenagers who left all their litter behind.

So the news arrives from work that we are finishing with the Vaccination Programme on 31st March and restarting our old jobs after Easter. I have mixed feelings but do think now it is time to bid farewell to the Support team. It has been a crazy, exhausting and difficult few months which started with high optimism and ended in crashing pessimism. I have learnt a bit more tolerance, which will surprise a few people, I am not known for my patience. I now listen more before jumping in with an answer, again something that may surprise a few people. (Not my husband though, he can't see any difference in me!). And every email I ever respond to in the future will start and end the same way, regardless of the tone or content.

' Thank you for your email.'

'We will get back to you in due course'.

If you obey all the rules, you miss all the fun - Katharine Hepburn

April

We had two glorious days before Easter, out came the deck chairs and barbecues, then the fabulous British weather turned. It was so cold that it snowed here four days on the trot. It didn't settle but there were flurries all day long. Out came the Winter coats and boots again and the deck chairs went back in the shed.

Talk about yoyo weather, see what I mean about hating the British climate.

So we went back to our official jobs that we have not done for over a year on 6th April. It was great to be back together in the office, unfortunately it was decided for our first day back that we should have a day long online meeting.

That was 7 hours of my life I will never get back. Drawing stupid pictures as an icebreaker, an hour long wellbeing presentation that was very nice but which no-one will take any notice of and I am not sure about the rest of it as I zoned out completely. One of my colleagues actually fell asleep. There were the usual over enthusiastic people on there agreeing with everything that was said.

We all just sat and sighed.

The following day when we finally sat down in front of our computers we couldn't remember how to actually do our jobs and there was tonnes of it to be sifted through and processed, so it was slow progress. The Office Manager had just about coped on her own until two weeks ago when it went mad.

I am doing the whole of the North on my own and the task is overwhelming. If you think about it, this time last year there were 4 offices with over 20 staff, now there is only us 4. Yes, business is not up to the numbers they were in 2019, but blimey, it is too much for one person to deal with. My friend Kirsty definitely got the short straw with

London and the South, there were 151 new bookings on the South alone, I at least only had about 120.

The other thing with me covering the North of the country is that I do not know where anywhere is North of Watford Gap. And that is honestly true, I am not making that up. Ask me where Phnom Penh is (Cambodia) or Terengganu (Malaysia) and I can tell you, but where the hell is Sheffield? Or Doncaster? Or Blackburn? I even managed to mix up Durham with Cumbria, which bodes well.

As the month goes on we are in yet another situation where we cannot hold back the tide of emails and bookings. But we can only do what we can do, they are not getting anything else out of me, I have run dry. On that note I also have 42 days holiday to take (we were allowed to carry everything over from last year when we were redeployed), as I only work 4 days a week this equates to 10.5 weeks. I doubt very much if anyone will have the time to cover me when I am off, so taking any holiday will result in a huge backlog.

The Moderna vaccine has arrived in the UK. It has now been decided that the Astra Zeneca jab cannot be given to anyone under the age of 30, due to the blood clot issues. A week later the Moderna jab is also found to be causing a few blood clots and now some people are panicking again about having the vaccine, especially amongst the youngsters. There are also rumours going around about the Covid vaccine making you sterile or that women will give birth to Thalidomide babies. All utter rubbish and completely unproven.

There has been escalating violence in Northern Ireland over the last few weeks. 90 Police have been hurt and many civilians arrested or charged with rioting. The protests are over keeping NI as part of the UK. On the 7 April, the fighting went over a so-called peace wall in Belfast that divides predominantly Protestant loyalist communities from predominantly Catholic nationalist communities who want to see a United Ireland. Once the wall was breached photographers and press were attacked and a bus set on fire.

This is not over. And probably never will be.

I was driving to the supermarket to do the weekly shop when a news flash came over the radio. The Duke of Edinburgh had died at Windsor Castle. I don't think it was a particular shock to anyone but most people felt very sad for the Queen. At least they were together when he went and had their chance to say goodbye privately. The media and TV goes into overdrive with tributes with all the presenters wearing black unlike when Princess Diana died and they all got caught out. Due to COVID, the funeral is reduced to 30 guests from the 860 which was in the original plan. In a way I think it will be better for Her Majesty to be surrounded only by her family and not a load of dignitaries. Even Boris doesn't get a look in.

The funeral is held in St Georges Chapel at Windsor on a beautiful Spring day. There is no state funeral but the Dukes Regiments are all in attendance wearing their finest dress uniforms lined up on the Quadrant of the castle. Prince Philip is taken by a specially built Landrover to the Chapel, followed by his children and other family members. I was willing the pallbearers not to drop him, the coffin is made of lead and weighs over a tonne. The poor soldiers that carried him up the three flights of steps into the Chapel were sweating like buckets. But they managed it with military precision and flair.

I must say sometimes us British cannot organise a piss up in a brewery, but boy can we put on a display of pageantry. We truly know how to bury a member of the Royal Family.

The Queen looked a tiny stooped figure, like a little black sparrow, sitting alone, keeping her distance from everyone else with her head bowed for much of the service. Who knows what was going through her mind.

Anyway it was a very beautiful and fitting family service and I would imagine the Queen preferred it that way. And I think Philip would have approved.

I get some emails from several vacation companies informing me that all holidays to Burma have been cancelled in the near future due to the deteriorating situation within the country. They are not taking any bookings for this year or next.

The poor Burmese people are definitely back to square one.

The American policeman who knelt on George Floyds neck for nine minutes and 29 seconds cutting off his breathing and killing him which sparked huge riots and protest across the USA last Summer has been found guilty. The jury deliberated for 10 hrs before finding Derek Chauvin guilty of Murder and manslaughter. He is now awaiting sentence.

I have at least been out a few times. I went to LTFC several times during the month, unfortunately both days were freezing, but at least I got to see some of my friends: Lisa, Rachel, Jane and my favourite Paramedic. It was great to have a really good chin wag.

I have also seen my mother and my sister, everyone is OK.

All done nothing and been nowhere.

The shops and hairdressers re-opened on 12th April along with 'outside hospitality'. All three of the pubs in our village have invested in huge marquees and patio heaters. Every time I drive past they are packed out. Desperate times indeed.

My favourite shop is now one big jumble sale. I went to Debenhams in my lunch hour and they were literally giving everything away, it was so cheap. The problem for me was that there was so much stock that it was totally overwhelming and I only bought one item. I then went back on my day off and the queue to get in was 400m long so I didn't bother. I have been scouring the Internet to find a company that caters for my age group, as apart from M&S I have no idea where I am going to purchase my clothes in future.

I did manage to order some carpet and a new mattress which I have to wait several weeks to be delivered. Now the stores are open, everyone has gone shopping and everywhere was very busy. £1000 spent by myself in one day but huge excitement all round, I will be able to organise my upstairs rooms and get rid of the clutter. (I will sell most of it on Ebay).

While going about my usual business now everything is open, I have noticed a definite increase in prices.

My usual hairdresser charged me an extra £2.50 for a cut and blow-dry (£46.50 - a months wages in Vietnam).

The dental hygienist charged me another £5.50 (£52.50).

To get my car washed cost another £1.00 (£6.00).

And to have my windows cleaned was another £3.00 (£18.00) which I did find a bit puzzling. He doesn't have to use anything extra nor wear PPE and certainly he was working all throughout Covid. As everyone was at home, they all wanted their windows clean to watch the world outside. He did a roaring trade.

Oh well, it is what it is, everyone is desperate to make up some lost income.

It was my wedding anniversary and 57th Birthday this month. How quickly did they come round again? They were marginally better days than last year. I received 4 huge bouquets of flowers which made my kitchen look and smell like a florists shop.

Peter brought me a new lap top case, a vegetable spiraliser and an avocado cutter. Who says romance is dead?

Joe Biden has vowed to tackle Global Warming. Not a subject that Donald Trump was particularly interested in. Mr Biden has pledged to cut US emissions by a half by 2030. Pollution is one thing that this Pandemic has improved: people not using their cars so much and there being no airplanes in the skies.

On the subject of flying, there is still no firm news regarding being able to travel abroad in the Summer. Covid passports are being talked about but the Government are being very cautious regarding foreign travel. And as much as I hate to admit it, we should not be travelling yet. We in the UK are more or less all vaccinated but some countries have not even started and they do not need us British, who are desperate for a holiday, bringing the virus or mutations in and spreading it around.

On the subject of Trump: he appealed against his ban from using Facebook and Instagram. It has been upheld and he is still not allowed to use either channels.

Some countries have obviously not been that cautious about travel when you look at the enormous problems in India where Covid is utterly out of control. The daily infection rate is in the hundreds of thousands and they have recorded 219,000 deaths. I did wonder how they had got away with so few cases in such a populated country, it is now catching up with them. And I bet that is not the correct figure, it will be a lot more than that. There is a new Indian variant that has been transmitted back to the UK (I wonder how that happened?) and Boris suddenly decides it is a good idea to put India on the RED travel list. Honestly after all this time, with the huge amount of passengers going backwards and forwards to India from the UK every week, he now decides it's time to stop it. This should have happened months ago.

Gate, horse, bolted. Again.

India is in such a Covid mess that they are running out of essential medical supplies, Oxygen and ventilators, so it is up to the rest of the world to help them out. Britain and the USA promise to send more equipment. I repeat my earlier point; it just goes to show, we are coming out of the other end of Covid due to the enormous success of the vaccine rollout here, but the rest of the world are only beginning.

Mind you, am I the only person who watched the news showing the festivities and huge unmasked crowds at a religious festival in Amritsar, (Northern India)?

I rest my case m'Lord.

On the subject of Boris Johnson, he is in trouble again. It has been leaked that at a very heated cabinet meeting late last year, he allegedly made a comment that bodies could pile up high in the streets rather than have him order a third Lockdown. Naturally he has denied the remark.

There then follows another scandal concerning Sir James Dyson, who allegedly promised to make Covid ventilators for the UK if Boris sorted out his tax bills for his Singaporean staff.
Naturally Mr Johnson has denied this too.
Thirdly there are rumours that Boris allegedly had illegal plans regarding the payment for renovating his Downing Street flat.
Again indefatigably denied.
Hmm, all of this around the same time that the sacked Dominic Cummings has called for an urgent inquiry into the Prime Ministers handling of the Covid situation and is questioning his competence and integrity.
Revenge & sour grapes? I will say no more.

The vaccine roll out is going extremely well even if it has slowed a little. By the middle of April over 11 million people in the UK have received both jabs and there has been a 95% uptake from the over 50's.
By the end of the month the 40 plus group can get their first jab.
There is talk amongst the Scientists that everyone over the age of 50 will need to have a booster jab in the Autumn which could be combined with the flu jab.Yes, Covid is going to be something we will have to live with.

Worldwide there has been recorded 152 million cases of Covid and 3.2 million deaths. Here in the UK we have had 4.4 million cases and 128,000 deaths.
Meanwhile back in Locked down Vietnam they have had 2985 cases and 35 deaths among a population of 90 million. They still do not have the vaccine there and it will be a long time coming.

As we start to emerge from the Lockdown, there is a trial in a Liverpool nightclub which allows 3000 people to congregate and dance together without masks. They do have to provide a negative Covid test before admittance. Scientists are using this event to look at whether crowds mixing and dancing indoors increases transmission of the virus.
Not sure what to make of this. Having a night out, which is one long scientific experiment which could result in a large part of the crowd passing the infection around? Oh well I suppose it has to start somewhere.

There has been a huge stampede at the annual Jewish Pilgrimage to Mount Meron in Northern Israel. Government officials had said 3000 pilgrims could visit at any one time, but it was flooded with worshippers, up to 100,000 people, and the catastrophe happened when they all tried to leave at the same time causing 45 deaths and 150 injuries. It is a terrible thing to happen when they feel that they are so close to their God.

I will admit I had a bit of a wobble around mid April. I am fighting down the rising panic that I might not see my girls in Vietnam for at least another year, if not more. They are both extremely unhappy and sad at the moment, having lost their financial independence and their livelihoods. The future for them looks grim, that's two business seasons gone now without any tourists and without any wages. What is alarming is that there have been a few isolated cases of Covid in their area and they have gone into full Lockdown for two weeks and the schools, bars, shops and restaurants are closed again.

In a way, they are now in a more desperate situation than we were last year. At least we have vaccinated half of our population, they have not even begun. That means that they will stay fluctuating in this state of limbo, backwards and forwards, in and out of Lockdowns until the vaccine arrives.

No tourist dollars until then.

I made an executive decision to stop drinking and go on a proper diet at the beginning of this month. I found a diet called' *the Human being Diet*' which is a scientific approach to healing the inside of the body as well as losing weight. It explains about the hormonal and menopausal changes as we get older and how we struggle to lose the pounds as we age. I decided to give it a try.

Well, so far I have lost my spare tyre, part of my arse and around 10 pounds, so I look better and not so much like Mrs Blobby.

I now fit back in all my clothes which gives me a choice of what to put on rather than just wearing the stuff I can get into. A fab result all round.

If I ever let my head down again, it will be just to admire my shoes -
Anon

May

My new carpet was fitted and I spent a lovely (but freezing cold) Bank Holiday weekend sorting out and arranging my study. All Peters crap has gone in the bin, a load of stuff has gone on Ebay and it felt good for the soul to shed a load of possessions. A massive bidding war went on on for one of Peters old jumpers and I ended up making £35 profit on it. Honestly the things that people buy on there. But I am not complaining, all the cash in is my girls bank account and seems to be growing every week. All of this from stuff I would have sold at the car boot for £1, given to the charity shop or taken to the tip.

We had a fight to get rid of our old mattress. The council will pick up an old mattress from your house for the grand sum of £46, but we don't want to pay that. It was too big to fit in the car so Peter decided to dissect it. There were bits of fluff and old springs littered all over my lovely new carpet. It filled 12 bin bags which then got taken to the tip. So that's it, all the old carpet and mattress out of the house.
Pure bliss.

There is a huge rumpus going on in Jersey. 60 French fishing boats sailed into St Helier harbour complaining about their fishing licences with regard to Brexit being on unfair terms. The French have threatened to cut off all the power supply to the island and Britain sent in 2 Royal Navy ships to keep the peace. Why are the French so argumentative about the waters around Jersey? France has an enormous coastline that they can fish the length and breadth of, why kick up about a relatively small piece of the sea? The fishermen withdrew the following evening with a parting shot that it is not over.
To be continued.

The long awaited 'Green' travel list was revealed. There are only 12 countries which we can travel to and return from without having to quarantine. Unfortunately some of the countries still have their own internal restrictions and three countries: Australia, New Zealand & Singapore are still closed to visitors. So basically it is a choice of Iceland, Portugal, The Falklands or Brunei for this years Summer holiday.
All of this will be closely monitored and there is also an 'Amber' list of places which you need to isolate for 10 days after returning from. All passenger will have to pay out for three COVID tests which are not cheap. Turkey is now on the 'Red' list and we cannot travel there at all. That is a bit of a bugger for everyone who booked their holidays there, Turkey was the 'safe' place to go last Summer.
Honestly who is going to bother? It's so much hassle and will you be safe anyway?
Later in the month some European countries impose heavy quarantine restrictions on any travellers from the UK. Austria has banned all

incoming flights and any tourists from the UK. This is all to do with the Indian variant which is spreading like wildfire in some countries.

The good news is that the Scientists have proved that the Astra Zeneca vaccine lowers the death risk by 80%. They have also said two doses work against this new Indian variant.
Boris has confirmed that there will be a full public inquiry into the Government's handling of the Pandemic which will start in the Spring of 2022. The Opposition parties and organisations of bereaved families have asked for it to begin sooner. This all follows a damning report by the World Health Organisation who said a quicker International response could have stopped the outbreak in China becoming a global disaster. Not really sure how anyone was supposed to know what was going on in such a secretive country. And we still don't know what happened and how the virus got into the food chain. Will we ever know? I don't think so.

Israel is the only country in the world to have vaccinated all their population in record time, so they are more or less safe from dying of Covid. So what do they do now? Start up an age old grievance between themselves and the Palestinians who believe the Israelis are trying to push them out of Jerusalem. The violence is escalating and by the middle of the month 197 are dead are dead and 1235 have been injured. If you believe the news reports they are on the brink of war after these recent confrontations. South East of Tel Aviv, the town of Lod has called a state of emergency. Tel Aviv is a lively seaside town full of funky bars and cafes, a bit like any Costa resort, I cannot imagine it under missile fire. By the 17th May, 3000 rockets have been fired into Gaza, causing mass destruction and the Israeli Prime Minister, Benjamin Netanyahu, says they will continue with full force.
I know my understanding of politics is sketchy at best, but throw in religious beliefs to any conflict and there will never be an end to it, not as long as the earth keeps spinning.
Anyway back to my original point, the Israelis are all vaccinated from Covid but are now killing each other with missiles and shells.

Good news though for my friends in Greece, they have managed to get their vaccinations booked after weeks of trying. And even better, it looks like they may be able to finally get their boat in the water and actually start their retirement dream later this month. The interesting thing is that they have been in Lockdown with curfews for nearly five months and all of a sudden the Greeks are opening everything up this month; they need a Summer season to make some dosh.

Suddenly Covid has disappeared in Greece. Yeah right.

On the 17th of this month more restrictions were lifted. Indoor hospitality, cinema's, museums - all reopened and you can now have two families mixing inside your home. Groups of 30 can meet up outside. Music venues are starting to open albeit with less crowds than usual.
It really feels as if we are on our way back to some sort of normality. Maybe, just maybe, the new James Bond film will now be released. I have been dying to see it since it was shelved last April (2019).

So along with the rest of the country I went out to lunch four days in a row, which gave the diet a bit of a battering. I took 4 of my 42 days holiday off and met up with friends & family and did a lot of shopping. I have to say I was in dire need of a break from work. It is the first time in 23 years (except for Christmas) where I have taken a week off and not actually gone away on holiday. Shame I couldn't get on a plane and go somewhere but it's not going to happen.
My friend Rachel came round under the pretence of restarting our Monday evening pilates classes: all we really did was a few stretches and then sat gossiping on the sofa drinking wine and eating chocolate. We want to go away together for a few days in July, ideally Salzburg or Rome, but they are still off the menu, so it might be Birmingham or Sheffield instead.
See what I mean: where has all the glamour gone?
I invited some other friends, who we haven't seen since last July, round for dinner one night. Having been on this diet for 5 weeks and not drinking, I somehow managed to get absolutely plastered. I have no recollection of them leaving or how I got into bed. But I did take my makeup off, so even in my inebriated state my beauty regime still kicked in. I paid for it the following day with the hangover from Hell. Every time I moved I thought I was going to be sick. Serves me right.

After a massive logistical and bureaucratic nightmare to do with the new Brexit rules, where he nearly conceded defeat, Peter went off to NI to deliver a machine and then to a couple of jobs in Dublin. He was gone for three days and the dog sulked for England. When he came home, she suddenly came back to life, running and jumping around like an adoring puppy.
She really is a two faced little bitch.

So it's May. This time last year we were all locked indoors but at least the weather was lovely. I think it has rained every day this month, at least the grass is green, by this time last year our lawn was a dust bowl. And it has been so cold, we had turned our heating off to then turn it back on again.

Peter has even started wearing his pyjamas again (I'm still sweating buckets at night time). There was a huge disturbance at 5.30 am one morning when he started screaming like a banshee. When he took his PJ bottoms off, a live moth fell out of them which had been in his pants all night long. What is that telling him?

It looks like this Indian variant has got a real hold in Bedford. The town has the third highest rate in the country. One of the schools which has 900 pupils has 350 off because of Covid, so they have shut the school completely. Back to square one with the kids education in that area. New pop up walk in Vaccination Centres are opening in town to try and encourage the communities in these areas to have the jab. I just don't understand their reticence. It is the only solution, there is no other answer.

I was beginning to feel slightly optimistic about the return to ' normal' but will it ever really be over?

I've spent part of the month re-jigging my photo albums. Condensing them down from 30 albums to a much smaller number. Starting in 1999, when Peter and I first met, up to 2014 when I went all digital and started keeping them on the computer.

It is a real walk down Memory Lane, and it's such a shame we don't look at our photos anymore unless you log onto the computer or look at the tiny pics on your phone. Flicking through an album of actual pictures is a really joy. I was also reminded of how gorgeous we all were when we were younger, which was the slight down side to it! There was also pictures of our 2000 wedding. Both our fathers, both of our paternal grandmothers, Maureen's husband and Peters cousins husband are in the photographs but are all now sadly departed.

A real reminder of lives gone by.

So the saying goes: Revenge is a dish best served cold.

Dominic Cummings is up before a parliamentary committee, giving 7 hours of evidence of the Governments alleged failings over the Covid response. It is a damning indictment from him and he also adds in a vicious swipe that claims Boris is unfit for the job. Mr Cummings openly admits that we should have closed our borders last year and not waited until February 2021. (I am in full agreement with this). He cites Taiwan as a case, they closed their borders in January 2020 and made everyone wear face coverings back then.

Matt Hancock is also called before the Beak to answer some of Cummings allegations that he lied to Parliament and the public regarding the Covid care home policy, PPE procurement and the disastrous test and trace system. Of course he denies everything. (As it turns out later in June, he obviously was not concentrating properly on his job at the time!)

All I can remember was Boris muttering about herd immunity and clearing off to the rugby and races in March 2020.

Other news this month:

There has been a terrible accident near lake Maggiore, where a cable car crashed into the side of a mountain travelling at as speed of 100 km an hour, 14 people are dead. Investigators say that the emergency breaks had been disabled and the operators knew. 3 company people have been arrested.

A Ryanair plane was intercepted on a flight between Greece and Lithuania by Belarus' forces and was pressurised to land in Minsk in order for them to arrest a journalist who is a prominent critic of their countries leader. Western Governments are calling it a Hijacking but seem reluctant to get involved with a country which has a shoddy human rights record.

The other piece of news that registered in my tiny brain, was that three officers involved with the Hillsborough disaster, have been ruled as no case to answer regarding altering police statements. The bereaved families are livid.

My spiritual home, Vietnam, is still locked down.

My girls are beginning to get desperate now. Poor Anna went for an interview in a bank but as she had no experience and there were zillions of candidates, she didn't get a look in. I can't go into what is going on with Greenie as she told me some horrendous things lately and I promised not to tell anyone. But it was VERY BAD.

I feel so helpless that I cannot help them (they are still refusing monetary help), we think we have it bad here.

The Vietnamese have so far vaccinated 1% of the population and despite it being a Communist country I bet is was the wealthier individuals who received it. Only 990,000 people have received the vaccine out of the 90 million population.

It also looks like they have some sort of mutated Indian/UK virus which is starting to cause problems within the country and they have now had 47 deaths. What I don't understand is how that mutation occurred in the country in the first place, you cannot get a visa to gain entry and that's

only if you can get a flight there anyway, so how did it occur, or am I being a bit thick? People smuggling across the borders no doubt.
It is blatantly obvious they still have a really long, long, way to go. Interestingly though, they have generously given a portion of their vaccine allocation to Laos, which is the poorest country in the whole of South East Asia.
I don't know what is happening with my friend Danny, he has gone completely off the radar, I hope he is OK. I am sure he will pop up somewhere along the line, on a day when he is sober!

My friend Mary is still in France, she can't return to her house in Dublin as they are still in full Lockdown. She says she is now putting her life in reverse. Whereas the Flat in Nice was a holiday home and she lived predominantly in Dublin, she has now decided to live in France and just go back to Ireland for a couple of months a year. The decent weather helps with that decision and the fact that she has a delicious French boyfriend. Go Girl.

My friends in Greece have managed to get their boat in the water and are now living aboard full time. They spend their days sailing into picturesque harbours through crystal clear water with fantastic (but very hot) weather. Unfortunately all the harbours are devoid of tourists so there is no-one around. Our plan was to go sailing with them for two weeks in September but who knows? I hardly know what will happen next week let alone in three months time.

It's the end of May and yet another Bank Holiday. It ends with a few gloriously warm and sunny days which lifts the spirits after the horrible weather we have had recently. Everyone is busy in their gardens and the waft of lighted barbecues drift across the garden.
It also ends in a slightly more sinister way with the Covid infection numbers in the UK starting to creep up again.

It is also the perfect weather to get married; Mr Johnson and his girlfriend tie the knot in a top secret ceremony in London. I am not particularly interested except for one historical fact. He is the first PM in 200 years to get married whilst in office.

Some women fear the fire, some simply become it - R.H.Sin

June

The first day of the month and it is announced that there have been no deaths from Covid today. HURRAH!
By the third of the month the news comes out that the Covid infection rate is definitely increasing again due to this new Indian variant. NOOOOO!
By the fourth of the month, speculation starts to rise regarding whether we will be able to end the restrictions on 21st June.
OMG, PLEASE NO !

Bad news for all those smug people who rushed off on holiday to Portugal when it went on the Green list. It has now been moved back onto the Amber list and anyone returning from there has to isolate at home for 10 days. It transpires that there may be more countries coming off of the Amber list to be added to the Red list as this Indian variant carries on causing havoc. The Green list might get even shorter. I don't know whether it is naivety or stupidity but Covid is not going to be over on 21st June and all those people hoping to get away this Summer may end up disappointed.
I have given up any hope of going abroad this year now. Talking to someone who did get to Portugal; they had to shell out an extra £700 for Covid tests, that's a huge amount of cash to fork out on top of the cost of flights & accommodation. Then what with all the waiting at Immigration etc, I cannot even begin to think about putting us through the hassle, Peter would have a meltdown in the airport. I would love to go and see my friends in Greece or South of France, but I have finally conceded defeat that it is not going to happen.
I AM GOING NOWHERE.

Well that's not completely true. My friend Rachel and I have booked 4 days in Central London. To go to the British seaside in July costs an arm and a leg at the best of times let alone during a Pandemic when no-one can travel abroad, leaving Great Britain as the only holiday destination left and everyone is cashing in on it. A fortnight in an English cottage will cost the same as fortnight in the Spanish sun, if not more. London is currently devoid of tourists, so getting around the Capital will be easy and most of the sights will not be swarming with millions of people. Four nights in a Central 4 star hotel with breakfast included came to the grand sum of £360 for both of us. So look out London, lock up your sons, the ladies are coming!
Don't know why I said that, we will probably both be in bed by 10pm!

I spoke to Greenie who was in the middle of cooking 10 courses of a family lunch for 50 people in 40C heat. Apparently they are having a bit of a heatwave in Vietnam, the high temperature is bad enough but the humidity is through the roof. The Viets are all staying indoors during the day, keeping out of the sun. Eric has a new job working for a Telecommunications company, whatever that means. Anna was pleased as punch that she has come up with a way of making some cash. She has created a special drink to help quench the thirst during these hot temperatures. She said it was going really well. I asked how much money she had made in a week, the thrilled answer was 75,000 dong - £2.50!! At least she seemed happier and had a bit of purpose about her. All three of them are constantly fretting about the rising Covid rates there. They have now had 8063 cases and 45 deaths. Yes I know it is a drop in the ocean compared to the UK, but they are all worried sick. The Viets have ordered the Russian vaccine; SputnikV, but it is yet to arrive. One thing you can count on is that when the vaccination finally arrives in Vietnam, they will have everyone vaccinated in record time, they are so efficient.

If they want any volunteers to assist, Peter and I will be there in a flash.

Relief has arrived at work in the shape of two male temps who are like chalk and cheese. Both lovely lads, one is very laid back and the other one will be running the company by the end of the month.

Work is still manic, there have been more resignations that have reduced even further the amount of staff we have, which doesn't really help the whole situation. We are keeping an eye on things as a lot of organisers are starting to get a bit jittery about the restrictions maybe not being lifted and we are anticipating a flurry of cancellations.

So 'just call me Harry' and his wife have just had a baby girl. For two people who want to be disassociated with the royal family, they have called her Lilibet Diana. They have just named their child after two of the most famous women in the whole world, the Queen and Princess Diana. Why didn't they just call her Chardonnay if they want her to be normal and un-royal?

Have any of you watched Toyah & Roberts Sunday Lunch? Basically the pop star Toyah and her husband, legendary guitarist Robert Fripp, obviously got very bored during Lockdown. So each week she sings a song somewhere in her house, with Robert accompanying her on guitar. Every week it's getting madder and madder with Toyah wearing sexier and slightly odder outfits. Peter is completely captivated and watches it with his tongue hanging out.

I just think the pair of them have lost the plot after being locked up in the house for a year and not being able to perform on stage.
(Secretly I think she has been extremely clever, she now has a mass following of people who probably had never heard of her before. And she looks fabulous for 63).
Don't tell Peter I think that though.

My husband took me out for the day to Bicester Village. It's a cut price designer village that is very pretty and has lots of lovely flora dotted about and a very classy feel to it. The only problem was that for the first time since Covid arrived I actually felt slightly alarmed by the amount of people crowded together in some of the narrow shops. Multiple nationalities all breathing over each other, I did feel a bit nervous.
Peter spent a shed load of money but to be honest I didn't see one thing that I really liked except for a dress in *Ted Baker* that was a size 6 and would just have fitted over one leg. Peter spent £65 on the most hideous flip flop/sandals you have every seen. He has a very eclectic taste in clothes and always buys the weirdest thing in any shop.
Even the dog hated them when he put them on at home and kept attacking them.
Not surprised, they are vile.

The weather has been surprising warm and sunny so far, and there is a treat in store for us girls in the office. Our manager we worked with on the Vaccination Project is coming to the area and wants to meet us all for lunch. It's a weird feeling to see someone in the flesh you have worked with so intensely for 4 months but have never actually met. She is as lovely as we all thought, but blimey is she tall. I am always the tallest woman in my social and work group but she was even taller than me, which was a shock to us all as we only ever saw her sitting down on TEAMS.
Lunch was a blast as we reminisced over some of the peculiarities of that particular project. It was a reprieve from the constant bombardment of emails and phone calls in the office which seem to be increasing day by day.

The Euro's football tournament kicks off to partially filled stadiums but strangely enough without the huge media hype that normally goes with these competitions.
It must be a good sign, as normally dismal England win their first game, the first time in ten attempts in this competition. Peter doesn't watch much of it, he is only interested in Luton Town and doesn't really enjoy football on the TV. What does interest him is when a Danish player,

aged 29, suffers a full cardiac arrest during the game with Finland. It looked really bad and his wife was brought down to the side of the pitch but somehow he pulled round in hospital.

Shocking, that an extremely fit young man in his prime can suffer a heart attack; a warning to us all.

By the middle of the month the cases of the Indian variant, Delta as it is now called, are spiralling upwards, we are having up to 10000 new cases per day in the UK. Boris calls for drastic action and basically delays the Lockdown easing until the 19th July. It will be reviewed after two weeks, they are hoping that this will enable everyone so far not vaccinated to get their first shot in the next few weeks and they are also reducing the gap between the 1st and 2nd shots to 8 weeks. By the 14th June 77% of the population have had their 1st dose and 55% the second. By 19th July they are hoping that 2/3 of all adults in the UK would have received their second dose. Certainly all the Vaccination Centres have stepped up to the plate and even I have managed to get some shifts on Fridays.

Unfortunately a lot of very naive (or stupid) people were not expecting the delay in easing the Lockdown and are moaning across the country that it's not fair, they have not been given enough warning, etc etc. For God's sake people look at the figures, we cannot risk completely opening up yet, it would be suicide. And let's face it, it is the people who are spreading it to each other because they won't follow the regulations or refuse to believe that it even exists. Yes the Government should have closed the borders months ago, but you only need to go out on the street in certain area's to see the public disregarding all social distancing rules.

The delay causes a catastrophic delay in the opening of theatres and dance venues. It also causes utter carnage with our business. Lots of our customers have cancelled events that we have spent the last two months organising and everything is up in the air again. We've all been here before.

Long awaited rescheduled weddings are allowed to go ahead but no-one is allowed a dance floor inside, if you must dance it has to be outdoors. I'm going to a wedding next week, thank God I am not allowed to dance. Two glasses of wine inside me and I turn into Beyonce. Well maybe a bit more Bouncy than Beyonce.

(As it turns out I ended up outside the venue, on the wet grass minus my 4 inch stiletto shoes, boogieing on down with a load of Peters teenage cousins. We had a total blast.

I also awoke next morning with a pain in my right hip and both knees, accompanied by an enormous hangover that lasted two days).

If you don't like the road you are walking, start paving another one -
Dolly Parton

Conclusion

I've decided to call it a day now with this diary, we are nearly at the end (I hope). I cannot go around in circles yet another time. And you don't want to hear it again.

I have a new book buzzing around in my head which I need to get written down before the whole idea departs my brain and I can't remember what it was going to be about.

So what does the future hold?

Will there be a third wave this Summer or later on in the Autumn? I am no scientist but I think we are going to have to live with Covid. Like flu it will come back every Winter and some of us (old people) will probably have to be vaccinated annually. I also can't see the mask wearing being eased in certain places, but I'd love someone to prove me wrong and it all go away after the 19th July.

Unfortunately, with the sky high figures of this Delta variant, I don't think it's over until the fat lady sings. And that particularly obese lady has lost her voice.

What have we learned?

Well, most of us don't like being locked up indoors, we are social animals and enjoy a bit of human interaction.

We don't really like doing exercise, even though we pretend we do.

It doesn't matter how hard you work, nobody notices.

We all drink too much and eat badly when we are bored. A consequence of Covid is that we now have much bigger bums and tums.

All most people want now is a holiday in a far off climate, a long, long way from here, a complete change of scenery.

The English love of football makes people behave in a bizarre way.

Politicians make complete tits of themselves over women. And other things.

What about me?

Well, I can still walk in vertiginous high heels.

I still have long hair which I am persevering with.

I'm still applying my lipstick on every occasion.

I still think I am 18 inside whilst the rest of my body behaves like it is 80 years old.

My marriage is still in tact.

I dream every day about returning to Vietnam and seeing my friends who are very important to me; one day it might even come true.

I've acknowledged that I will never snog Pierce Brosnan (that will never come true).
In reality I am so over Covid, and apart from the hot flushes, I am pretty much over the menopause.
Lucky me.

I am proud of the woman I am because I went through one hell of a time becoming her - Anon.

Printed in Great Britain
by Amazon

65608300R00163